Books and Reading Development

The Bradford Book Flood Experiment

DATE DUE			

Books and Reading Development

The Bradford Book Flood Experiment

Jennie Ingham

Heinemann Educational Books
on behalf of the British National
Bibliography

Heinemann Educational Books Ltd
22 Bedford Square, London WC1B 3HH
LONDON   EDINBURGH   MELBOURNE   AUCKLAND
HONG KONG   SINGAPORE   KUALA LUMPUR   NEW DELHI
IBADAN   NAIROBI   JOHANNESBURG   KINGSTON
EXETER (NH)   PORT OF SPAIN

ISBN 0 435 10451 9

British Library Cataloguing in Publication Data

Ingham, Jennie
 Books and reading development: the Bradford
 Book Flood Experiment.
 1. Bradford Book Flood
 2. Developmental reading
 3. Reading (Elementary) – England
 4. Reading (Secondary education) – England
 I. Title
 428.4'3'071242817   LB1525

 ISBN 0–435–10451–9

Cover photograph courtesy of Staff and Pupils
of Handsworth School, London Borough of Waltham Forest

Printed and bound in Great Britain by
Biddles Ltd, Guildford and King's Lynn

This book is dedicated to my husband, David, and to my children, Francesca and Raphael, all avid readers.

'The ability to read may be regarded as the basis of education and communication and as an essential possession for success in life.'

George Th. Pavlidis

Contents

Foreword   vii

Acknowledgements   ix

List of Appendixes   xi

List of Tables   xii

1   Why a Book Flood?   1

2   The Schools   24

3   Reading Records   73

4   Case Studies: Reading in School   113

5   Case Studies: The Homes and the Children   150

6   Results of the Tests and Other Comparisons   209

7   Conclusions and Recommendations   225

Epilogue   247

Appendixes   249

References   270

Index   273

Foreword

As Director of the National Book League, I am particularly happy to write the foreword to this book. The NBL has been closely concerned with the project it describes. It has acted as co-ordinator between the City of Bradford Metropolitan Council Libraries and Schools Divisions, the Postgraduate School of Studies in Research in Education of the University of Bradford, the British National Bibliography Research Fund, and the publishers who generously provided more than 8000 books free to make the whole experiment possible.

A large body of educational opinion throughout the world firmly believes that the adequate provision of books, coupled with the desire to read them, is an important element in every child's upbringing. However superficially exciting – or indeed useful in very real senses – new sorts of electronic media and gadgets may be, books provide a child with a medium to stir the imagination, develop comprehension, and perfect communication at *his or her own speed* in a manner not yet equalled by any other form of learning. For many years now surveys have shown that children coming from homes filled with books embark on education and life with positive advantages.

Having stated this, we are still left with the large question: How many books? Would there always be children who read a lot and others who read little whatever the provision or ease of acquisition of books? This project was one attempt to find the answers to these questions. Clearly one experiment in four schools (two flooded and two control) cannot give us answers that would apply everywhere in England. But what has been learnt in Bradford, described in the pages of this book, can help us flesh out the picture more accurately.

I do not want in any way to belittle the generosity of the British National Bibliography Research Fund, which made the research possible, or the publishers who contributed so many books, or Bradford Libraries from which came the initial drive, and much else besides, by stating that a great deal has been achieved on comparatively small resources. We spend millions to perfect new arms or warships, hundreds of thousands to develop new machines; in comparison, the tens of thousands devoted to trying to find out whether our children are getting enough books is small. But it is a start. It means that educational debates on the value of books and reading can be that much better informed.

As Director of an organization whose sole purpose is to persuade more people to read more books, I welcome this report wholeheartedly and hope that all those connected with the education of young people will find the time to read it.

Martyn Goff OBE FRSA
Director of the
National Book League

Acknowledgements

In any project of several years' duration, which involves an external funding body and representatives of a local education authority, in addition to research staff and samples of teachers and children, many people contribute in a diversity of ways to its progress and successful completion.

This experiment would not have taken place unless Martyn Goff, Director of the National Book League, had proposed it and undertaken to obtain generous supplies of books from publishers, or if the British Library had not agreed to give financial support through the BNB Research Fund. We are grateful to all those who helped to initiate it, and for support throughout the four years 1976–80, from Martyn Goff and from the BNB Research Fund Chairman, Peter Stockham, and its successive secretaries, Hugh Pinnock, and Margaret O'Hare, with her colleague, Richard Snelling. Initially, too, the experiment could not have been funded without the leadership of Louis Cohen, who wrote successive proposals in consultation with the Chief Librarian, Bill Davies, and English Adviser, the late Alan Leake, and Adviser Eunice Beaumont of Bradford Metropolitan Council. Promises, subsequently fulfilled, of generous support by Bill Davies and his colleague, Bob Wilkes, the principal librarian of the Education and Young People's Services, in sorting, shelving and adding to books supplied, and by the English Adviser in selecting schools, were also essential to the setting up of the experiment.

Throughout the first three years of this experiment, our greatest debt of gratitude is, of course, to the headmasters, teachers and pupils in the four schools for giving their time so freely, and to the teachers for allowing such ready access to their class-rooms. In addition, parents of children who were the subjects of case studies deserve especial thanks for allowing me to tape-record interviews. Headmasters have also served on the Consultative and Core Committees, chaired by Bill Davies, the former committee representing all interested parties including a publisher's representative, a councillor from Bradford's Education Committee, and a local HMI. We greatly welcomed the interest and support of them all. In addition, we appointed as consultant specialist in reading Peter Pumfrey of Manchester University, whose conscientious reading of papers and perceptive comments have often delighted us and always helped us.

When Louis Cohen left at the end of the first year of the experiment to take a Chair at Loughborough, we were most grateful to Gajendra Verma for tiding us over a difficult transitional period by interviewing headmasters and helping to organize the final posttesting. We have to thank Stephen Clift, Research Assistant from 1976–8, for contributing substantially to the statistical work, for sharing in designing the Reading Record Form, and for preparing the Book Flood Reading Attitude Scale. In the first and third years of the experiment we were also very grateful to the numerous people who assisted with testing in schools: postgraduate students and staff of Bradford University and students of Bradford College assisted by their tutor.

My own personal thanks go to Margaret Marshall of Leeds Polytechnic School of Librarianship, and to Peter Pumfrey, for their support when I applied for additional funding in 1978; to the staff of Bradford University Computer Centre for their help with statistical work on the Reading Record Form, especially to Pat Rushforth, David Butland and Jack Yerkess; to the clerical staff of the School of Studies in Research in Education, Bradford University, particularly to Georgina Coates, Margaret Stefanuti and Jean Lonsdale; and to Kathy Gale, who transcribed tapes at home.

Most special thanks to Ruth Beard for her continual help and encouragement, practical assistance with statistical work and writing up of Chapter 6, as well as in a multitude of ways too numerous to mention.

Finally, I am most thankful to my family – to my husband, David, for his patience and understanding; and to my children for revealing to me the joys of children's books.

List of Appendixes

Appendix I   The Reading Record Form   249

Appendix II   Final category system for coding children's reasons for book choice   252

Appendix III   Reasons and final comments from the Reading Record Forms   253

Appendix IV   Descriptive statistics   256

Appendix V   Favourite authors and titles   258

List of Tables

1·1   Matrix of Book Flood measures   13

2·1   Outer city experimental school: count of school and class library books   27

2·2   Outer city experimental school: results of school-administered reading tests – September 1976   31

2·3   Outer city control school: count of school and class library books   40

2·4   Outer city control school: results of school-administered reading tests – September 1976   43

2·5   Countries of origin of ethnic minority children and their parents   50

2·6   Inner city experimental school: count of school and class library books   51

2·7   Inner city experimental school: results of school-administered reading tests – September 1976   57

2·8   Inner city control school: count of school and class library books   64

2·9   Inner city control school: results of school-administered reading tests – September 1976   68

3·1   Number of Reading Record Forms completed: outer city schools (matched schools paired)   75

3·2   Number of Reading Record Forms completed: inner city schools (matched schools paired)   76

3·3   Number of individual titles recorded in each school in each year   76

3·4   Number of individual authors recorded in each school in each year   77

3·5   Location, with matched schools paired (percentages)   77

3·6   Reasons given for choice of books recorded on the Reading Record Forms (percentages)   81

3·7   Percentages of books recorded on Reading Record Form that were taken home/not taken home   83

3·8   The extent to which books, recorded on the
      Reading Record Form, were completed,
      with matched schools paired (percentages)   83
3·9   Children's expressed opinion of the books
      recorded on the Reading Record Form, with
      matched schools paired (percentages)   85
3·10 Children's experienced degree of difficulty with
      the books recorded on the Reading Record
      Form, with matched schools paired (percentages)   87
3·11 People to whom children talked about the books
      recorded on the Reading Record Form, with
      matched schools paired (percentages)   88
3·12 Whether child told friends that the book
      recorded on the Reading Record Form was
      a good book, with matched schools paired
      (percentages)   90
3·13 Whether child wanted to read another book
      by the same author, with matched schools
      paired (percentages)   90
3·14 Type of book, with watched schools paired
      (percentages)   92
3·15 Books available in school and class libraries   94
3·16 Number of times books rated as 1 or 2 on
      Question 5 – opinion – set against total
      Reading Record Form returns, and expressed
      as percentages of the latter, for each school,
      each year, for boys and girls together and
      separately   94
3·17 Favourite authors: location, with matched
      schools paired (percentages)   96
3·18 Favourite authors: reasons for book choice,
      with matched schools paired (percentages)   97
3·19 Favourite authors: type of book, with
      matched schools paired (percentages)   99
3·20 Favourite authors: type of book, for boys and
      girls separately (percentages)   100
4·1   Sample of case study children in outer city
      experimental school   117
4·2   Outer city experimental school: places from
      which case study children obtained books
      recorded on Reading Record Forms and
      numbers of books obtained from each location
      plus (in brackets) numbers of books completed   119
4·3   Sample of case study children from outer city
      control school   127

4·4   Outer city control school: places from which
        case study children obtained books recorded on
        Reading Record Forms and number of books
        obtained from each location, plus (in brackets)
        number of books completed   130
4·5   Sample of case study children from inner city
        experimental school   134
4·6   Origins of 'ethnic minority' case study children   135
4·7   Inner city experimental school: places from which
        case study children obtained books recorded on
        Reading Record Forms and number of books
        obtained from each location, plus (in brackets)
        number of books completed   136
4·8   Sample of case study children from inner city
        control school   144
4·9   Inner city control school: places from which
        case study children obtained books recorded on
        Reading Record Forms and number of books
        obtained from each location, plus (in brackets)
        number of books completed   145
5·1   Avid readers: the sample of boys   151
5·2   Avid readers: the sample of girls   152
5·3   Infrequent readers: boys and girls   152
5·4   Age on leaving school of parents of avid and
        infrequent readers   153
5·5   Further education of parents of avid readers   154
5·6   Occupations of mothers   154
5·7   Occupations of fathers   155
5·8   Number of children in families of avid and
        infrequent readers   156
5·9   Position in the family of avid and infrequent
        readers   156
5·10   Numbers of books at home, belonging to
        avid readers and infrequent readers   157
5·11   Membership of public library by avid and
        infrequent readers and their mothers and
        fathers   157
5·12   Truancy, illness or disabilities   157
6·1   Some initial measures (mean quotients or scores
        and numbers of children)   210
6·2   Changes in attitudes: ratings and scores   211
6·3   Schonell Reading Age and chronological age   213
6·4   Edinburgh Test raw scores and Cattell Culture
        Fair Test quotients   214

6·5   Four-way analysis of variance using Edinburgh
       Test scores   216
6·6   Scores of fourth-years 1978, 1979   217
6·7   Significant results in analyses of co-variance   221
6·8   Regression analysis   223
7·1   Increases and decreases in total number of
       books recorded, in number of individual authors
       recorded, and in number of separate titles
       recorded, between the first and final years of
       the experiment   228
7·2   Type of book, boys and girls separately
       (percentages)   233

Additional tables in Appendix V

3·I   Favourite authors: outer city experimental
        school: 10+; favourite titles: outer city
        experimental school: 10+   258
3·II   Favourite authors: outer city experimental
        school: 11+; favourite titles: outer city
        experimental school: 11+; favourite authors:
        outer city experimental school: 12+   259
3·III   Favourite authors: outer city control school:
        10+; favourite titles: outer city control
        school: 10+; favourite authors: outer city
        control school: 11+; favourite titles: outer
        city control school: 11+   260
3·IV   Favourite authors: outer city control school:
        12+; favourite titles: outer city control
        school: 12+   262
3·V   Favourite authors: inner city experimental
        school: 10+; favourite titles: inner city
        experimental school: 10+; favourite authors:
        inner city experimental school: 11+;
        favourite titles: inner city experimental
        school: 11+   263
3·VI   Favourite authors: inner city experimental
        school: 12+; favourite titles: inner city
        experimental school: 12+   264
3·VII   Favourite authors: inner city control school:
        10+; favourite titles: inner city control
        school 10+; favourite authors; inner city
        control school: 11+; favourite titles:
        inner city control school: 11+   266

3·VIII   Favourite authors: inner city control school: 12+; favourite titles: inner city control school: 12+   268

1 Why a Book Flood?

. . . research is always a venture into the unknown, so there is no ultimate 'should be' Ary, D., Jacobs, L.C., and Razawich A., Introduction to Research in Education, *(Holt, Rinehart & Winston, USA, 1972).*

What are the ingredients of reading success? Is there a recipe, a formula, which, if mixed in the correct proportions, can be guaranteed to produce perfect results every time? This question has taxed the minds of reading researchers and, indeed, all those involved in the teaching of reading, for so long now that one thing, at least, is clear – there is no simple, straightforward answer.

When we try to make sense of the growth of reading skills and interest in books, when we try to tease out the conditions which are prerequisite if a child is to become a skilful or avid reader, we must be prepared to grapple with human nature and human society, with all their intricacies, contradictions and paradoxes. For instance, how do we explain the child who apparently reads and watches television simultaneously? Or the avid reader who watches more television than the non-reader? How do we pigeon-hole the child whose parents never read a book, but who is a skilful and avid reader?

There are dangers inherent in the tendency to package and label reading behaviour, or any other aspect of human behaviour, too neatly. It is human nature to seek security, to look for patterns in behaviour so that we may predict with greater accuracy; certainly, as educators and parents, we *need* to do so. But we must not be tempted away from the complex realities of the situation, realities which are familiar to every classroom teacher. The natural tendency to grasp *a* solution to the problem of teaching children to read in school, for instance, has led many people up many a blind alley.

Yet clearly, we do need practical but flexible guidelines. So let us examine what we *do* know about the correlates of reading success, putting the Book Flood in the context of that knowledge, and underlining the ways in which we were able to extend that knowledge, or at least provide another piece of the jigsaw.

The Bradford Book Flood Experiment

The aim of the Experiment was to examine the effects, upon children's reading skills, habits and interests, of 'flooding' or saturating their classrooms with books in addition to their school text-books or such reading books as might already exist in their classrooms.

Advisers selected two matched pairs of schools, all 9–13 years middle schools. One pair of schools was in the inner city, where the intakes include quite a large proportion of children whose parents had been born in India or Pakistan. The other pair was in the outer city in an 'estate desert' area. One school in each pair was randomly designated the experimental school, thus receiving publishers' donations of approximately 4,500 books per school, in the proportions 1/3 non-fiction to 2/3 fiction. The other two schools automatically became the controls. The Book Flood was lodged with the second year cohort of children, initially aged 10+, and, with some adjustments, remained with them until they left their middle schools at the end of their fourth year, aged 12+.

The books which were housed with the six classes of children (three in each experimental school) varied to some extent during the experiment because some of them were deemed by the teachers to be too difficult for the children at the beginning of the experiment, and were, therefore, saved until the children were able to cope with them; whilst, conversely, others were judged to be too easy or too babyish at the end of each year, and so were left behind for other younger children to enjoy. How exactly the books were distributed, displayed and used was deliberately left to the teachers, for the ways in which teachers used the books was one of the most important variables which we wished to monitor, as being highly likely to affect the impact of the influx of books.

The core of the original experimental design was a series of tests, chiefly of reading ability (described in detail in the second half of this chapter), which were administered at the beginning and again at the end of the experiment. The idea behind such a pre-test/post-test design is to assess the effect, if any, of whatever new variable is introduced – in this case the additional books – by measuring the 'change scores', i.e. assessing the significance of any changes in test scores during the period of the experiment.

Such a technique would probably be sufficient in itself were we not dealing with human beings in constant interaction with other human beings – teachers, parents, siblings, friends and other children. If we could, in truth 'control' all other variables, and if we were really able to 'match' schools, including their Headteachers and staff, then educational research would be far simpler than it is.

Quite clearly the effect of the books would be governed by a whole host of other factors, including personal and environmental factors, and those relating to school organization. Since we were not involved in a large scale, statistically-generalizable survey, in all aspects of the research it was important to exploit the advantages peculiar to the small-scale, in-depth, longitudinal study, which Frank Whitehead had suggested was needed in order to complement the survey reported in *Children and Their Books* (Whitehead *et al*, 1977). Both types of research are equally essential if we are to arrive at a total picture; the advantages of the two approaches are quite different and complementary.

The home environment

In examining the effect of the home environment upon reading, therefore, we decided to take advantage of our small sample and conduct in-depth case studies with a small number of families, building up detailed pictures of life-style and values, and pin-pointing the place of reading in each picture. Because the interviews were completely open-ended what emerged was a picture of the *relative* value of reading for each member of a family, and the rôle, if any, which reading played in the life of the family.

It is interesting to place this aspect of the research in the context of previous research and to compare the sorts of findings which have tended to emerge from large-scale surveys with those which have emerged from smaller, often longitudinal studies. There is no doubt that the socio-economic status of a family correlates highly with the degree of a child's reading success. On the basis of many reliable research studies we are able to state with some conviction that the child of a professional or non-manual worker is *more likely* to achieve a high level of reading attainment than the child of a manual worker. This kind of global generalization is particularly common to such large-scale studies as Davie, Butler and Goldstein's National Child Development Study (1972), or Whitehead *et al*'s survey (1977). Such studies are particularly useful in that they *are* statistically generalizable and point us towards factors which are more commonly to be found in the professional family than the family of the manual worker.

But of course such studies, valuable and necessary as they are, are unlikely to be educationally productive unless we take the trouble to look beyond the 'what', to the 'how' and the 'why'. It is, therefore, important to examine in detail *across* socio-economic barriers the factors which operate in the homes of those children who are skilful and avid readers. Of course, the authors of the large-scale surveys were not ignorant of differences within socio-economic groups. Although Davie, Butler and Goldstein state categorically that, 'The chances of an unskilled manual worker's child (Registrar General Group V) being a poor reader are six times greater than those of a professional worker's child (R.G.I.)', they do not omit to add the following rider:

> Family and home influences operate in complex and subtle ways . . . a large-scale study is not well-equipped to search out the subtleties. These can best be dealt with in smaller studies with their sharper focus and more detailed information.

And Whitehead et al gave us a timely reminder that '. . . there are philistine middle class homes as well as working class ones'. How right they are, but they forgot to add that there are cultured working class homes as well as middle class ones! Of the smaller scale studies one of the earliest was conducted by Dolores Durkin in California. Amongst her sample of 49 early readers only seven were from professional families. Five-year-old John, the subject of Jane Torrey's (1969) case study of a child who taught himself to read, was the son of a trucker and a hospital maid.

More recently, Margaret Clark, in her study of young, fluent readers (1976), stressed parental factors other than education, occupation and income. Since then Barbara Tizard (1981) has shown how parental involvement in children's reading can affect the children's achievement in school. Certainly, the avid readers in the Book Flood were almost entirely from working class families.

Perhaps one of the most fascinating studies in progress is that led by Gordon Wells at the University of Bristol, the Bristol Logitudinal Language Development Research Programme. Fascinating because, although the study is primarily concerned with child language development, the researchers have found a strong correlation between 'the extent to which parents accept and develop children's verbal initiations' and 'reading achievement after two years in school', especially as verbal interaction emerged as one of the most important correlates with interest in reading in the Book Flood case studies. Wells also found considerable variation *within* social class.

There is an increasing tendency amongst reading researchers, and a most productive one I believe, towards a holistic approach to the child as reader. This approach places the child in the context of total environment and experiences; it also places reading in the context of communication skills generally. This tendency is typified by a book which is not strictly research, Leila Berg's *Reading and Loving* (1977). Her memorable vignettes bring home forcibly the total unreality of attempting to isolate reading as an activity and putting it, dry and gasping for breath, under the microscope.

What then are the parental factors, other than socio-economic status, which correlate with reading ability and frequently with an interest in books? They divide readily into two clusters: those relating to the parents' interest in books and reading; and those relating to the parents' interest in the child:

A. Parental interest in literacy and promotion of books:
1. The parents read, and obviously enjoy, books, usually including public library books.
2. The parents read to the child regularly.
3. The parents provide the child with drawing and writing materials.
4. The parents take the child to the public library.
5. The parents provide books for the child.
6. The parents take some quality newspapers into the home.
7. The parents are willing to teach the child to read, if the child shows an interest, rather than leaving it to the 'experts' when the time comes at school.

B. Quality of parental (or other significant adult) interaction, with the emphasis on verbal interaction.
1. 'Mutuality' of language interaction (Gordon Wells, 1979), i.e. the parent responds to the child's initiations of conversation, parent and child working together to achieve mutual understanding.
2. The parent finds time for the child, especially for talking, listening and reading to the child.
3. The parent treats the child with respect, as an individual with needs and rights.
4. The parent is on hand to give help and attention when needed, but does not stifle independence of choice and selectivity, especially of books and television programmes.

Of course, no one is suggesting that if a parent falls short on one or two items their child cannot be an able and avid reader; these are simply factors which, on the basis of many small and large-scale studies, tend to correlate highly with reading ability and an interest in books.

The way in which the Book Flood case studies were able to add to this particular area of knowledge was by approaching the home interviews in a totally open-ended manner, allowing the pattern of life and the values which permeated it to emerge, so that reading was in no way isolated. This approach facilitated an examination of the relationship between personality, leisure activities generally and reading in particular. In describing the relationship between reading and television we were able to break new ground. Talking to parents we were able to uncover a relationship between interest in reading, attitudes to education and child-rearing generally, and the parents' perceptions of the extent to which they were able to control their own and their children's lives (i.e. whether they perceived a mainly internal or external locus of control).

The example of the relationship between television and reading illustrates perfectly the complementary nature of large-scale surveys, and small-scale, in-depth studies.

When I came to examine the previous literature on this subject it appeared to be contradictory. Himmelweit, Oppenheim and Vince (1958) had found that, although initially children in those families which decided to buy televisions at that time read less, as they got used to viewing they gradually reverted to books; so that after a few years the viewers were once again reading as many books as the controls, and the duller children had even increased their share. These findings are in line with those of Whitehead *et al* (1977) in their large-scale survey for the Schools Council:

> When one remembers the other demands made on children's time on a weekday evening during term time it seems clear that the amount of television viewing accomplished by most children cannot help but reduce the amount of time available for reading, and in fact we found that for each sub-group there existed an inverse relationship between amount of television viewing and amount of book reading.

However, in addition to their large-scale survey, Whitehead *et al* conducted a series of follow-up interviews with 576 out of the total sample of 8000 children who completed the original questionnaires. Here they found indications of a somewhat different pattern of behaviour:

> . . . our interviews lent little support to the stereotype sometimes offered of the bookish child as one who is immersed in books to the exclusion of all other interests. On the whole, the children in the 10+ group who read a large number of books seemed also to be children who were busily engaged in reading comics, *watching television,* playing games, and pursuing a variety of hobbies and interests, both active and sedentary. . . . Indeed we were led at times to feel that our interviewees tended to polarize themselves into two groups, those who were hyperactive in a great many directions, including reading, and those who were in general somewhat lethargic or apathetic and displayed a low level of involvement in any of their activities.

Whilst these findings are not necessarily contradictory to those resulting from the initial survey, which was of a global nature, they certainly present a very different picture of the leisure-time activities of children at the extremes of the continuum: avid – infrequent readers.

The findings from these follow-up interviews are, in fact, in keeping with those of other researchers in the field (e.g. Clark, 1976, *Reading in America,* 1978, 1979), and it might well be that the findings *are* contradictory to some extent, as a result of the different methodological approaches adopted. It seems likely that if one carries out ethnographic research, exploring the relationship between television viewing and reading one will uncover patterns of behaviour which do not emerge from a large-scale survey based upon a series of closed questions, requiring a negative or affirmative answer, or requiring a simple response to a multiple choice question. Thus, if one asks infrequent readers to indicate on a questionnaire how they have spent their evenings, particularly in winter, they are likely to record having watched a great deal of television, as that is likely to be the only identifiable 'activity' going on in the house, even though, most of the time, nobody is actively watching it. If one questions these children closely, however, as I did, one might well find that they know very little about the programmes they claim to have watched, and even might not be able to identify which channel was on when they are presented with a list of programmes in the *Radio Times* or *TV Times.*

Very few questionnaires include open-ended questions, for the simple reason that the responses are very difficult to analyse and code up for the computer. In fact, such a question was included in the Reading Record Form as part of the Bradford Book Flood Experiment, and the result was extemely rewarding, but necessitated a great deal of hard work in terms of agreeing on a category system, and subsequently categorizing thousands of responses. Nevertheless it was a thoroughly worthwhile activity as the responses were substantially different from those obtained during a pilot study when children were presented with a multiple-choice question instead. I well remember an occasion when I was administering an individual attitude test to an 11-year-old boy, one which offered a forced choice between pictures of a number of pairs of activities (Askov). Instead of giving me a definite answer, the boy insisted that whether he would, for example, choose to watch television or read a book *depended* on what was on television and what the book was about. Even more complicated and more difficult to record except by detailed transcription of a case study is the situation where a child reads in the room with the television on, looking up from the book actively to watch those programmes or parts of programmes which are of interest!

Reading habits and interests

In this area also we were able to exploit the small scale of the study to gather detailed information over the entire three year period of data collection. This record of the children's reading was important for monitoring the effect of the Flood; for instance, we wondered whether it would affect their criteria for book choice, or the ways in which they set about choosing books. And, of course, we needed an accurate record of what they actually read in relation to what was available, how the boys' reading compared to the girls', how their interests varied with increasing age, and so on. The longitudinal record was also intrinsically valuable in that it is unique, both in the detail and length of the record for such a relatively large sample (by small-scale study standards); and in that it is methodologically unique, because of the ways in which we set out to avoid the pitfalls which this type of questionnaire often encounters.

Many previous studies of children's reading interests have employed the 'one-off' survey approach, which, by its very nature, is descriptive rather than diagnostic, dealing with the 'what' rather than the 'why' (e.g. Jenkinson, 1940; Carsley, 1955; Yarlott and Harpin, 1970/71; Whitehead *et al*, 1977). Although such a study, particularly if conducted on a large scale and employing rigorous sampling procedures, will certainly yield results which are statistically generalizable, inevitably, it will fail to provide detail, or a developmental picture, just as the smaller scale longitudinal study cannot provide the statistically generalizable results. The problem is basically financial, for a large-scale longitudinal study would be vastly expensive. In the absence of funds for such a study, educational researchers have to content themselves with using the two complementary procedures on different occasions; and with generating hypotheses from the more detailed studies, on which they are then able to base, for example, formulations of questions for use in subsequent large-scale surveys. Whitehead et al, recognizing the complementary nature of the two approaches, acknowledged the need for '. . . a longitudinal study of a much smaller number of children in order to follow through their reading over a period of several years'.

In particular, one of the disadvantages of the survey approach is that it does not reveal the possible wide variety of reading undertaken by an individual child, since children are typically asked to record what they have read during the previous few weeks. It is no exaggeration to say that a thirteen-year-old might read a *Paddington* book one week, several books by Judy Blume the next week, following *It's Not the End of the World* with *The Ogre Downstairs,* read nothing but comics for a few weeks, dip into encyclopaedias

and books on sport for perhaps half a term, read *Watership Down*
and *Plague Dogs* in rapid succession, and return to something like
Roald Dahl by way of a breather. The return to old favourites in
times of academic or emotional strain is well-known. The wide
variety of some children's reading is beautifully parodied in Peter
Hollindale's citation of *The Journeying Boy* by Michael Innes
(Hollindale, 1974):

> Please deliver at once by special messenger one pair of binoculars
> for bird-watching and a good camera (not box). Please also send
> these books: *Biggles Flies East, Biggles Flies West, Biggles Flies
> North, Biggles Fails to Return,* Bertrand Russell's *History of Western
> Philosophy,* George Moore's *Daphnis and Chloe, Biggles and the
> Camel Squadron,* Bleinstein's *More and More Practical Sex,*
> Blunden's *Life of Shelley,* also *Atlanta in Calydon, Biggles in
> Borneo, Women in Love,* and any close translations of Caesar's
> *Civil Wars.*

Awareness of this particular limitation of the survey approach led
us, in the Bradford Book Flood Experiment, to design a questionnaire which the child completed each time he or she read a book, on
which was recorded, amongst other data, the title and author of the
book, so that by the end of the experiment we had a detailed,
longitudinal record of the reading interests of 360 children.

The Reading Record Form also nicely illustrates another
advantage which the longitudinal study of a relatively small
number of children can have over the large-scale survey. Since
asking children what they are currently reading does not always
yield highly reliable results, because of the variety just described,
many researchers employing the large-scale survey approach have
resorted to asking children, when completing questionnaires, to
tick broad categories of books preferred (Jenkinson, 1940; Smith
and Harrap, 1957; Butts, 1963; Inglis, 1969; Yarlott and Harpin,
1970/71), such as 'school stories', 'animal stories', 'love and
romance' or 'adventure'. (Whitehead *et al,* 1977, reached the same
conclusion in their final report, pp. 110–111.) The chief problem
with the category approach is the over-simplification inherent in
such an approach; whilst some books fall readily into topic or
subject categories such as science fiction (e.g. the *Dr Who* series) or
'detective stories' (e.g. the *Hardy Boys* or the *Nancy Drew* series),
many others defy categorization at this simple level. For example, I
wonder how one might categorize *The Shrinking of Treehorn* or *The
Ogre Downstairs*? Are they 'fantasy', as in the former a child
gradually shrinks and later turns green, whilst in the latter children
fly, and toffee bars, a pipe and doll's house people become animate?
Or are they 'social realism'/'family life', since they treat of painfully

real situations encountered by many of their readers? One might ask similar questions about, for example, *There's No Such Thing As A Dragon, The Blah, Freaky Friday, A Billion For Boris, The Ghost of Thomas Kempe* and myriads of others which cross subject boundaries, but which all use fantasy in order to illuminate and contain realistic problems, usually involving human relationships. In *Freaky Friday* and *The Ogre Downstairs,* for instance, empathy is portrayed at the level of concrete operations by means of magic, just as budding hypothetical thought is given a helping hand in *A Billion For Boris.*

By avoiding the category approach in recording children's reading interests one also avoids lumping together diverse books, which have only one common feature and which would be likely to fall into the same category. For example, within the single category of 'animal stories' we might well find *Mrs Frisby and the Rats of NIMH, Dogsbody, Tarka the Otter, Charlotte's Web, The Midnight Fox, Watership Down* and *Animal Farm,* only one of which is purely and unconditionally an animal story. Possibly even more disparity would be found within the category of 'school stories', which might include *What Katy Did, The Eighteenth Emergency, Jennings* and *Pardon Me, You're Stepping on My Eyeball!* There can be as many differences *within* a subject category as there are *between* categories. Therefore it is preferable if time and money allow to record actual titles read. However, the coding and computer analysis of the amount of data for the 360 children involved in the Book Flood was such a huge task that it is obvious why one rarely finds data collected in this way. More details are given in 'Recording Children's Responses to Books' (Ingham 1980).

Finally, on the subject of categorization, it is worth mentioning that it could cause a distortion of results if, in their responses, children conform to sex stereotypic responses or succumb to peer group pressure. For example, a boy who might respond favourably to, and record having read, *The Midnight Fox* or *Dogsbody*; or to *A Very Long Way From Anywhere Else,* or any of Paul Zindel's books, would be unlikely to express a preference for 'animal stories' or 'love stories'.

It is apparent that the appearance of respectability with which statistics resulting from large-scale surveys are endowed, can easily be misleading. They do not necessarily present an untrue picture, but can only faithfully record the answers to those questions which were asked in the first place. This is a limitation which we should bear in mind at all times. 'Quantitative' is not a synonym for 'objective', nor is 'qualitative' a synonym for 'subjective'. The questions we ask and the ways in which we ask them to varying degrees determine the answers which we are given.

The role of the school

As every teacher will realize, one of the most important variables in this experiment had to be the classroom teachers, not in isolation, of course, but in the context of school organization and ethos. The teachers and Headteachers, like the children and parents, were treated as whole people with histories, values, beliefs and personalities, all of which affected, and were affected by, the particular school of which they were a part. Therefore, again taking full advantage of the small scale of the study and the fact that we were working in four schools only, we decided to conduct a case study of each school, its Headteacher and all other members of staff involved in the Book Flood.

The data for this part of the study were collected by means of participant observation and tape-recorded interviews with staff, as well as by collecting information from advisers and education officers. The aim was to record those factors in each school which might affect the ways in which the children responded to the books. These included the extent of the teachers' knowledge of children's books and their degree of enthusiasm for them; the various ways in which teachers displayed, promoted and used books; the attitudes of the Headteachers towards reading; and, related to this last point, those aspects of school organization which might be expected to affect reading habits, such as the allocation of staff to the teaching of English, the timetabling of English lessons and allocation of classrooms, the organization of school and classroom libraries and the distribution of capitation allowance.

To my knowledge this type of approach has not been taken with regard to reading before, and rarely in any other area of educational research, although a similar approach was applied extremely successfully by Elizabeth Richardson in *The Teacher, The School and the Task of Management* (1973). The scarcity of such studies is not really surprising when one considers the frequent and sometimes justified distrust of researchers by teachers. It takes a great deal of time and dedication to build up the level of trust where teachers are prepared for a researcher to wander into their classrooms, often unannounced, and even greater trust is needed if teachers and Head-teachers are to be as forthcoming as they were in the Book Flood interviews; I cannot say how grateful I am to them, not least for the service they have done for education. The approach is certainly extremely time-consuming, and requires the researcher to be present in school in person on a very regular basis – in this case an average of one morning per week in each of the four schools. No one can get a true picture of a school, by making a formal visit two or three times per term. I can only say that the effort expended paid dividends.

The testing programme

Pre-testing

Towards the end of the autumn term 1976, the second-year children in the four schools were tested on several psychological measures to provide information on their general intelligence, reading skills, reading attitudes and self-esteem. This information constitutes a baseline from which the impact of the book flood can be assessed. The measures used were: Cattell's Culture Fair Test of 'g' (the general factor of intelligence); Schonell's Word Recognition Test, using the revised word order (Shearer 1975); the NFER Reading Test AD (sentence completion); the Edinburgh Reading Test Scale 3; the Sharples–Reid Self Assessment of Reading Interest; the Book Flood Reading Attitude Scale; the Askov Reading Inventory; the Coopersmith Self-esteem Inventory.

In addition to the measures of reading interest, form teachers were asked to give an assessment of reading interest for each child on a seven–point scale (from favourable to very unfavourable).

When choosing the reading tests, criteria adopted were that tests should have been constructed recently or recently restandardized, that they should have British norms, acceptable levels of validity and reliability and that they should be concerned with assessing general level of achievement in reading, rather than with diagnosing the possible sources of reading difficulty. They were also suitable for the age group under study, remaining appropriate over at least two testing sessions, and had different formats covering a variety of reading skills.

The three reading tests listed above were selected on the basis of these guidelines. It should be said, however, that only the Edinburgh Test meets all of these criteria. The Schonell is quite an old test, of course, but norms obtained in 1971 are available and it seemed advisable to include a word recognition test as measures of this type are widely used in schools (e.g. Burt and Vernon). The Reading Test AD is suitable for the age range 7·06 to 11·01, and could only be used for the initial testing. It was included because the Edinburgh Test was considered rather difficult for many children in the study, and it seemed likely that it would not discriminate very accurately among children at the lower end of the ability range. The NFER Test, however, would be found much easier by most children and would discriminate more accurately among the lower ability pupils, although it was considered a possibility that the test would

Table 1·1 *Matrix of Book Flood measures*

I TESTS Date:	Total sample Nov. 1976 April 1977	Approx. 10% Nov. 1977	Total sample April 1978	Previous fourth year	Total sample April 1979
General intelligence	Cattell's Culture Fair Test of 'g'				
Reading skills	1 Schonell (indiv.) 2 NFER AD 3 Edinburgh Scale 3	1 Schonell re-test	1 Schonell 3 Edinburgh Scale 3	4 NFER EH2	1 Schonell 3 Edinburgh Scale 3 4 NFER EH2
Reading attitudes	1 Sharples–Reid Book Flood Reading Attitude Scale 3 Askov Reading Inventory		1 Sharples–Reid 2 Book Flood Reading Attitude Scale		1 Sharples–Reid 2 Book Flood Reading Attitude Scale 3 Askov Reading Inventory

II READING RECORD FORMS	Given to total sample from November 1976 to June 1980.
III CASE STUDIES	Approx. 10% stratified, proportionate, random sample of 'avid' and 'reluctant' based on year Reading Record Form returns from the first year of the experiment.
IV SCHOOL PROFILES	Information collected *mainly* during January–June 1980.

show an upper ceiling effect, and so fail to discriminate accurately at the upper end of the ability range.

The use of several reading tests is justified on the grounds that while described as tests of reading ability, we cannot be sure that they in fact measure the same psychological functions or, if they do, whether they measure them equally well. It is clear that one test involves reading a list of words and another answering comprehension questions, and they may draw on different psychological processes. Equally, as we have seen, tests may vary in their efficiency with respect to a given sample. If a test is too hard for most children we would obtain a distorted picture of the degree of individual variation within the group. The same point applies if the test is too easy.

A further advantage derives from the use of more than one test. No matter how well designed and carefully administered a psychological test is, it is always fallible to a certain degree. The score obtained by an individual may not reflect his 'true' ability due to the operation of 'error' factors. Such factors may lead to his ability being overestimated, as when a comprehension exercise happens to be on a subject the testee finds particularly interesting, or is taken from a book he has read recently. Alternatively, it may underestimate his ability if he feels ill on the day of the test, or has had some kind of emotional upset.

A non-verbal measure of the general factor of intelligence was included to provide additional information about the psychological characteristics of individual children and the groups as a whole. It has been argued that working-class children tend to show a discrepancy between their general intelligence and academic performance in areas that require proficiency with language. If this is the case we might expect to find relatively higher levels of performance on the non-verbal test than is found on the highly language-based tests of reading. We may also find individuals who show particularly marked discrepancies between general intellectual ability and reading skill, and the Book Flood may influence such children differently from those who have similar reading skill but show no such discrepancy.

Re-testing on the Schonell Reading Test six months after pre-testing
During the first term in which books were arriving at the experimental schools, it became clear that such a quantity of new and varied books generated much interest and enthusiasm among the children. It was felt, therefore, that a small-scale assessment of reading performance several months after the Book Flood had

begun would be of some interest. A stratified random sample (by reading ability and sex) of children from each school was re-tested on the Schonell during the first week after Easter.

First post-test, November 1977
The first post-testing took place at the end of November 1977. The date of the testing was brought forward slightly in order to allow more time before the end of term to follow up absentees. The battery administered consisted of the Schonell Reading Test, Edinburgh Reading Test Scale 3, Book Flood Reading Attitude Scale, and Sharples–Reid Self Assessment of Reading Interest.

We also asked English teachers of third-year pupils to give us their assessment of each child's degree of reading interest on the same seven-point scale used by the second-year teachers. The first post-test battery thus contains a smaller number of measures than the pre-test battery. This reduction was one result in part of a lack of personnel for administering the tests, and of the fact that some of the measures used initially were no longer suitable for the third-year children. We also wished to minimize disruption in the schools and aimed to complete the testing in one morning rather than in two, as in the pre-test. Finally, the pre-test battery took a long time to mark and it seemed advisable to reduce the time spent in marking, making more time available for other activities.

The final post-test, March 1979
In the final testing that took place in spring 1979, all the initial tests were used with the exception of the NFER Test and the Cattell Culture Fair Test of 'g'. A few absentees were tested at the beginning of the summer term in order to obtain as complete results as possible.

Results of the testing are reported in Chapter 6. More detailed accounts of the tests follow.

Reading tests
In the present research, since our purpose was to obtain data on the reading abilities of children in the four schools, we required descriptive, standardized tests of reading abilities. The variety of possible kinds of these tests include word reading tests, sentence reading tests, continuous prose reading tests, sentence completion tests, comprehension tests based on continuous prose passages and 'Cloze' tests that consist of prose passages in which words are deleted at regular intervals – say every fifth or every tenth word – and the testee is required to fill in the blanks with suitable words.

We chose tests to cover the range currently available for the middle school age group and an account of each test follows.

Schonell's Graded Word Reading Test (5·0 to 15·0)

This test is the first in a battery of seven tests developed by Schonell between 1942 and 1955. Tests 1 to 4 assess reading attainment and tests 5 to 7 were designed to aid diagnosis of reading difficulties. The word reading test (R1) is widely used in Great Britain although reservations have been expressed about its usefulness in view of the limited area of reading attainment it covers and its age. The age of a test influences results in two ways: first, if reading standards have improved generally in the population since the test was first standardized then the test will give an optimistic assessment of the child's ability and, secondly, the relative difficulty of the words contained in the test may have changed. In order to meet these difficulties Shearer (1975) has recently carried out a large-scale restandardization of the word reading test on children aged 5 to 11 and has produced new norms and a revised order of words.

In the revised list, easy words in large print include: 'tree, egg, little, sit, milk, playing, train'; words of medium difficulty include: 'angel, nephew, appeared, university, gnome, ceiling, smoulder'; while examples of difficult words are: 'satirical, evangelical, tyrannical, belligerent, enigma, preferential and terrestrial'.

The test is administered on an individual basis and is very straightforward. The child reads the words printed on the card and is credited with all the words correctly read. Testing continues until ten consecutive words are failed. The test provides an assessment of the child's ability in terms of a reading age. A given reading age signifies that the child is able to read the same number of words as the average child at that age. Thus, if 9-year-old children (9·0) on average are able to read fifty-four words on the test, then a child of any age who reads fifty-four words is said to have a reading age of 9 (9·0). Reading ages (RA) can be converted to reading quotients (RQ) by dividing by the child's chronological age (CA) and multiplying by 100:

$$RQ = \frac{RA}{CA} \times 100$$

A quotient of this kind expresses the discrepancy between the child's reading age and chronological age. If a child is average for his age he will obtain a quotient of 100, and if he is above or below average he will score above or below 100 respectively.

NFER Reading Test AD (7·06–11·01)

This test, prepared by A. F. Watts, is a measure of reading comprehension since it involves choice of words to complete sentences. A few examples serve to show the range of ability it covers:

1 Come with me to the shops to buy some (fire, water, stone, sweets, motors)

12 Television cannot be enjoyed by people who are unable to (see, touch, smell, stand, sing)

23 John is an ambitious young musician who is determined to (exceed, intercede, proceed, recede, succeed)

35 The political dangers of monopoly seem to have been much (exasperated, excised, exaggerated, expropriated, expostulated)

The test was standardized by obtaining results for nearly 8000 boys and girls. A conversion table provides reading coefficients corresponding with scores and ages. In marking, a correction for guessing is obtained by discounting answers after five consecutive incorrect answers have been given, since this seems effectively to segregate chance scores due to guessing from scores measuring reading ability. Test re-test reliability (i.e. correlations between two sets of scores for the same children) lies between 0·91 and 0·97 for the four yearly age groups 7·06–8·01 to 10·06–11·01.

Edinburgh Reading Test Stage 3 (ages 10·0 to 12·6) (Moray House College of Education: J. F. McBride and P. C. McNaught)
This test is the third in a series of four (Stages 1 and 4 are yet to be produced) that will eventually cover the ages 7·0 to 16+. Each stage is in three parts: a practice test and the two parts of the test itself. The test is divided into five timed sub-tests that have been designed to assess different areas of reading competence. The Edinburgh Tests thus differ from earlier tests that have tended to be confined to limited areas of reading ability.

The test provides an over-all score for the whole test and separate scores for each sub-test. The over-all score can be converted into a standard score which indicates where the child stands in relation to children of the same age. Sub-test scores can be converted to standardized scores on the basis of the total standardization sample performance. This means that valid comparisons between children of different ages on individual sub-tests are not possible, but a useful profile of a child's 'strengths and weaknesses' can be obtained. The sub-tests are as follows:

A   *Reading for facts*
This sub-test presents four passages which the child is asked to read carefully. He is then asked to decide on the basis of his reading whether a number of statements are true or false or whether the passage does not say. This sub-test was 'designed to sample some

of the processes involved in the type of reading used in referring to books and other sources of information, for example, in connection with project work'.

B   *Comprehension of sequences*

Nine sections consisting of four or five sentences in the wrong order. The child has to decide on the correct sequence. 'This section is intended to assess the child's ability to comprehend sequences of events, as in narrative material, or to follow the steps in a piece of reasoning.' E.g. 'The four parts of this passage are in the wrong order. Write A B C D on the lines below to show the correct order:

A   The handle turned silently in her hand
B   As she entered the house the clock struck ten
C   Very cautiously she pushed the door open
D   Margot reached the front door of the old house

FIRST....... SECOND....... THIRD....... FOURTH.......'
  1   2   3   4

C   *Retention of main ideas*

The child is asked to read three passages carefully, and then, without referring back to them, answer a number of multiple choice questions about the passages. 'The intention of this sub-test is to assess the child's ability to learn through reading as he would be called upon to do in individual study.'

D   *Comprehension of points of view*

This sub-test consists of four passages that give statements made by several people about a given subject, or statements about their points of view, e.g. re Mr Allen, Professor Banks, Miss Cook and General Dodds: 'Mr Allen thought that too much money was being spent on space travel when there were many people on earth who had no homes and were undernourished' . . . 'Miss Cook said that people wanted to venture into space for the same reasons as they wanted to climb high mountains – for the thrill of it all'.

A number of specific statements follow and the testee is required to decide which person would have made that statement in a discussion, e.g. 'The space race is *not* sport, it is part of a serious struggle for power.' This sub-test is said to be designed to assess the extent to which the child is capable of building up clusters of ideas that represent different points of view on topics that could be classified as 'mildly controversial'.

E   *Vocabulary*

This sub-test requires the child to complete unfinished sentences with a suitable word, replace words in sentences with suitable synonyms, e.g. choice of a synonym is required in the example:

'The dog barked ferociously at the postman' (fearlessly/defiantly/ fiercely/frantically)

while suitable completion of a sentence is required in the example:

'The new boy in the office was often late and careless in his work. The manager decided to . . .
A   make his blood boil   B   face the music   C   burn his boats
D   haul him over the coals   E   lose his head'

Other items require children to replace words or phrases in a continuous prose passage with alternative phrases or words. The sub-test is intended to assess '. . . the extent of the child's familiarity with the meanings of words and phrases . . . and his ability to use the context to predict possible meanings of words and phrases and to select an appropriate meaning from several possibilities . . .'
Question 4 follows:

4   Six boys came over the hill half an hour early that afternoon, running hard, their heads down, their forearms working, their breath whistling. They swept by the house and cut across the stubble field into the barn. And then they stood self-consciously before the pony, and then they looked at Jody with eyes in which there was a new admiration and a new respect. Before today Jody had been a boy, dressed in overalls and a blue shirt – quieter than most, even suspected of being a little cowardly. And now he was different.

A   The best title for this passage is:
    Six Boys at Play / The Change in Jody's
    Fortunes / A Red Pony is Born / A Race over the
    Hill / Horses for Sale   A
B   What was it that the boys came to see:
    the barn / the house / the pony / Jody's sister / Jody's new
    clothes   B
C   Why do you think Jody is said to be different? Is it because:
    he couldn't walk / he didn't live in the town / he had become
    a singer / he had grown up / he owned a pony   C
D   Which words in the passage suggest that the six boys went
    regularly to Jody's home?
    They are .... D

E   What do you think 'their forearms working' means?
    making digging movements / moving like pistons / waving
    hello / swinging loosely / linked together   E

Reading attitudes

A number of instruments for determining the attitudes of children
towards reading have been developed in England and the United
States. In general the scales developed in the United States are
inappropriate for use in an English setting. All scales developed so
far are based on the assumption that attitudes towards reading can
be expressed as a score on a single dimension stretching from
'highly interested – to – highly uninterested'.

In the present study we employed a number of indicators of the
extent to which the children enjoyed the activity of reading:

1   The child's response to the 'reading' item on the 'Sharples–Reid'
questionnaire.
2   The child's score on the Askov Non-Verbal Reading Inventory.
3   Teachers' assessments of the child's interest in reading.
4   The amount of reading the child actually does in his leisure
time.
5   The child's score on a reading attitude scale devised by our
Research Assistant.

The following qualifications concerning these measures should
be noted:

1   The 'Sharples–Reid' scale simply mentions reading without
specifying a particular reading content or situation in which reading
is taking place. It is unclear therefore how the child is interpreting
this item. If the school has specific reading lessons the child may
dislike them or dislike reading aloud to the rest of the class but
enjoy the reading he is required to do for another subject or the
books he has at home. Depending on how the child interprets each
'reading' item, therefore, he may give it a favourable or unfavourable
rating. Two-month test–re-test reliability with samples of 30, 28
children proved to be only 0·56, 0·51, i.e. overall 0·53, perhaps
because children interpreted its items rather differently on the two
occasions, and because the section of the scale relating to reading
consists of only eight items.

2   The Askov Scale consists of a number of items in which pictorial
representations of a number of activities are paired and the child is
required to choose which of the two activities he would rather
engage in if given the choice, e.g. swimming or climbing on a
frame. Reading is one of the activities included and is usually

illustrated by a picture of a child sitting reading a book under a tree. The child's score is the number of times reading is chosen as the preferred activity. The Inventory involves a forced choice and does not recognize the possibility that both activities represented in a given pair may be equally liked or disliked. Thus a child who enjoys reading and reads a great deal, but who equally enjoys the other activities pictured in the test, may actually obtain a lower score than a child who is indifferent to reading but dislikes the other activities included in the Inventory. Again the meaning of the pictures is open to wide interpretation by the child and in particular there is no specification of what is being read. Its internal consistency reliability of 0·91 measured with a sample of sixty-six children is good. It is the validity of the test that is questionable.

3   Two problems are presented by the use of teachers' assessments. First, the assessment may be coloured by the teacher's general evaluation of the child's ability and behaviour and affected by his knowledge of the child's behaviour in other settings; secondly, there is no guarantee that different teachers are operating with the same standards. Behaviour that indicates high interest to one teacher may elicit a judgement of moderate interest from another depending upon the general levels of ability and interest in the class or school as a whole.

4   Inferring interest from amount of reading actually done would appear reasonable but there is always the danger that children are giving inaccurate information.

5   The Bradford Book Flood Reading Attitude Scale was devised by our first Research Assistant, Stephen Clift. Initially he used seventy-four statements that were rated by thirty-five judges for favourability to reading. Their judgements led to scale values, e.g.:

I do not like reading at all	1·22
I hardly ever read a book at home	3·06
Comics are the only thing I like to read	5·11
I like reading in school when I can choose my book	7·81
Reading gives me a lot of pleasure	9·90

A shortened scale of sixteen items representing the entire range of scale values from 1·1 to 11·0 was used finally after preliminary tests in one school. With samples of twenty-nine and twenty-eight children reliabilities of 0·80 and 0·59 were obtained on re-testing after two months. This gives an over-all test reliability of 0·70, which is modest.

The supply of books
The 'flood' of books was obtained for the two experimental
schools by a joint effort involving the National Book League and
Metropolitan Bradford Libraries. The National Book League
contacted publishers and sought donations. Purposely no guidance
was given to publishers as to which titles were required, but a blanket
request was made for a broad selection suitable for a middle school
(9 to 13 years). Fiction and non-fiction was requested and emphasis
was placed on the wide range of reading ability to be covered,
much wider than chronological age.

This first sounding of the publishers produced nearly 5600
books. Even without precise guidance the range of titles donated
was very wide in reading level, subject content and style of creative
writing. Most titles were in multiples so that the schools had an
equal number and at least one copy could be distributed to each
class in the appropriate year group. This first stage produced a
creditable basic collection to enhance the schools' existing book
resources. Any titles with inappropriate reading ages were
exchanged volume for volume with more appropriate titles from
the Libraries Division's stock. Over 400 volumes were exchanged.
Some publishers sent Bradford Libraries their catalogues so that a
selection of relevant stock could be made. This facility allowed the
basic stock to be balanced out so that areas of interest and ability
not covered could be corrected.

All books received were handled by Bradford Libraries: non-
fiction was classified by the first three places of eighteenth-edition
of Dewey. The top edges of the pages were colour coded to
distinguish between the schools. A brief stock card record was
made out for each title which included quantities and distribution
details. For the initial stages of the project a student from Ilkley
College assisted by classifying fiction by genre as part of research
into this topic he was undertaking quite independently of the
'flood'.

The next stage in the processing before the books were sent to
the experimental schools was made possible through the generosity
of certain library suppliers. The library sent all the books to the
suppliers so that date labels could be attached, a book card typed,
and a plastic sleeve fitted wherever possible to increase durability of
the binding and cover.

All these processes took time and parallel with it an appeal was
launched by the library for additional shelving to be donated to
accommodate the books in the schools. Shelves were obtained, but
the framework to fit them into had to be specially made. This
caused a slight delay but eventually produced over thirty extra bays

of shelving for class-rooms. In addition some moulded plastic display stands were donated.

Two more stages remained in the process of obtaining books. Once the initial influx of books had been assimilated by the schools a party of teachers from each was taken by Bradford Libraries to a local library supplier and the Yorkshire Joint Library Services School Library Book Exhibition Collection at Wakefield. They selected 1150 books they considered necessary to fill gaps in their stock.

The final stage was a further appeal by the National Book League to publishers half-way through the project for more books to 'top up' the flooded schools; in response, publishers generously donated another 450 volumes. In addition, Bradford Libraries provided another opportunity for the teachers to buy specifically to fill gaps.

At the conclusion of the experiment the National Book League again appealed to publishers for more books, this time to repay the control schools for their patience in being guinea pigs during the experiment but without having the advantage of a large quantity of books. In addition to these donations the remaining 'flood' books in the experimental schools were redistributed with the paired control schools.

2 The Schools

When my eyes stop staring at the stars, so long as my feet are on the ground . . . then it is time for me to retire (headmaster to his staff).

Introduction

The information for this chapter was gathered in the following ways: the details about school organization during the first year of the experiment, and about second-year teachers was provided by Dr Stephen Clift who was a researcher with the experiment at that time; part of the data on the headmasters was provided by Dr Gajendra Verma (Postgraduate School of Research in Education, University of Bradford), who interviewed every headmaster at the beginning of the experiment and jointly with me interviewed each one again in autumn 1978. These two sets of interviews were taped.

I collected the remainder of the information myself between September 1978 and June 1979 as follows:

1 I interviewed each of the case study children individually in school.
2 I talked with groups of children in each school about their reading habits.
3 I interviewed each headmaster just before the end of the experiment.
4 I interviewed each head of English, where they existed, or fourth-year staff involved in the teaching of English, as well as every teacher responsible for the school library.

Discussions with case study children and with their parents were fully transcribed, while discussions with school staff were précised because of shortage of clerical assistance for such a time-consuming task.

In addition to this fairly normal method of data collection, I spent a good deal of time in every school including, on average, one day a week in each from September 1978 until June 1979 as a participant observer. I was often in staff-rooms during breaks and lunch-hours and sometimes arrived to sit in on lessons unexpectedly.

Obviously it would be totally impossible for teachers to carry on as though there were no one there, but I believe we came as close to that state as is possible in this type of research. This was partly because it would have been difficult for teachers to keep up a performance, particularly outside the class-room, for three years; partly because I had regular discussions with pupils as well as teachers; and partly because they knew that my own teaching experience gave me insight into the practical difficulties that many of them had to face.

The advantage of the small scale of the experiment was that it made getting to know the staff and many of the pupils a realistic possibility, but inevitably the interpretation of the findings presented in this chapter is my own subjective interpretation, and should be considered in conjunction with the findings presented in other chapters. The other disadvantage, in addition to subjectivity, of a small-scale study is that one feels loath to make criticisms of people who have such a difficult job and who have offered so much in terms of time; on the other hand, I believe I know the headteachers and teachers well enough to feel sure that they would be the first to criticize *me* if I did not draw conclusions and make recommendations.

Concerning all four schools, it should be stated at this point that we were not dealing with a cross-section of Bradford middle school children, since most of the pupils were from working-class families, with perhaps a few from higher up the social scale. It was not possible to collect sociological data on these families in any detail without attracting undue attention to the experiment, but it was possible to collect sufficient information for our purposes by visiting 10 per cent of the homes during case studies, and by talking to LEA officials, headteachers and teachers. Both of the control schools are designated SPA schools.

The outer city schools
Both of the outer city schools in the experiment began their middle school reorganization in 1971. Originally, they had been two-form entry junior schools, before becoming two-form entry middle schools, by stages, as follows:

Until July 1971 the ages of the pupils were 7–11.
From September 1971 to July 1972 the ages of the pupils were 8–12.
From September 1972 onwards the ages of the pupils were 9–13.

Gradually, from September 1978, the schools took in additional children, until they became full three-form entry middle schools in

1976, at the start of the Book Flood Experiment. Both schools are situated about 4 miles outside the centre of Bradford in 'estate–desert' country where the housing consists mainly of council houses and council flats, but also includes a few privately owned homes.

The outer city experimental school

The school was built in 1955, fractionally after the occupation of the council estate, on the edge of which it is situated and which it was built to service; 93 per cent of the pupils live on this estate, the rest coming from private housing. The head said he thought that the school would benefit from a broader catchment area and a less homogeneous intake, particularly in terms of parental attitude.

At the beginning of the experiment there were only two children in the school who belonged to ethnic minority groups, whereas now the school has about thirty such children arriving each year – mostly second-generation Asian immigrants. The head looks upon these children as British, which they are; however, in order to do justice to their language development, he would like to be able to limit the intake of these children to between 10–15 per cent of the school population.

School and class libraries. While school and class libraries will be referred to at various points throughout this chapter, it is useful at this stage to draw together a few points about their history, location in the school building, and the contents of the libraries.

Since the junior school prior to middle school reorganization had class libraries, but no provision for a school library, the head decided that the *middle* school should have a central resource area, which would be best incorporated in an extension. This was built, at the front of the school, at the time of reorganization, in order to create both extra space and an entrance for the middle school separate from the entrance to the first school.

The school library is an attractive room with fish tanks and plants, easy chairs, and octagonal tables with upright chairs set in areas divided by bookcases. Unfortunately, however, the room serves the additional purpose of office for the school secretary, complete with telephone and typewriter; it can be rather cold and draughty because of its open-plan connection with the entrance; and it can be noisy, again because of open-plan connections – first with the dining-hall, which is adjacent to the library, and, secondly with the assembly hall, which is regularly used for PE and indoor games. Nevertheless, the room is aesthetically pleasing and quite comfortable, as well as being in a central position and easily accessible.

Table 2·1 gives a breakdown of the categories and approximate number of books actually available on the shelves in this school in spring 1979. The figures were arrived at by a team of people under the direction of Mr R. Wilkes (Education and Young People's Services, Bradford Central Library) during a school holiday. Obviously, some books were out on loan, but we believe that the figures give a realistic indication of the number of books usually available to the children, and of their location. It is noticeable that the school library contained roughly equal proportions of fiction and non-fiction. The Book Flood books were put into class libraries so that the figures for class libraries are inclusive of the Book Flood books, of which 63·7 per cent were fiction and 36·3 per cent non-fiction. A colour coding system is used for the school library as the Dewey system was thought to be unnecessarily complicated; easier readers are separated from the rest of the stock. In addition to books, the school library also houses audio-visual equipment, including facilities for recording both radio and television programmes, and a range of visual aids, for all of which the head of English is responsible.

Table 2·1   Outer city experimental school: count o' school and class library books

School library		%	Class library		%
Fiction	1521	49	Fiction	4013	61
Non-fiction	1586	51	Non-fiction	1729	27
	——		Reading scheme	789	12
	3107			——	
	——			6531	

(Approx. 4450 Book Flood books)

Prior to the Book Flood, the head had thought that a school library providing a centralized stock of books was preferable to a series of class libraries (although reading schemes and remedial readers were kept in a class-room). This was partly because a wider and greater choice of books was thus available to *all* the children in the school, and partly because of the organizational difficulties concomitant with making books available for borrowing from different areas in the school. However, by the end of the Book Flood, although perhaps not totally convinced that change was desirable, the head felt that it would be churlish to return to the previous system.

The Book Flood books began to arrive at the beginning of 1977, with most of the remainder coming fairly rapidly during the following months, so that the 10+ children were able to read a large number of them in that year and could feel that their class-rooms were 'flooded' with books. A few books had to be 'put by' until the children were older and some, which were felt to be totally unsuitable in terms of difficulty, were exchanged. In addition, a small amount of money was made available for filling any gaps that teachers felt were glaringly obvious, and so that 'specialist' teachers could buy a few books, e.g. on art, cookery, science, music, etc. While the result was an unsatisfactory mixture of publishers' donations and a few books chosen by teachers, many teachers admitted that, without lengthy training, they would have been *unable* to choose 4500 suitable books by themselves. Unfortunately, quite a lot of the books, and not only the easy ones, were retained in the second-year class-rooms after the Book Flood children had moved up the school, and yet more were subsequently retained in third-year class-rooms, so that there were fewer books available in the fourth-year class-rooms than would have been desirable.

In the class-rooms the books were kept on open bookshelves that were easily accessible. However, they were rarely deliberately displayed, although there were exceptional cases of teachers who did take advantage of display techniques, which seems to be particularly necessary when dealing with thin paperbacks. The head was probably aware of this deficiency as, in the first year of the experiment, he had invited a senior adviser in 'to talk to the whole staff about art in the middle school and display because our standard of display isn't quite up to scratch – again it is because we have so many new members of staff'.

In the final year of the experiment, Bradford Libraries offered each fourth-year teacher in the experimental schools a swivel stand for display purposes and, in this school, in two classes out of three, they were accepted and used enthusiastically.

The school bookshop. This was begun by the head of English during the final year of the experiment. It opens in a fourth-year class-room on a Friday lunch-time; books are attractively displayed according to author or subject matter, with accompanying posters around the walls.

The organization of English teaching. The head of English decides on the broad outline of English curriculum in consultation with the headteacher, after which the head of English discusses the curriculum with the class teachers, each of whom is responsible for teaching English to his or her own class; some teachers expressed the wish for more detailed guidance than they were given, but most seemed reasonably satisfied with the arrangement.

Children are not streamed as the head believes that streaming 'is not acceptable in this day and age'; he also sees streaming as 'stagnant' because both pupils and teachers become 'labelled'. However, children are 'set' for maths. The fact that English is taught throughout the school by class teachers may be in part a reflection of the junior school origin of this particular middle school. However, children are extracted for remedial work (see following section); in addition, the head of English sometimes takes a group of the most able children and sometimes a group of the least able, for perhaps half a term at a time, for part of their English work, so that most of the children in the school receive the benefit of his expertise at some time in their career, albeit in small doses.

Unfortunately, this system did not operate as effectively as it should have done for a period from about the end of May 1978 until the end of June 1979 (i.e. for more than an entire academic year and including the whole of the final year of the experiment). During that time the head of English became acting deputy head because the deputy head was involved in a serious car accident and was unable to resume his duties effectively before September 1979. This is the kind of incalculable and unpredictable event that happens in most schools at some time or another and which teachers, and researchers, have to take in their stride. Of course, we shall never know how this affected the Book Flood children in the final year of the experiment. Perhaps it should be stated at this point that one group of 12+ children in the final year of the experiment was doubly deprived, because their usual teacher was away ill for half a term, from January 1979, so that their usual programme of English lessons was disrupted (I do not intend to diminish the efforts of the temporary teacher).

It is the policy of the head of English to suggest an author for class reading in each year group. For the Book Flood children in the first year of the experiment, the author was Roald Dahl, in the second year Alan Garner, and in the third year Henry Treece (the 'Viking' books). The head is aware that some of the teachers who are neither 'all-round' junior trained teachers nor English 'specialists' feel a bit lost teaching English at all. He realizes that to some extent, to use his own words, the middle school teacher is 'Jack of all trades, master of none', yet he dislikes the idea of specialists teaching nothing but their own subject. At the same time, he is well aware that some teachers take the attitude that 'reading should have been dealt with at junior school' and possibly resent teaching the subject. Unfortunately, there are teachers at the upper end of the school who frankly would prefer *not* to teach English. My contention is that English cannot be well taught by a person who is lacking in enthusiasm, and that it is a pity to put teachers who have no interest at all in children's literature or the English language into a situation where they are expected to convey their non-existent enthusiasm, and usually minimal knowledge, to their pupils. To compound the problem, many children come to a reluctant English teacher at a stage when they are in danger of becoming reluctant readers and are, therefore, particularly in need of sensitive and informed help with book choice.

Assessment of reading and remedial provision. At the time of the experiment, the first- and second-year children were given the Burt Graded Word Reading Test once a term, while the third- and fourth-year pupils were given the Vernon Graded Reading Test once a term. The Book Flood children were tested with the Burt Test in September 1976 (see Table 2·2). Children with obtained reading ages of 8 years 6 months or less were placed on remedial reading schemes. A great deal of emphasis was placed upon attempting to ensure that children were able to read with competence and understanding before they left the middle school (but this applies to all four schools). The head did not take a *laissez-faire* attitude if the children came up from the first school without the mechanics of reading, or without the ability to read with understanding. He saw it as an important part of the job of the middle school, certainly in the first two years, to continue this work, but this attitude concerned reading skills rather than reading interest and I doubt whether the two can often be separated. Also, I think we should ask ourselves to what extent this expressed attitude is consistent with the policy of having some teachers, with neither training nor interest in the subject, teaching English, and, therefore, responsible for the continuing development of pupils' reading skills and interests at the upper end of the school.

There was no specialist teacher for remedial English at the time of the experiment; this work was the responsibility of the head of English and the 'school librarian' (not an English specialist), who kept the remedial reading schemes in her class-room, where books were graded according to reading age. The head said remedial

English was taught on the basis of 'I'm here to help you', not 'You're the dregs and I haven't much option but to teach you'. This is why he did not stream or set the children for English but used the extraction system which is possibly temporary or reversible.

Table 2·2   Outer city experimental school: results of school-administered reading tests – September 1976

	(Burt Word Reading Test)							
Reading age	6	7	8	9	10	11	12	13
Boys	2	3	4	7	8	4	11	0
Girls	1	1	6	7	4	4	15	0
Total	3	4	10	14	12	8	26	0

N = 77.
Missing values = 3.
> *Note:* The missing values figure is based on the number of children in the second year at the beginning of September 1976.

Since I took over responsibility for the experiment in summer 1978, I found that I did not have time to interview second- and third-year class teachers in depth, nor to get to know them properly; in-depth interviews of staff had not been part of the experiment before that time. For this reason, I am able to write in detail only about headmasters, 'school librarians', fourth-year class teachers, and heads of English where they existed. The demands of case studies of children, computer work on the continuing reading records, and of the testing programme, made further staff interviews impossible. However, I shall refer to second- and third-year staff in less detail throughout the chapter.

The headmaster. The head became deputy head of the school in 1957 and head in 1966. Several times he expressed the view that he sees no great advantage in children taking up reading as a hobby; he is more interested in children leaving the school with the ability to read with understanding so that they can cope with the demands of the upper school and of the 'world outside' after school. So far as 'avid' readers are concerned, the head revealed the suspicion that they might be the less active, less 'sporty' children who had turned to reading instead and who might be missing out on other aspects of life.

He is particularly aware of the dangers of labelling or categorizing either pupils or teachers, whether it be as less-able pupils, teachers of less-able pupils, or as immigrants, for he realizes the debilitating effects of these categories. He is also aware that labelling a child as less able can be seen by that child, and the child's teacher, as a description of an immutable fact, and that teachers unwillingly labelled as teachers of the less-able 'C' stream can themselves partly cause the continuance of the lesser ability. However he is aware that some of the time the least, and most, able pupils need a different approach, as do children for whom English is their second language. He tries, therefore, to make available to these children some of the *best* of his staff, but not *all* the time, and to ensure that the children believe that the aim is to help, not contain, them.

Similarly, he is reluctant to label the children's homes in terms of social class; he sees the 'bad' homes as ones where the parental attitude is one of non-involvement in the child's development; he sees some homes as being 'bad in terms of books, interest, attitude, parents not taking the right attitude towards their children, allowing them to do as they want, letting them choose what they want, allowing them to go where they like. At night they don't construct anything for them. During the week-end some of them don't construct anything for them!' He tries not to label children as belonging to broken homes (some of his best pupils do!), but believes that about 50 per cent of his pupils come from homes where parents have either remarried, or are divorced or separated and have remained single-parent families.

The head organizes about three formal staff meetings per term, but, since the school is small (332 pupils at the beginning of the experiment), informal staff meetings are readily organized should they be necessary.

During the experiment, he timetabled himself to teach two half days and one whole day per week but felt this to be an unsatisfactory situation because, if there were some point to be dealt with at local education authority level or if a parent came in urgently, he had to leave his class.

Finally, when asked to outline his philosophy of education, he replied:

> The philosophy of education here is, first of all, to set up an environment which cares for the children; to have working in it teachers who are committed to all the children in the school; to reinforce what success children have had with further success; serving these children in a way that *challenges* the estate's attitude – not to deride them but to offer something else – to offer a kind of loving-kindness to children so that they grow up in an atmosphere where people are interested in them, where people will do their utmost to help them, where people set standards of the highest so that children can achieve them: politeness,

consideration and all other human qualities, moral qualities, spiritual qualities that are necessary if a community is to thrive at its best level.

The head of English. The head of English took English and history to 'A' level and specialized in English at college, reading contemporary political sociology as a subsidiary subject. He described the college course as an extension of the 'A' level syllabus, with no mention of children's literature. The post held at the present school is Scale 2 with English as his main subject and some environmental studies.

He draws up the English syllabus, which, for fourth-years, consists of two lessons for language, two for creative work and two for literature, literature including the prescribed class reader. He believes in 'a positive sales campaign', especially of literature beyond the children's ordinary experience.

His knowledge of children's books began when he took up his present post and realized the children's need for advice on book choice; and he has also learnt a good deal by reading to his own children at home. He says that he usually manages to read about three children's books a week.

As far as the respective advantages of school and class libraries are concerned, he appreciates the convenience of a centralized stock, but also welcomes the accessibility of book stocks in class-rooms because he believes it important for children to be able to change their books with the minimum of fuss in a less daunting situation than that presented by a school or public library. He considers that both have their complementary roles to fulfil.

He claims that he *has* noticed an increased interest in books, among both staff and pupils, since the Book Flood, but feels that it would have had more impact had an entire, possibly changing, stock of 4500 books remained with the Book Flood children throughout the experiment.

Here we have a teacher with a firm grounding in English language and literature, as well as with an acquired knowledge of children's literature, appointed with responsibility for English, but in practice playing a multiplicity of roles – particularly in the final year of the experiment, when he was acting deputy head, as well as head of English, with responsibility for audio-visual equipment and some remedial English; in addition, he took on the responsibility of initiating the school bookshop! Possibly, with the help of a remedial specialist, and with the deputy head present, the picture would have looked different.

The 'school librarian'. I put this title in inverted commas advisedly since the teacher concerned was also a class teacher, with most of the responsibility for remedial English.

This teacher did Biology, English and Art to 'A' level, followed by a teacher-training course in main biology. Maths and English were compulsory subsidiary subjects and, in addition, she chose art, craft and music from a list of optional subsidiary subjects. Her first post was at the present school, where she was appointed in 1969 when it was still a primary school, as a fourth-year junior teacher to 11-year-olds. After reorganization she taught throughout the school for a couple of years before becoming a first-year class teacher.

When the previous 'school librarian' left in 1974, she was given responsibility for the school library because she had a scaled post and, I suspect, because she is conscientious and energetic in her work; nevertheless, she was 'petrified', feeling totally unprepared and inadequate. I should add that the library is always attractive and well-organized and the accession register up to date.

Although she is not an avid reader and does not read a great deal of children's literature, she does read during school holidays and takes the time to visit book exhibitions and book suppliers in her own time during the vacations. She believes that she is *now* quite well informed about children's books although she finds it totally impossible to keep up to date with the fiction and needs help in finding short-cuts.

She sees the coexistence of school and class libraries as basically an organizational problem that they have solved by having each class teacher keep the tickets for borrowing from anywhere in the school by children in his/her class.

The amount of money available for school library books was adequate a few years ago but is no longer because of the effects of inflation.

She stressed the importance of making children comfortable when they read. She has noticed how much better they concentrate in the armchairs in the school library than when sitting at their desks. She tries not to notice the positions the children get into when reading in class provided they are quiet and genuinely engrossed! This observation is confirmed by the children's comments made during case study interviews.

This teacher left the school at the end of the experiment as her husband was moving to a job out of the area.

Fourth-year class teachers. **A** Teacher A did English, history and geography to 'A' level, followed by a course in geography with prehistory at a college of education, where the basic English course included a 'few lectures' on the teaching of reading. However, an awareness of the importance of a school library and resource centre, adequately staffed, developed during teaching practice, when this teacher was able to compare schools with and without this facility. No instruction whatsoever was given about children's books and their use during the initial training period. However, the teacher has a love of books that developed as a child; there were plenty of books both in the parental home and, subsequently, in the marital home. This was fortunate, but this teacher nevertheless expressed the view that neither the study of literature to 'A' level nor personal reading had given her sufficient knowledge of suitable books for today's middle school pupils.

The present post as fourth-year general teacher was this teacher's first appointment. A double lesson each week was set aside for the study of the Henry Treece class reader, when she usually read aloud one chapter and a child read another; discussion of vocabulary and content also took place at this time. This teacher did not believe in setting aside a special time for pupils' personal silent reading, but instead preferred it if children read voluntarily when they had finished a piece of work; this was a practical possibility for all but the slowest workers, since the children spent a good deal of time in their own class-room. She encouraged them to discuss their reading with her and the other pupils and to display the books that they had really enjoyed. This teacher had a particular flair for display of all kinds.

On the subject of school and class libraries, she wished that the school library could be more 'fully available', and believed that difficulties arose because it was also used as an office and because it was a long way from the class-rooms: children were therefore tempted to get into mischief if they went alone. She felt that class library books, on the other hand, were more readily available and accessible with the result that children were *coming into contact with books more than ever before* and were not dependent for reading material on bringing school library books to lessons; nor were they limited to changing them, at the most, once a week.

B Teacher B spent some time as a professional musician before deciding to go into teaching as a music specialist, offering maths as a subsidiary subject. The teacher training course that he did was mainly in music and education, but included minor components of history, geography, science, English and maths. English was taught for half a day a week for a year; the course included studies of and discussions about children's books, for example Rosemary Sutcliffe's *Warrior Scarlet* and Leon Garfield's *Black Jack*, which may have been a somewhat conservative choice but at least a deliberate attempt was made to familiarize the prospective teachers with literature suitable for the age group that they were intending to teach.

This teacher enjoys teaching *creative* English in particular and, together with Teacher A, developed the idea of *The Wardrobe*, based loosely on the beginning of C. S. Lewis's *The Lion, the Witch and the Wardrobe*. Children were given the beginning of the first chapter of a story which they were expected to complete; if they needed them, they could also have the beginning of subsequent chapters. This activity tended to take up two periods a week.

Although this teacher had gained some knowledge of children's books by reading to his own children at home, he freely confessed to a frequent inability to recommend an appropriate book, a need for advice from an expert, and a need for continual updating of his knowledge of children's books. He encouraged discussions about books, and this was particularly fruitful as the class included a group of four really 'avid' readers who always contributed energetically to the talks; the teacher felt that the discussions were of benefit to both the less-able readers and to himself.

He also set aside a double period for the class reader, but tended to read one chapter aloud himself after which the pupils would read two chapters silently.

The reader will realize that little time was left for pursuit of individual reading interest, a fact that was corroborated by the pupils.

The teacher made a point of stressing how important he believed it to be to encourage children to read something in school in free moments, even if it were a comic or the sports page of a newspaper; he believed that teachers should not despise this kind of reading, but should accept it and lead children on from there – for instance from comics to *Asterix* or from the sports page to *Goals in the Air*.

C   Teacher C did French, Latin and geography to 'A' level followed by a degree in French and geography. A *small* amount of English was included in the Dip.Ed. course, but 'nothing was discussed in any depth'. One lecture was set aside for school librarianship. This teacher freely expressed a lack of interest in the English language and in children's books. His intention had been to teach French as a specialist subject, offering maths as a subsidiary topic; he had not expected to teach English at all. He believed that the pupils were fully aware of his lack of interest in books, which he realized was a disadvantage since it resulted in an inability to recommend books, as well as an inability to make an informed contribution to any discussion about books, which his 'avid' readers in particular looked forward to.

While he appreciated the advantages of a class library, this teacher believed that the *choice* of books in the class library was restrictive – *more* books and a *changing* supply were needed, because keen readers exhausted the stock of Book Flood books and were borrowing instead from the school library – a point confirmed by pupils and other teachers.

Had staffing permitted, this teacher would have preferred not to teach English at all, especially not to the reluctant reader. It should be stated that this teacher had a great deal to offer to the pupils in terms of verbal skills; the quality of dialogue that he had with them was obviously advantageous in itself.

These profiles should illustrate the problems that can arise when class teachers are almost totally responsible for the teaching of English at the upper end of the middle school, as they are usually secondary-trained teachers who wish to specialize in one, or possibly two, subjects. This is a situation that perhaps will be remedied when middle schools are better established.

The problem is that middle schools at present contain a mixture of junior-trained and senior-trained teachers, rather than staff specifically trained for the middle school. There is also a degree of confusion about whether children should be taught entirely, or partly, by subject 'specialists' at the upper end of the school. This is an area with which heads need guidance, as the quality of English teaching for 11- to 13-year-olds in this sample of schools seemed to be very much a 'hit-and-miss' affair.

Final discussion. At the end of the experiment, in June 1979, all the teachers who had been involved were invited to meet together, either at school or in my home, to say what *they* believed had been the effect of the Book Flood.

The following main points were made:

1 The teachers agreed that the 'children's enthusiasm' had 'exhausted the supply' of Book Flood books. Initially, when children saw all the new books they 'couldn't wait to read them'; those who were able had quickly exhausted the supply and returned to the school library. However, there was a general desire among staff and pupils to continue the idea in principle – if possible with a larger and more varied supply of books and with greater movement of books between class-rooms.

2 The teachers expressed the view that the non-reader or poorer reader had not been well catered for by the Book Flood. However,

these children had probably become more familiar with the handling of books, and had improved their general knowledge by browsing through the non-fiction books; they were unlikely to have improved their reading ability. Children in the middle band of reading ability, who possibly did not have a great many books at home, were the most likely to have benefited. Teachers noticed that while less-able children were often attracted by the *covers* of paperback books, they were usually disappointed to find that they could not cope with the small print inside.

3 The teachers believed that the Book Flood, and more particularly the Reading Record Form, had encouraged children to make an effort to read a book from cover to cover; also, children's browsing and book choosing skills had improved. Teachers had noticed children reading silently in spare moments without prompting and with greater concentration since the Book Flood, as well as exhibiting eagerness to discuss both the class reader and individual reading books.

4 Most teachers felt that they had not been adequately prepared for recommending authors and titles to children, and that the sudden influx of 5000 books had therefore put them at a disadvantage. They expressed a wish for more detailed advice, and discussed the possibility of apportioning the responsibility for keeping up to date with different areas of children's literature, both within the school, as well as with teachers in other schools and librarians via news-sheets, etc. Nevertheless, they conceded that their knowledge of children's books had improved to some extent during the course of the Book Flood; for instance, one teacher said that he had become familiar with a few authors, whereas he had previously known none; others said that certain authors in their class-rooms had been brought to their attention by children.

5 All the teachers had found that children were keener to borrow books if they did not have to go down to the school library; class-room libraries were agreed to be more convenient, less formal and closer to the circumstances that might prevail for children fortunate enough to have a generous supply of books at home. They expressed the view that the school library had an important, but different, role to fulfil, in providing a centralized stock of books that was available to the whole school on a more formal basis.

6 Finally, the teachers thought that their teaching practice had changed in that they were now more likely to give children *time* for selecting and changing books, and that this was facilitated by the existence of a class library. They were also more aware of the need for effective display of books and book-related materials.

The outer city control school
The school (which was built as an open-air school in 1951), like its matched experimental school, serves an estate on the edge of which it is situated. Most of the houses on the estate are council property (about 80 per cent), but there is a smaller number of private dwellings (about 20 per cent). About 75 per cent of the pupils come from this estate, the remainder coming from council or private homes elsewhere within the catchment area. On this estate, as on that served by the matched experimental school, the houses on the main road at the edge of the estate are generally the best kept, whereas those in the heart of the estate *tend* to be more neglected, although obviously there are exceptions. This school, unlike its matched experimental school, is a SPA school; however, both are middle schools, which originally developed from junior schools.

The school had only a small number of ethnic minority children at the time of the experiment; there were thirteen in the year group with which we are concerned.

School and class libraries. At the time when the school was a junior school and the present headmaster came as head in 1965, there had been no provision for a school library; the head decided to convert the medical room into a library, but he did not actually open it until three years later when he had gathered together enough books for them to make an impact and not look lost on the shelves. When the school first became a middle school, it was still two-form entry, but in 1976 when it became a full three-form entry middle school, the head decided that he needed to use the library room, which is about the right size for half a class, for remedial and other extraction groups. Therefore he decided to leave the fiction stock in that room as children would still be able to borrow books from it at lunch-time. The non-fiction stock, remedial books and reading scheme material, however, had to be housed elsewhere so that it would be available for use during lessons. The remedial books and reading schemes were placed in class libraries, where fiction was also supplied (see Table 2·3); the non-fiction/reference books were housed in the area adjacent to the assembly/PE hall. The reference library is pleasant, with some easy chairs, small areas created by the arrangement of bookshelves, small tables, plants, etc., but because of the open-plan nature of the area, children using the library are constantly distracted: classes need to walk along the passage between the library area and assembly hall in order to reach the fiction library or dining-hall, both of which are sometimes used as class-rooms; they also need to walk past to go to the hall for PE or singing, both of which can be clearly heard in the reference library.

Libraries in both outer city schools are very pleasant but neither cosy nor peaceful, despite every effort to make them so, because they are open, draughty and often noisy, a disadvantage of many modern buildings. It is an attitude that seems to carry over to the class-room furniture, where the use of tables, often without shelves for trays, rather than the old-fashioned desks which provided each child with a private storage place, restricts the use of personal reading material. I must stress that, in both schools, the heads have made the best of the available space in terms of library provision and display area. The researcher is well aware of the discomfort and distraction that is possible in these open-plan areas, since a good deal of the individual testing and interviews with children had to take place there. Perhaps, like a theatre, a school library can only be a library and cannot either be used as something else at other times or share a space with rooms built for other purposes.

Table 2·3   Outer city control school: count of school and class library books

School library			Class library		
	%	%			%
Fiction	813 (27)	21	Fiction	3126	54
Non-fiction	2222 (73)	58	Non-fiction	403	7
Reading scheme	816	21	Reading scheme	2284	39
	3851			5813	

The fiction library is staffed by pupils; the reference library is manned four lunch-times a week by members of the teaching staff. A colour coding system is used for the non-fiction books as Dewey is considered to be too complicated. There are no *timetabled* library periods, although staff may send individual children or small groups down to use the library during lessons. Apart from occasional exceptions, only fiction books may be borrowed. Material other than books, such as audio-visual equipment, is not housed in the library.

It has been the policy, at least under the current headship, for the class-rooms to contain bookshelves of fiction, including reading scheme material. On this point the two outer city schools differ; they also differ in that in the control school class library books are rarely taken home, although the Book Flood could have encouraged teachers to allow children to take books home from the experimental school because there were so many books and they were free! Certainly, it was not the norm for children from the control school to take class library books home; they were not actively encouraged to do so because of the danger of loss or damage.

As far as provision for class libraries is concerned, the older stock is mainly with the first- and second-year children, as it remains from junior school days; whereas at the time of middle school reorganization, third- and fourth-year children, in addition to the inheritance of books from the lower end of the erstwhile secondary school, were allowed additional money for new books. Subsequently, when the school became three-form entry, additional class library books were bought to cater for the extra classes, a greater proportion of these books being allocated to the top 'G' stream pupils, simply because there were few books already in school that were suitable for them. However, now that the middle school is established, differences in book supply have been eliminated as far as possible as the head is careful to allocate an equal amount of money for each class library. Marginal differences are bound to persist to some extent, though, for the books in the 'G' class-rooms *tend* to last longer and look attractive longer; because they are better cared for the stock in these classes is less likely to be depleted.

The books in the class-rooms are well organized, being divided into fiction, non-fiction, and reading scheme material, all with sub-divisions. The large proportion of reading scheme material is probably necessary here because although the children in the 'G' stream generally have reading ages at or above their chronological ages, the reading ages of about 75 per cent of the children in the 'F' and 'C' streams are below their chronological ages. The 'school librarian' claims that one result of having a good stock of fiction in class-rooms is that only about 25 per cent of pupils ever use the school fiction library.

School bookshop. There is no school bookshop in this school.

Organization of English teaching. On entry to the middle school children are put into four mixed-ability sets, as far as possible with friends from first schools. Partial streaming begins in the children's second year and continues throughout the school; a top 'G' stream and parallel 'F' and 'C' streams are created on the basis of teacher knowledge of the pupils during their first year at the middle school, continuous assessment, VRQ, and attitude to school work; reading ages are taken into consideration in borderline cases. There is some mobility between streams on the basis of ongoing assessments of the children. Since streaming is based, in part, on reading ages that are not absolute or unvarying scores, one wonders to what extent the lack of mobility between streams is the result of labelling and expectations. The effect of such almost permanent labelling on both staff and pupils might well be demoralizing; *perhaps* the effect of withdrawal for remedial work, *instead* of streaming, is less crippling as it is more readily reversible, a temporary measure the duration of which is dependent upon effort and improvement, and which need not cross subject barriers.

Wherever possible, younger children are timetabled to do some English, including reading, every day, on the principle that 'a little and often' will bring success; older pupils, on the other hand, are timetabled for double periods of English wherever possible, as the head believes that they need time to become involved in creative work or reading, and that generally they have a longer concentration span. Also, where possible, pupils are kept in class bases, so that some books are readily available to them. This is a comparable situation to that in the matched experimental school, except that without the Book Flood there would not have been class libraries in the experimental school at all.

Most of the teachers in the outer city control school set aside regular times for children to read aloud, for the teacher to read to the children and, less frequently, for children to read to themselves; the latter activity was most likely to occur in the 'G' stream class-rooms. Unfortunately, children in 'F' and 'C' streams, who were less likely to be familiar with books than 'G' stream children, generally less able as readers and with shorter concentration spans, were presented with books which, although not unsuitable, were *unappealing* and did not include much *modern* fiction. The problem was compounded by the lack of teaching staff with detailed knowledge of the wide range of children's literature now available.

Finally, it is obvious that many of the 'Book Flood' pupils in the 'F' and 'C' streams must have read *only* reading scheme material, whereas the equivalent children in the experimental school were able to take advantage of the easier Book Flood books in addition to the set reading schemes, thus coming into contact with 'real books'.

Assessment of reading and remedial provision. The Burt and Schonell Graded Word Reading Tests were used to determine which children needed additional help (see Table 2·4); those who did need assistance were withdrawn for remedial English work. Neither of the teachers responsible for the teaching of remedial English was a specialist. It was disturbing to find that the teacher responsible for remedial English for the lower school did not feel confident in her work and did not regard herself as a 'literary person'. The situation may have changed by the present time, of course; also, in fairness one must add that headmasters frequently have a battle before they are allowed to replace valuable staff who leave and that existing staff are, therefore, often forced to take on a multiplicity of roles. A further result is that new staff, when they are taken on, are often appointed because of their willingness and ability to diversify, if necessary taking on new responsibilities when other staff leave, rather than for their expertise in a particular area.

*Table 2.4   Outer city control school: results of school-administered tests –
September 1976*

(Burt Word Reading Test)								
Reading age	6	7	8	9	10	11	12	13
Boys	2	11	9	3	3	10	6	1
Girls	1	10	5	7	7	8	2	1
Total	3	21	14	10	10	18	8	2

N = 86.
Missing values = 4.
   Note: The missing values figure is based on the number of children in the second year at the beginning of September 1976.

The headmaster. The headmaster came from a previous headship of seven years' duration, to a headship at the primary school in 1965, prior to middle school reorganization. He told me that he was very much aware of the fact that the pupils' home and school lives could not be viewed separately. The school is on the edge of the estate, which the headmaster believes is deteriorating – in terms of the mobility of the population, the high proportion of 'broken homes', and in terms of problems created by such factors as family size (average 4–5 children) and poverty because of unemployment. There is a suggestion that recently people have not *chosen* to live on the estate and that they do not stay if they are able to move. Certainly, I found the children in this school remarkably responsive to individual attention and desperate for conversation. This probably reflects lack of time available for discussion in their homes and lack of time in school, when teachers are dealing with both academic and pastoral problems.

   The headmaster is concerned that books are suffering as a category for use of capitation allowance, because of the increased cost of stationery, pencils, etc., as well as the increased cost of books themselves. Of course, the situation will be worse this year because of capitation cuts. Again, I feel bound to reiterate that the majority of these children do not have books at home and are unlikely to be introduced to the habit of using the public library. There is no doubt that the head finds the situation a very serious one; indeed, one reason for being involved in the experiment was that he knew the school would receive at least 2500 books at the end of the three years.

He describes his staff as being 'on the young side', most of them having joined the school as probationary teachers; the average length of service is 7–8 years, staff usually leaving either for promotion or to have families. The head believes that it is particularly important to have the support of his staff in any decision-making. Formal staff meetings are held two to three times a term, but informal staff meetings are easily arranged should they be necessary.

The head teaches small extraction groups, usually of more able pupils, who *can* be left to get on by themselves in an emergency, for about fifteen periods a week; he uses the fiction library which adjoins his office at one end and has a connecting door; thus, to use his own phrase, he is able to keep his finger on the pulse of what is going on, and to relieve some of the pressure on class teachers, who are therefore able to give more attention to less-able pupils. He also substitutes for absent teachers, when he keeps an eye on book stocks available in various class-rooms.

Undoubtedly a keen reader himself, the head believes that 'Reading Maketh Man', and insists on new members of staff being 'literate' as well as 'qualified'. He explained that the member of staff who teaches more than two-thirds of all fourth-year English, and is not an English specialist either by training or experience, was appointed and thus used because of his 'experience with older children' and 'formal training'.

There is no doubt that the head is a well-read man; he did a vocational course in English literature while in the forces, after which he specialized in music and mathematics. He does not, however, have the backing of informed staff in the areas of reading and children's literature and one wonders to what extent this is the result of the necessity to appoint someone to fill various rôles, of lack of choice among applicants for a middle-school post in an SPA school, and to what extent it is the result of priorities. The strength of the English teaching staff seems to be a very hit-and-miss affair rather than top priority, perhaps as a result of the head over-estimating the abilities of the average member of staff and under-estimating the background knowledge necessary for the adequate teaching of English language and literature to this age group.

There is no head of English as such, all the fourth-year English being taught by two of the fourth-year teachers; the third of the fourth-year teachers is the deputy headmistress, who is a Belgian national, and specializes in the teaching of French.

The 'school librarian'. The teacher responsible for the school library during the experiment read main geography with English literature and outdoor pursuits as subsidiary subjects. He joined the school in 1971 as an 'all-round' teacher, subsequently applying for responsibility for the school library when the position, a Scale 3, became vacant in 1972. At this juncture, he decided to take the Library Association and School Library Association's Joint Certificate for Teacher–Librarians, involving his attendance at lectures two evenings a week for one year. This course has now been completely rearranged as the Certificate in School Library Studies.

He told me that his college English literature syllabus was like an advanced 'A' level course, only applicable to sixth-form teaching, yet intended for all teachers – including prospective primary school teachers. At no time did any of the lecturers talk about children's literature. Even on the librarianship course he thought that the books recommended for children were 'very out of date' – such as *Swallows and Amazons* and *The Famous Five*; he did not learn anything *new* about children's books. A great deal of time on the course was spent in describing complex classification systems that are totally inappropriate to the needs of the average school.

This teacher does read children's books on his own initiative; he attends book exhibitions; he takes the School Library Association's Newsletter and he attends courses on children's literature whenever possible. However, he emanates the feeling that he is fighting a losing battle most of the time with the majority of the children.

He has no control over class libraries and is unaware of the stocks of books in other teachers' rooms. He told me that it was his belief that the vast majority of books in school were never read; that most of the pupils had little interest in books and had to be 'harassed' to read, with the result that a silent reading lesson was a real chore. Since I asked children to read silently when they had finished tests and some of them finished very early, I can vouch for the fact that creating an atmosphere both quiet and relaxed, where concentrated reading is a viable proposition, is quite an energetic task. The fact that I succeeded probably had a great deal to do with the novelty of the situation; teachers have to succeed about forty times a year.

Fourth-year class teachers.
A Teacher A is the fourth-year leader and 4G class teacher. He

takes 4G for all their English except for creative English, which they do with Teacher B. Teacher A did main art and maths subsidiary at a small teacher training college, with the aim of becoming an art teacher. He passed 'A' level art after leaving school, by attending evening classes. English was a compulsory part of his college course. He told me that he thought the English course was an adequate preparation for teaching English, including children's literature; the students were expected to read and discuss children's books in depth. Thus we have our second example of a non-English specialist being given a sound introduction to children's books.

Before his appointment at this school, which was initially a Scale 2 with responsibility for art, he taught 8–11-year-olds in a junior school, followed by two years in a middle school teaching maths. After a year at the present school, he also became fourth-year leader. He teaches mainly maths and art, plus English to his own class, 4G. When I asked him how he felt about teaching English, he replied that he had always taught some English, adding, 'I think all teachers are expected to teach English'. He enjoys it, especially reading aloud to the children and stimulating their imaginations; his art training influences his approach particularly towards the display of books, and the creation of a colourful and comfortable atmosphere in his class-room.

When he was allocated money to choose books for 4G, he decided to buy paperbacks '. . . because I could get more and they were more colourful . . . . They were about 50p each so I bought about a hundred books for £50 or £60.' These books were carefully selected – he asked me to help – and attractively exhibited, with regular changes of display, among a variety of art work and written work. The atmosphere in the class-room was both homely and workmanlike whenever I visited it – which was often unannounced.

This teacher knew a great deal about traditional children's books before he went to college, because he had a lot of books in his home as a child. He said to me, 'Well, *obviously,* I would read to her [his mother] and there would be the *usual* bedtime stories, and so on.' (My italics.) His attendance at a college where a grounding in children's books was considered important was fortuitous, and his wife, a primary school teacher, is an avid reader who specialized in English at college. He was also intelligent enough to realize that his job would be pleasanter and easier if he familiarized himself with the books in his class-room and chose new ones carefully, so that he could make recommendations, which he felt he needed to do for the boys in particular. Nevertheless, with only four boys and two girls who had much difficulty in choosing books while the vast majority had little trouble in finding books to interest them, encouraged by the belief that they were the most intelligent and capable children in the school, his task was more likely to be rewarding than that of Teacher B, who had the responsibility of teaching English to the 'F' and 'C' stream children. The expertise of Teacher A in teaching English seems to have been very much a matter of chance; it should also be added that he left for promotion elsewhere at the end of the experiment.

B   Teacher B worked in the civil service on first leaving school, obtaining 'A' levels in history and English at evening classes. He read main history with subsidiary English at a teacher training college; the course was specifically for middle school teachers. Before teaching at the present school, he taught history and geography in an upper school in Bradford (14–16-year-olds). His present post is for English and the humanities.

Three-quarters of his timetable is devoted to the teaching of English, the rest being divided equally between maths and geography.

Although this teacher was an avid reader as a small child, his interest dwindled until he became involved in the 'A' level literature course at school. His college course did not include any work on children's literature at all. He does not usually read children's books. This teacher does set aside one lesson a week during which children are expected to read silently and during which he expects them to conduct themselves as they would in a public library. He finds that in order to create a peaceful atmosphere for those who want to read, he has to insist on all children being silent, if necessary with the threat of extra work as punishment. At least in this way, he believes he is giving every child the chance to read quietly, an opportunity that many of them never have at home.

He thinks that the stock of books in his class-room includes too much hardback material with poor covers – 'many children judge a book by its cover'. The display of such material would not be very effective. This teacher does not actually encourage children to take home books from the class-room because of the number of losses, but does occasionally make exceptions.

Teacher B is aware that less time is given to reading as children approach the end of the middle school because of the demands of the upper school curriculum in the areas of grammar, spelling, comprehension, etc. Nevertheless, he continued with at least one period of reading per week. He is also aware of the disadvantages created by the fact that most middle school teachers are junior trained and have no subject specialism. Despite his lack of training as an English specialist, he has made a real effort to train himself and we must realize that his task is an extremely difficult one when he does not teach the most able children and does not have the most attractive up-to-date book stock. Perhaps he is better off this year!

Final discussion. Teachers were not available for a discussion at the end of the experiment as there were so many end-of-term activities taking place.

Summary of the similarities and differences between the two outer city schools

   Similarities
1   Both were previously primary schools.
2   Catchment areas and types of intake are similar.
3   Buildings are similar.
4   School populations are of a similar size.
5   English is taught throughout the school by class teachers (although an English specialist does exist in the experimental school).
6   Both remedial and more able groups of children are withdrawn for some of their English work.

   Differences.
1   There is no streaming in the experimental school and remedial withdrawal is usually of a temporary nature at the upper end of the school; in contrast, in the control school a top 'G' stream and two parallel streams are in operation after the first year. There is virtually no movement between streams.
2   There were no class libraries in the experimental school prior to the experiment, and the head was not favourably disposed towards them; there had always been class libraries in the control school, though, and the head wished them to coexist with the school library.
3   Children in the experimental school were encouraged to take class library books home, whereas children in the control school were not.
4   There was a far larger stock and far greater use of reading scheme material in the control school than in the experimental school.
5   At the control school, there was a far larger proportion of non-fiction in the school library, the bulk of fiction material being housed in the class-rooms and, therefore, not available for borrowing; in contrast, proportions of fiction and non-fiction were more

or less equal in the school library at the experimental school.

The inner city schools

Both inner city schools were secondary schools prior to middle school reorganization; and both are close to the centre of Bradford, catering mainly for children from working-class families including quite a large proportion of second-generation immigrants, mostly of Indian and Pakistani origin.

The inner city experimental school

This school was built in 1878 and was a girls' secondary modern before it became a junior high (11–13 six-form entry) in 1964. It continued as a junior high until middle school reorganization began in 1972, with the intake of 10+ children. However, the development of the school was dramatically interrupted in 1966 when the building was almost completely destroyed by fire. The building had been on two levels, on a sloping site, and the lower level survived, but about 90 per cent of the school had to be rebuilt and currently consists of well-planned terrapin-style buildings, but linked in such a way that they appear to be one complete building from the inside. The school became totally a middle school (9–13 three-form entry) in 1973, although the top stream had been part of the original junior high until 1974.

The catchment area for this school is very large, or rather long – about 3 miles – taking in a wide variety of types of housing but, nevertheless, is a very solid working-class area. About two-thirds of the intake is from private housing, this being mainly fairly close to the school, and the remaining one-third is from council estates, mostly farther afield, although there are one or two children from private houses at the far end of the catchment area. Some of the parents are unemployed, and many of the children belong to one-parent families. However, the headmaster felt that the intake had been 'relieved of some problems' by slum clearance.

While at the beginning of the experiment, in 1976, the percentage of ethnic minority children was about 14 per cent, by the end of the research, in 1979, it had increased to 25 per cent. The non-indigenous children, or children whose parents were non-indigenous, who were actually involved in the experiment, were mainly of Asian origin. Details of their origins are shown in Table 2.5.

This school is the only one of the four that is not classified as SPA. In any case, there was never a fixed addition to capitation allowance for SPA schools but, instead, a central pool that has now ceased to exist as a result of recent cuts.

Table 2·5   Countries of origin of ethnic minority children and their parents

Inner city experimental school

Number of children	Sex	Child's country of origin and place if known	Father's country of origin	Mother's country of origin
1	Male	Huddersfield, England	Cyprus	England
1	Male	Bradford, England	India	England
1	Female	Bradford, England	Pakistan	England
1	Male	Kenya	India	India
4	Male	Bradford, England	India	India
6	Female	Bradford, England	India	India
3	Male	Bradford, England	Pakistan	Pakistan
1	Female	Bradford, England	Pakistan	Pakistan

18 Total

Inner city control school

Number of children	Sex	Child's country of origin and place if known	Father's country of origin	Mother's country of origin
3	Female	India	India	India
4	Male	Pakistan	Pakistan	Pakistan
2	Female	Pakistan	Pakistan	Pakistan
1	Male	England	India	India
3	Female	England	India	India
5	Male	England	Pakistan	Pakistan
2	Female	England	Pakistan	Pakistan
1	Male	England	W. Indies	W. Indies
2	Female	England	W. Indies	W. Indies

23 Total

School and class libraries. Table 2·6 shows a breakdown of the books actually available on the shelves in school and class libraries in spring 1979. The school library contained slightly more non-fiction than fiction. The proportion of fiction to non-fiction in the class libraries was very close to that within the Book Flood as a whole, a proportion similar also to that of fiction to non-fiction in the outer city experimental school. Actual numbers of books in the two schools were also similar.

At the time of middle school reorganization, extra money was made available to middle schools of junior-school origin, so that they could cater adequately for the 11–13 age group. However, schools of secondary origin were eventually granted an additional £1000 each, which, in the case of this school, was claimed by the present head soon after he took up his post in 1974; he decided to spend it entirely on providing books for the school library, as he felt that they were sorely needed.

Table 2·6   Inner city experimental school: count of school and class library books

School library		%	Class library		%
Fiction	1372	42·5	Fiction	4026	61
Non-fiction	1853	51·5	Non-fiction	1950	29
	——		Reading scheme	649	10
	3225			——	
	——			6625	

(Approx. 4450 Book Flood books.)

Until 1976, the head of English had been responsible for the school library but this was felt to be too heavy a burden when added to other pastoral responsibilities, so in 1976 the present 'school librarian', a young second-year class teacher with a scaled post for extra-curricular activities but no special academic responsibility, took over the school library, which he immediately reaccessed. He used the £1000 grant for both school and class libraries; the latter were almost bare at the time. Money allocated to the school library in subsequent years was as follows:

> 1977: £450
> 1978: £300
> 1979: £350, plus a set of encyclopaedias

Inevitably, this spending was affected by the influx of approximately 5000 books into the class-rooms in 1976 (now halved, of course).

There is not the clear-cut distinction between the organization of school and class libraries in this school that is to be found in many others. Stock is flexible; borrowing is encouraged from any area and recorded in a uniform card index system regardless of the location from which books are borrowed. Most staff believe that mobility of books and of borrowers should be encouraged, the most important consideration being that books should be *used* rather than stored.

The other major change, apart from the appointment of a new headteacher and of a new 'school librarian', that affected the school library during the time of the experiment was a change of location for the library. Under the previous head, and at the beginning of the experiment, the library had been situated in the far corner of the assembly/PE/dining-hall, thus limiting access; this room is now the upper school English base. The room had been used extensively as a class-room, as well as a television room and a holding place for naughty children. The head believed that the library should occupy a central position in the school, should be easily accessible at all times, should be a pleasant and quiet place to be, and should be *used as a library* for as much of the time as possible. The school library was, therefore, re-sited during the first year of the experiment in a room off the main central corridor of the school, payment being made by the local authority. The room is pleasant and well equipped, with plentiful display units of various kinds. It is usually kept free of other lessons and almost every class has a weekly library lesson, with the exception of the fourth-year top stream at the time of the Book Flood. Unlike the libraries in the outer city schools, it has the advantage of being self-contained so that children are able to read undisturbed provided that the teacher ensures the kind of atmosphere conducive to quiet reading.

The school library is open every lunch-hour, staffed by pupil librarians on a rota basis, but the 'school librarian' is usually also available and is very willing to offer help or to receive suggestions, which he usually acts upon, for further buying. The library is a friendly place to be; trouble-makers are reasoned with and rare individuals are discouraged from borrowing temporarily only as a result of repeated losses or deliberate damage to books. Books are colour-coded, and are bought through the Schools' Library Service. Audio-visual materials are not located in the school library.

It is noticeable that *all* the class-rooms in this school, not only the Book Flood ones, are well-stocked with books. All the first- and second-year class-rooms, and the English base for the upper school and many of the specialist areas like the art, woodwork and home economics rooms, demonstrate the teachers' awareness of the importance of book display, as part of a general understanding of the need for display all around the school, whether of pictures, children's written work, models, or live animals, in an attempt to create an atmosphere at once lively and homely, stimulating and comfortable, which is maximally conducive to work. Furthermore, it is obvious to a visitor to the school that books are a 'natural' part of the environment, 'friends' found not only in 'special' areas, but throughout the school; they are never isolated or inaccessible. Display is facilitated by the use of sloping shelves around the walls, made by the woodwork department soon after the beginning of the experiment with money partly from the Advisory Service and partly from the school. Initially, they were built for the Book Flood children only, but soon everyone wanted them and they are now to be found in most class-rooms. Displays are frequently changed and, although class libraries are well used, books are kept in an order that facilitates this use. The fact that all first- and second-year class-rooms are close together, having been reorganized in that way by the present headmaster, makes the interchange of books among first- and second-year children relatively easy, especially as this practice is encouraged by teachers – for instance, if a child wants to read all the books available in school written by a particular author. The head, and most of the staff, accept up to a point that books will be lost, damaged and stolen. However, a universal system of recording borrowing, and an order underlying and facilitating the superficial flexibility, keep such loss and damage at a manageable level.

School bookshop. There was no school bookshop in this school during the experiment, but children are encouraged to buy books through the *Lucky Scoop* and *Chip* clubs (Scholastic Publications). At present (February 1980) the head of English is considering the possibility of organizing a school bookshop.

The organization of English teaching. In their first and second years at the school, children are taught English by their class teachers in their class bases, apart from additional remedial lessons for some. The first- and second-year classes are all mixed-ability groups. In the third and fourth years a mixture of streaming and setting is in operation. For most subjects, children are grouped into one top stream and two parallel streams; for English, however, and recently for maths also, the two parallel streams are reconstituted into three groups, the bottom group effectively becoming the remedial group – thus creating four sets for English, the top set being identical to the top stream. The head believes that such a system at the upper end of the school facilitates effective teaching and is therefore to the children's advantage. Teaching in the third and fourth years is entirely subject-based and English teaching is limited to a small number of class-rooms in order to maximize display areas and units within those class-rooms, although the use of subject bases is more restricting upon book use than are class bases. In fact, the mobility of the third- and fourth-year children, along with the existence of new-styled tables instead of desks, detracts from the amount of 'spare moment reading' undertaken by these children in all four schools. On the other hand, the use of an upper school English base means that books can be concentrated in one main area for 11+ and 12+ children, and displayed and organized by one person. Indeed, in this school, wherever possible, English in the upper school is taught by English specialists; in one case, by training as well as by knowledge and experience and, in the other case, by extensive knowledge and long experience.

The head of English is responsible for the organization of English teaching throughout the school and actually teaches four out of the eight groups in the third and fourth years. In the final year of the experiment, two out of the four groups of Book Flood children were taught by the head of English. She is quite clearly *not* working in isolation; the headmaster has strong, positive views about reading and about the teaching of English, views of which the staff are well aware; the second-year class teacher who is responsible for the school library, the two other second-year class teachers, the first-year class teacher who is responsible for remedial English, and many others, all make a significant contribution to the work of the English department. Indeed, it is outstandingly noticeable that many of the teaching staff are well-acquainted with both adult and children's literature and are well able to hold their own in discussions on the subject. Space will not permit me to say a great deal about teachers involved in the teaching of English other than the head of English and the 'school librarian', but I feel bound to give one or two examples of the depth of knowledge of children's books possessed by some of these teachers. One of the second-year class teachers, who also teaches English to the third and fourth years, has been with the school since 1951, has 'always' taught some English, and is able to discuss a wide variety of children's authors from first-hand knowledge of reading either to herself, to pupils in school, or to young relatives. Like most of the teachers involved in the Book Flood, she acquainted herself with the books when they arrived and, rather than reading an entire book to a class, she would often '. . . read a little to everyone and say, "There it is on the shelf!", or, "It is one of a series"'. This is *typical* of the class teachers of English in this school in that they *used* the books, as they would have used any other educationally valuable windfall, rather than merely giving them house room. Also typical are the positive expectations for the Book

Flood expressed by this same teacher and her enthusiasm when the books arrived, an enthusiasm that hardly seemed to wane during the three years of the experiment, although obviously the task of encouraging children to read is more difficult at 12+. This teacher expressed her positive expectations as a result of the availability of the Book Flood books in the following words:

> The fact that there is a selection of books wider than our own school library, obviously means that they will be able to find more to read. I think a lot of the children who are fairly interested but don't have a lot of encouragement at home, would not join a public library, if it was not at the end of their street. To go out of their way to the library is something they would probably not do, *so I suppose we should expect an improvement* [my italics] – they'll read more, they'll begin to read more fluently, and, as they have exhausted what is first of all suitable for them, then they'll begin to search through the shelves and begin to be a little more selective.

I must emphasize once more that this teacher's knowledge of and enthusiasm for children's books was typical of most of the English staff at this school, although obviously some had more extensive knowledge than others.

Another English teacher at this school expressed the following point of view:

> I always supposed that, if I was going to introduce literature with a capital 'L', I would have to make the bridge – the bridge is in the teacher reading what the children read and what they chose for themselves. If you are going to make evaluations, and if you are going to present the evaluations, you have to move from where *they* are to an area where *you* are, through their position. And so you have got to build the bridge . . . you are making judgements from the other side if you don't go over.

In the area of language development also she is widely read, having taken a particular interest in Bernstein. She is interested in the connection between one's ability to express one's feelings and situation, and the ability to cope with the feelings or the situation. Many of the pupils, she believes, and their parents, are 'passive'. The way of life '. . . means being passive to experience, passive to ideas, allowing others to label your reality for you. . . . I want to give them more choice'. This she attempts to achieve both through literature and through conversation. In literature, ideally she would like to introduce the children to a wide variety. She would also like the literature to help them to see from another's point of view – to 'stand in another's place' – which hopefully might facilitate the far from inevitable development of abstract and hypothetical thought.

She does not expect children to swallow whole her choice of books, but prefers them to reject, if reject they do, from a knowledgeable rather than an ignorant standpoint. She said, '. . . the idea is that you present some form of literature and they have the choice to reject it but on different terms this time . . .' From a linguistic point of view, she believes that most of the children *need* conversations with adults in school, preferably on a one-to-one basis, particularly if they are to benefit from their reading. This 'feedback' from the teacher she sees as being complemented by feedback from peers, particularly where recommendation of books is concerned.

Finally, both from her own point of view and that of the children in her care, she believes that reading can help us to 'know' other minds:

> I must become aware . . . of what other minds think. And because one can only be in one place at one time, therefore one's encounters with other minds are limited. Reading is the most obvious way, by proxy, of encountering other minds, and probably one of the greatest assets about being able to read is that the encounters with others cross time barriers.

I feel sure that the underlying concern and enthusiasm must communicate itself to the reader as it did to many of the children.

The policy of having a head of English, with over-all responsibility for the organization of English within the school as well as teaching half the upper school English, is partly the result of the school previously having been a secondary school, as the present head of English was, in fact, appointed as head of English to the girls' secondary school. Nevertheless, it is always possible, if not easy, to reorganize a primary-type middle school in the same way, rather than simply allowing things to continue.

In most classes children are read to by the teacher (sometimes an entire book and sometimes parts of books), read aloud to the teacher, and also read silently to themselves – although more of these activities, in the case of our present sample, took place in the second and fourth years than in the third year. All children have library lessons and are taught the 'mechanics of the library' in the first year. Children are given time to talk about books and other experiences, as the headmaster and the rest of the staff believe that conversation is important to language development and general personal development, particularly conversation with adults.

Assessment of reading and remedial provision. When the present headmaster took up his post, he called in the Remedial Teaching Service to assess the children's reading performance using Young's Group Reading Test (see Table 2·7) and to give advice on remedial teaching.

The Holborn Reading Test and the Richmond Tests of Basic Skills: Levels 1–6 have also been used in this school. The school is not allocated a remedial specialist and remedial work is shared among three or four teachers all of whom are informed about this type of work, have attended at least a one-week in-service training course and, in some instances, also follow-on courses dealing with specialist aspects of the teaching of remedial reading. The head believes that the labelling of one teacher as *the* remedial teacher would have a detrimental effect upon the performance of that teacher, unless it were a teacher who had deliberately set out to make a career of this aspect of teaching. In the upper school, the bottom sets of children are sometimes taught by the head of English, and sometimes by another teacher who expressed a desire to do this work, had previous experience, and undertook some in-service training; the head of English had attended numerous in-service courses.

Table 2·7   Inner city experimental school: results of school-administered reading tests – September 1976

Young Reading Test					
Reading age	6	7	8	9	10
Total	1	12	21	11	42

N = 87.
Missing values = 10.

> Note: The missing values figure is based on the number of children in the second year at the beginning of September 1976.

The head invites parents of the less-able readers into the school to help with their children's reading '. . . and would like to invite college students in were there a college in the vicinity'. First- and second-year teachers try to group children in such a way that each group of five or six contains children who can help the less-able readers within the same group. The remedial teacher for the lower school is well-informed, very kind, efficient and enthusiastic, utilizing a variety of games and other materials – it is a pleasure to watch her work. Above all, her kind manner and positive approach is totally appropriate. Indeed, throughout the school, the approach towards the less-able reader is one of positive encouragement and practical help.

The headmaster. The head's previous appointment was as a deputy head; he took up his present post in 1974 when the previous head retired after about ten years' service. The present headmaster, there-fore, joined the school just as middle school reorganization was completed. The teacher who is responsible for the school library expressed the view that the head is particularly sympathetic towards his requirements, as the head himself was responsible for a school library in a previous post. Certainly, the head is very positively oriented towards the expansion of both school and class libraries. He is a person with definite *and detailed* views about both the use of books and about the teaching of English, although I should make it clear that these views would be readily accepted by, rather than imposed upon, the teaching staff. For instance, the teachers are aware of the head's enthusiasm to take part in the Book Flood since the school was 'sadly lacking' in books when he took up his headship. He said, 'I was happy to get the books. This was one of my main interests, because at the time I felt the school was short of books and this was a way of getting more.'

He was anxious to spend the £1000 allocated to the school as a middle school of secondary origin, on books, and to appoint someone with energy and enthusiasm to be responsible for the school library, thus freeing the head of English to cope with the job in hand rather than over-burdening her with a variety of roles and responsibilities as can so easily happen in a small school.

This head told me that he believes that teachers are aware of his desire to see both children and teachers sitting and reading; he does not want children put in a 'pending tray' during reading lessons while teachers do something 'more important', but believes that teachers should themselves read and be seen to read, keep records of children's reading, and should offer help and advice during these lessons. He believes that punctuation and grammar should be taught directly and separately, *not* through literary extracts lest this destroys an enjoyment of the literature; he also holds the view that extensive reading improves children's vocabulary and sentence structure. He sees conversation as playing an important part along-side reading; he believes that in speech, as in one's choice and attitudes towards literature, one should not reject or despise what children have to offer, but that one should extend the range of choice by making children aware of the alternatives. He told me that it was his belief that, if children can read, talk or write about something, they can begin to cope with it; otherwise children experience 'an overwhelming feeling of frustration'. He does of course realize that conversation is difficult with large classes but believes that children should be encouraged to develop their linguistic abilities in this way wherever possible. He expects his staff to be literate and also accepting of children's linguistic and literary limitations.

The head said that he firmly believes that books should be treated as 'friends'; that they should be found *throughout* the school – in the staff room, corridors and specialist subject areas, as well as in rooms where English is taught. Ideally, he would like to see a wide variety of reference books in *every* class-room as he believes availability and accessibility to be of paramount importance, but rising prices and cuts in capitation make such aspirations unrealistic. What the head would *like* to be able to do is to provide children in school with the variety of books available to children in fairly well-off, literary homes; similarly, what he would *like* to do would be to give children the opportunity for one-to-one conversation with adults, such as a few fortunate children have with their parents.

The head does not timetable himself to teach, because he believes that he needs to be available to deal with emergencies and visitors, although he does frequently substitute for absent teachers. The head believes that it is particularly important, especially on their first visit to the school, that parents should feel the effort has been worth while. Therefore, he likes to be available and his impression is that the number of parental visits steadily increases as a result. He does not think it would be educationally desirable for him to be regularly leaving the same class. The emergencies generally take the form of children with problems in school which are closely related to problems at home; or visits from parents with problems at home that are affecting their children's performance and behaviour at school. He realizes that problems at home are often such that '. . . children cannot be blamed for having no interest in school at all. We know ourselves, if there is something worrying us at home, this is what comes uppermost and, as far as we can, work tends to be put on one side.' He is also aware that the school cannot solve all these problems, but does believe that a sympathetic ear can help to alleviate them and that knowledge of children's difficulties can prevent behaviour patterns from being misjudged.

In conclusion, the headmaster's knowledge of, but more particularly, attitude towards, books is apparent in his conversation and obviously permeates both the daily running and physical organization of the school.

The 'school librarian'. This teacher has qualities that complement those of the head of English and that are particularly appropriate to a teacher who is responsible for a school library.

He did geography, economics and British constitution to 'A' level, followed by a B.Ed. with geography as his main subject and education his subsidiary. His first appointment was to the inner city experimental school, in 1971, as a second-year class teacher; and he was given responsibility for the school library in 1976. He immediately embarked upon a part-time course leading to the Certificate for Teacher–Librarians. Unfortunately, he discovered that this course taught an inappropriately refined system of cataloguing and did not effectively increase his knowledge of children's literature. Nevertheless, he has acquired a wide knowledge of children's books, mainly by the good old-fashioned way of reading them, and takes an obvious pleasure in doing so. Perhaps the fact that he takes part in a variety of sporting activities with the boys encourages them to respect his views about literature, as also does the fact that *he* respects *their* views, demonstrated by his willingness to buy books that they request, and by taking magazines as well as books into the school library.

He believes that 'word of mouth' is very important in the development of an interest in books, so that he deliberately encourages children to talk about the books that they have read, which he believes helps pupils to articulate their ideas, and also helps other children and himself acquire information about books. The fact that he also has great faith in the power of display is illustrated by the organization of his class-room and of the school library.

Like the headmaster and the head of English, he believes in meeting the children on their own ground, but *not* in staying there. While he would never underestimate the value and significance of *Nippers*-type books, he would be worried if children did not read anything else because such books are so totally faithful to the experiences of many of the children; he believes that their experiences, ideas and language should be extended. However, in order for children to develop their reading skills, he believes that they need active encouragement in the form of hearing extracts well read, hearing books described by other children, having their attention attracted by display, and being directly taught the skills involved in choosing books. His aim is to give them the confidence and skill to choose and read books a little beyond their present ability and experience, although they obviously cannot be expected to sustain this all the time, and will need continual help and encouragement.

One of this teacher's chief assets is that he knows the children in his class so well and knows his stock of books – so he is rarely at a loss to recommend something. He is also able to do this in a more general way in the school library, for example, by recommending football stories to boys who want to know about nothing else.

What we can learn from this case study of the organization of English and use of books in one school is that, in addition to a large stock of books, a supply of teachers who are informed about and skilled in the use of books is also essential if children are to develop their reading skills and develop a permanent reading habit. I say teachers in the plural, as it would be quite impossible for one teacher to know all the books and to feel at home with the entire age and ability ranges within a school.

Final discussion. Unfortunately, due to illness, the head of English was unable to be present at the final discussion that took place in June 1979, in my home – the participants giving up an entire evening in order to attend.

The main points that emerged from the final talks were as follows:

1   The teachers said that the children's reactions had been positive throughout the experiment; the novelty of the Book Flood had not worn off. Whereas before the Book Flood children had been able to exhaust the supply of books available to them in school, since the arrival of the books they no longer could. Children had commented on the fact that their school was much better supplied with books than were other schools attended by friends or siblings. Nevertheless, these teachers stressed the importance of rotating the stock of books available in each class library if interest is to be sustained; the way in which the children instigated the practice of wandering into other class-rooms and asking to borrow books from them, initially made the teachers aware of the need for flexibility of borrowing and mobility of book stock.

2   The staff felt that the Book Flood had provided the less-able readers with a variety of books to choose from, rather than being confined almost exclusively to reading schemes, with the result that a quiet reading period had actually become pleasurable to some of these children for the first time.

Ethnic minority children, who, the teachers believe, sometimes had difficulty in developing their reading skills because they lacked books in English at home, and because of problems created by the need to operate in at least two languages, had frequently developed into avid readers as a result of the 'flood'.

In the fourth year, previously an awkward time for less-able readers who want maturity of content from books but often cannot tackle the form and level of difficulty of more 'adult' books, the variety of books available had sometimes made it possible for these children to continue to read and to develop their reading skills further.

Less-able children had been more likely than usual to ask for help with both reading and book choice, as a result of seeing so many attractive books available and hearing their peers talk about them.

3   Staff had noticed that pupils, particularly the keen readers, were developing a greater facility with the manipulation of words and

phrases, both in writing and in conversation, since the advent of the Book Flood.

4   Children had become increasingly aware of authors, of series, and of sensible criteria for book choice. Teachers had also noticed children attaching greater importance to other children's recommendations of books, as well as themselves recommending to the teachers the use of some of the Book Flood books as class readers.

5   Most teachers had previously kept a record of children's reading and had some awareness of children's literature. However, they had been excited and encouraged by the influx of books and believed that their enthusiasm must have affected the children. In particular, the new stock meant that teachers were able to become acquainted with modern children's authors, both by reading books for themselves and by listening to children talk about them. Whereas previously their knowledge of modern children's books had been largely restricted to those that were recommended by librarians or had won awards (books that were frequently unsuitable for children in their care), they were now aware of a wider range of modern fiction and were therefore in a better position to make recommendations. They particularly felt the need to do this when children were 'stuck with' an author or series and did not know where to go from there.

6   Staff agreed that they were more 'pro class library' than they had been before the 'flood', because of the degree of 'flexibility' that class libraries allow. Whereas previously children had associated a single period a week with reading a book, they were now, in addition, able to read before assembly, when work was finished, and so on, although they admitted that this applied to the first and second years more than to the third and fourth years, who could only do this if they took care to carry a book around with them. They said that this type of reading habit would be a realistic possibility for every child in the school if money would permit a large book stock in every class-room. The library lesson, although necessary, had connotations of artificiality; the class libraries, on the other hand, had encouraged a more casual and comfortable acceptance of books in an atmosphere something akin to that which exists in the home of the child fortunate enough to be well supplied with books at home.

The teachers had, in fact, kept track of class library books by the same ticket system as that which pertained in the school library so that it did not matter from which room a book was borrowed; they added that borrowing from other rooms had not occurred in the pre-Book Flood era.

The inner city control school

The school was built in 1877 and was a secondary modern until it became a junior high in 1964, and, subsequently, a fully fledged middle school in 1974. The building is typically Victorian with narrow corridors and self-contained rooms. Although various 'huts' are in use outside the main school, there were still not enough class-rooms for each first- and second-year class to have a permanent base, nor for each subject to have a permanent base, so that at least one teacher was always peripatetic within the school – this teacher being the head of English during the first two years of the experiment. The school has recently been given an additional class-room so that the problem has been eased.

The catchment area contains a good deal of very poor housing; the most poverty-stricken homes that I visited during the course of the case studies were in this school's catchment area. In the 1950s most of the pupils had come from back-to-back terrace houses, closely surrounding the school; these houses were later replaced by *small* flats in tower blocks housing few children because of their size, so that, until about 1970, approximately 90 per cent of the intake had been from a nearby housing estate, part of which has a reputation as a 'dumping ground' for problem families from other estates. However, with middle school reorganization, two other middle schools began to draw pupils from this estate, allowing the inner city control school to take in some children from an estate a little farther afield, not a corporation estate, but a trust estate that is outstandingly selective with its tenants. Therefore the intake is now more mixed than it was before middle school reorganization.

Another recent change affecting the intake has been the inability of a nearby school to cope with any more 'ethnic minority' children, with the result that the usually Asian parents of these British children, second-generation immigrants, can now opt to send the children to the inner city control school. At the beginning of the experiment, the intake of ethnic minority children had been approximately 5–6 per cent in the third and fourth years, and about 20–25 per cent in the first and second years (the 'Book Flood' children being second years) – at least 6 per cent more than in the matched experimental school. By the end of the experiment, the over-all intake was 25 per cent and the new first-year intake for 1978 was about 28–30 per cent, with the result that the school had been allocated a full-time qualified teacher to work with these children. The intake of 'ethnic minority' children is at present down to about 20 per cent; the specialist has left and is not to be replaced.

Apart from the homes owned by these Asian families, very few homes were owner-occupied. I visited quite a few of the Asian homes while I was doing the case studies and found that they and the homes on the trust estate were the better cared for and usually the ones that were a little better-off materially.

One of the results of the increased intake of 'ethnic minority' children has been the need to spend a large proportion of the English department money on materials for these children, at a time when the school was also trying to build up its resources for the 9- and 10-year-old children who had recently joined the school. This should be borne in mind when appraising the school and class library resources.

School and class libraries. At the time of middle school reorganization, it was decided that in order to make available the best possible non-fiction and reference materials to *all* first- and second-year pupils, the school library should be developed as a centralized resource area, since it would not be possible to buy sets of all the necessary books six times over. Wherever possible, any new teachers appointed to the school, once the head had been made aware of plans for middle school reorganization, were junior-trained teachers, who now entirely teach the 9- and 10-year-old children, and who designed their curricula in order to make maximum use of the library as a resource centre. Thus, the library contains a preponderance of non-fiction material (see Table 2·8). By the end of the experiment, the headmaster and the 'school librarian' felt that they were in a position to begin to build up the fiction stock of the library. The 'school librarian' experienced a certain amount of disappointment that the upper school teachers made little use of the library as a resource centre, apparently preferring traditional class-based resources.

Table 2·8   Inner city control school: count of school and class library books

School library		%	Class library		%
Fiction	297	9	Fiction	606	13.5
Non-fiction	3073	91	Non-fiction	974	21.5
	——		Reading scheme	2910	65
	3370			——	
	——			4490	

Most fiction is housed in the class-rooms rather than in the school library, being kept mainly in the first- and second-year bases and, now that it exists, in the upper school English base, as teachers feel that it is easier to keep track of the books in these rooms than if they were spread throughout the school. Although the librarian who organized the 'book count' separated reading schemes from fiction, the staff regard the reading scheme material as fiction and believe that this is essential material in a school where so many children have reading ages below their chronological ages and where there are so many for whom English is their second language; and, of course, the vast majority of reading scheme books *are* fiction. Books on loan from the school library service are also fiction and housed in the first- and second-year class-rooms and the upper school English base.

The almost total split between non-fiction in the school library and fiction in class libraries will not continue, however, as the aim is to build up a stock of 'real literature' to be shelved in the school library, so that it will be accessible to all pupils throughout the school, for instance in library lessons when, previously, children had been confined to reading mainly non-fiction, and in lunch-hours, when class libraries are often inaccessible. Fiction books are taken home from the central area under a loan system.

The school library, which is a typical large square room in a typically Victorian school building, is very well organized and houses, in addition to books, audio-visual materials, maps, posters and information folders. The 'school librarian', who left for promotion in July 1979, had devised a cataloguing system that linked books and audio-visual materials around topics. The Dewey system is used to classify non-fiction material. The non-fiction books were available for borrowing during the experiment, but this policy is under review as it can create problems of availability.

Shortage of class-rooms during the time of the experiment necessitated the use of the school library as a remedial teaching base and as a television room. Nevertheless, *all* first- and second-year children had a library lesson, as did most of the third years, but only one fourth-year class did. The 'school librarian' expressed his personal opinion that some teachers tended to regard the library as a 'soft option'. However, all third- and fourth-year children were, and I believe still are, given time for silent reading during English lessons, a time that the head of English believes is valuably spent and in no way a soft option, in this case, as he takes considerable care over recommending and discussing books, hearing children read, and doing everything he can to encourage the growth of a reading habit.

Unfortunately, class libraries were inadequate in a number of ways: shelving was practically non-existent (most of the books being *stored* in beautiful Victorian cupboards that often cannot be opened until desks are moved); the fiction books *do* consist mainly of reading scheme material, books for reluctant teenage readers and shortened versions of classics; the supply of fiction material is very meagre. The reasons for these inadequacies are almost certainly financial: there is about £600 per annum available for school library books and all English books including reading schemes and remedial materials. Middle school reorganization meant that the £300 usually spent on the school library, was in fact for several years spent on stocking it as a resource centre, and that, for about five years, English department money was spent on junior-type materials. Of course, as already mentioned, the problem has been compounded by the vastly increased intake of children for whom English is a second language. At least now, as a result of the Book Flood, they have an additional 2500 books, accompanied by the necessary shelving, which should give the book stock a much-needed boost, thus freeing part of the annual capitation allowance for the purchase of new books.

School bookshop. This was opened in 1974, by the 'school librarian', and is continually active on a small scale. It is really remarkably successful if one considers the poverty of most of the families and the fact that the buying of books at all is alien to most of them; the other side of this coin, however, is that there is obviously a great need for a bookshop in a school where the vast majority of pupils have not been introduced to bookshops by their parents.

There is a display window at a point that most children pass several times a day, and the display, although small, is regularly changed. However, the lack of space demands that the books be stored away most of the time and be brought out in a man-high folding 'book jacket' when the bookshop is open. Certainly, some of the children who would not normally buy books do buy them if they are presented with the possibility of doing so at slightly reduced prices and on school premises.

The organization of English teaching. When the present headmaster took up his post in 1974, he made it clear that he wanted first- and second-year children to be taught English by junior-trained class teachers in class bases and, if possible, third- and fourth-year children to be taught English entirely by 'specialists'. Six years later he believes in this policy even more firmly and wishes to increase his specialist English staff. The head of English, who teaches *all* third- and fourth-year English, did this for the first two years of the experiment without a base and, in the final year, *with* a base, one of the rooms in a two-room hut outside the main school building.

The head of English has 'loose control' over the English curriculum for the lower school as he was secondary trained and is a secondary school teacher by experience; he is also a modest man who believes in letting people get on with things if they are capable of doing so. However, all book purchases are finally organized through him.

During the experiment, the headmaster increased the number of English periods per class from four and a half to seven, plus one library lesson. In addition, there are extra periods of English for the children in need of remedial help.

There is no streaming in the first and second year. Until July 1978, the third and fourth year were divided into a top 'A' stream and two parallel 'B' streams, but, from September 1978, the third and fourth years were streamed 'A', 'B' and 'C', the pupils in the 'C' streams not taking French as a school subject; instead these children had additional English lessons in half class groups, giving them a total of eleven English lessons per week. Wherever possible a double period of English is timetabled for the upper school children at some time during the week so that they can settle down to read; care has to be taken not to place these double periods of English too close to the remedial lessons in case children reach saturation point.

The fact that there is now an upper school English base, even if it is only a hut, has made it possible for the head of English to have materials available for the third and fourth years during English lessons. The hut is divided into two rooms with a foyer between. The foyer, an extremely grand name for a rather small, smelly entrance (the lavatories are behind it), houses a meagre stock of paperback novels. The cold, the smell and the depressing atmosphere hardly create an area conducive to browsing. It is a pity that the English base cannot be located in the main building, for such books as there are currently have to be locked up in breaks and lunch-hours to prevent loss and damage.

It is policy to allow all children throughout the school time for reading, although often of reading scheme materials such as the Griffin *Pirates*, or of books for reluctant teenage readers like the *Spirals*. SRA is also widely used in the lower school. The head-master and the staff involved in the teaching of English believe that time spent by children reading, or by the teacher reading to the children, is time valuably spent, although they wonder which subjects are going to have to give elbow room to such new additions to the curriculum as health education and moral education.

Assessment of reading and remedial provision. The Holborn Sentence Reading Test is used for purposes of assessment (see Table 2·9). This is an individually administered test and, as such, the previous deputy head felt that anxiety might affect some children's perform-ance; this resulted in the Young Group Reading Test also being introduced. Scores did in fact show some discrepancies. There is an awareness, among the staff, of the limitations of various tests.

Table 2·9   Inner city control school: results of school-administered reading tests – September 1976

	(Holborn Reading Test)							
Reading age	6	7	8	9	10	11	12	13
Boys	5	4	11	4	8	3	2	1
Girls	3	11	12	10	8	4	1	5
Total	8	15	23	14	16	7	3	6

N = 92.
Missing values = 1.
    Note: The missing values figure is based on the number of children in the second year at the beginning of September 1976.

At the beginning of the experiment, the person responsible for remedial English was a lady who, although she had not been trained as a remedial specialist, had attended several in-service courses and was clearly dedicated to her work, using a variety of approaches and often placing reading in the context of a game or some other activity. She was replaced by a teacher who had less confidence and enthusiasm and who, in her turn, was superseded in September 1978 by a full-time non-specialist trained teacher, assisted by a teacher seconded from the Immigration Department. Although she spent most of her time doing remedial work with both indigenous and 'ethnic minority' children, she did also do some ordinary teaching. The school had been allocated a specialist because of the large intake of 'ethnic minority' children, but there were a great many children whose mother-tongue was English who also needed her help. This specialist left in December 1979 and was 'replaced' by a half-time remedial specialist who deals with English for children of Asian origin, or whose parents are of Asian origin, so that another non-specialist teacher has to cope with all the remedial teaching of indigenous children.

The headmaster. The head trained as a craft teacher, his first appointment being as a general teacher in a Leeds school, followed by an appointment as a specialist craft teacher. After four years in Leeds, he became craft teacher in his present school in 1955. In 1967 he was appointed deputy head with the same school and became headmaster in 1974. He believes that his long stay has the advantage of giving him detailed, and historical, knowledge of the local community. He is also very much involved in the daily life of the school, having worked his way up from the 'shop floor', and is often to be found in the staff-room, or sorting out the boiler, or on playground duty. Of course, all the heads do these things to some extent; it is a question of degree, though.

He stressed that when he became headmaster he set out deliberately to change the attitude of staff towards the teaching of English, and that this was one reason why he offered to involve the school in the Book Flood. He believed that some teachers regarded English as a '. . . convenient lesson to fill in the timetable', so he has aimed to concentrate the teaching of English with a small number of 'specialists' or committed junior-trained teachers, and to timetable efficiently. His *bête noire* is room allocation as there are quite simply not enough rooms to go round. All third- and fourth-year children now have a specialist teacher for English, whereas prior to his headship they had class teachers. The head emphasized and frequently reiterated that he is totally committed to the idea of one or more English specialists in the school, and stated that he would appoint another if the present one leaves, or when he retires. He is now also using a part-time teacher on his staff, who is an English graduate and has been a journalist, to teach English, in addition to the head of English.

He says that the Book Flood, even though he did not actually receive any books until September 1979, has caused him to look more closely at reading and has probably prompted him to give the head of English a base, but he is a little afraid of giving too much attention to English at the expense of other subjects, and *possibly* does not realize yet the implications for other subjects that will most certainly ensue as a result of the policies that he has put into operation. However, he does have to keep a balance and achieve the highest possible standards in all subjects.

The head teaches six periods a week simply so that he can keep in touch with the children; he describes these as 'one-off' lessons. He wishes the children of Asian parents to be well-catered for but does not want the differences to be over-emphasized. He said: 'They are first and foremost children and should be treated as individuals'.

Two of the staff have been at the school longer than the headmaster; the senior mistress thirty years, and the head of English thirty-five years, which helps to give the school a family atmosphere. There is also the kind of camaraderie among the staff, shared by the head, that I have heard people describe as existing in the trenches! The senior mistress was often heard to say, 'Well, you've got to laugh . . .'

The new class-room did arrive, and went into operation on 2 February 1980 – that's the good news; the bad news is that one and a half staff have been lost and are not to be replaced.

The 'school librarian'. This teacher became responsible when he was transferred to the school as part of middle school reorganization in 1972; before that he had been head of a local primary school. At college he specialized in English and religious education and trained as a primary school teacher. Towards the end of the experiment he was studying for an Open University degree and seeking promotion. Before his appointment at the inner city control school he had gained, in 1968, the Certificate for Teacher–Librarians; for a number of years he had been Secretary to the Bradford Schools' Library Assistants, and did in-service teaching on librarianship at the T. F. Davies Centre for Teachers.

In addition to being responsible for the school library, he was a second-year class teacher and second-year leader. He believed that in order to organize a school library efficiently, a teacher needs to spend about 75 per cent of his time on precisely that, including giving a weekly library lesson to each class in school.

He took over the school library in what he described as a 'dreadful state' and spent a considerable amount of time reaccessing it and developing a new cataloguing system so that it could be used efficiently as a resource centre. He believed that third- and fourth-year teachers did not take advantage of the resources available and bemoaned the extent to which the library had been used as an ordinary class-room due to shortage of space. In retrospect, he thought that he had probably made a mistake by almost totally neglecting the acquisition of fiction books, but was loath to begin reordering when he realized that he would be leaving, as he thought his successor should be allowed to take the responsibility for ordering fiction stock.

As far as the experience of reading on a personal level is concerned, he told me that he had always been an avid reader and that he is married to an equally avid reader. They have about 2500 books at home and regularly read to their own children. In fact, much of his knowledge of children's books has been gained from his family, an important contributive factor in many of these case studies. When he took charge of the school library, he deliberately set about familiarizing himself with children's books, which he obviously enjoys reading, as he is able to talk about them in detail and with enthusiasm; it is a great pity that he did not *buy* more fiction.

He used journals like *Growing Point* and *Children's Literature in Education* in an attempt to keep up to date with modern children's fiction but, nevertheless, felt that he failed to do so adequately.

He believes that teachers should introduce children to literature that deals with ideas beyond their immediate experience and environment, but that it is difficult, if not impossible, for pupils to make this kind of leap unaided; therefore it is important for a teacher to read to children. He claims that it is more difficult for teachers to hold pupils' interest since the advent of television, which requires of them less energy, but he believes that the attempt should, nevertheless, be made.

Head of English. The head of English has taught in the school for thirty-five years and is liked and respected by both staff and pupils. English was his main subject at teacher training college and he has 'always taught English', although he has also taught maths, history and music.

He became head of English while the school was a junior high. He taught 'O' level English and maths at evening classes for seventeen years and sees himself primarily as a secondary school teacher; he is quite happy to allow junior-trained teachers to take charge of the detail of English teaching lower down the school, although decisions about buying books, and changes in curriculum, always go to him for approval before they are finalized.

He sees his main problem in recent years as being the lack of a base as he has had to keep sets of books in cupboards all over the school. He still lacks space, as his room does not allow for display units and the large number of desks make it difficult to open the cupboards.

I think he would recognize that his weaknesses are in the areas of recommending books to girls, and knowledge of *modern* children's literature. He *is* usually able to recommend books to children, but told me that he would welcome guidance in choice of books for 12+ girls; it is a true sign of greatness to ask for guidance after thirty-five years of successful teaching! Perhaps his many strengths will be complemented by those of the young, female, part-time English specialist mentioned earlier. He believes in setting aside time for personal private reading during English lessons and in encouraging children to talk to him about their reading. He obviously loves reading himself and would like pupils to experience the same enjoyment as well as improving their reading skills. He finds the Asian children keen to read and aware of the value of education generally.

In conclusion, he said that his main problems were basically physical ones: the need for an adequate and permanent English base; space and money for display units and shelving; and money for a lot more books, as most of those he had were old and looked 'unattractive and uninviting'. The Book Flood will have gone a little way towards solving these problems and, in spite of them, he manages to encourage a remarkable number of children to read for themselves, and perseveres in introducing them to books like *The Silver Sword* as a class reader, or to shortened classics – and with success, as most of the children say they enjoy them.

Summary of the similarities and differences between the two inner city schools
1   There is a tremendous difference between the Victorian building of the control school and the modern airy building of the experimental school, although a similarity is that both have school libraries that are self-contained rooms – unlike those in the outer city schools.
2   The 'immigrant' population is greater in the control school, and was so at an earlier date, affecting the need for additional materials and allowing them an additional member of staff. The chief effect here was on money available for buying 'real literature'.
3   The experimental school covers a slightly 'better' catchment area in purely material terms, the very worst housing conditions being in the catchment area of the control school.
4   The policy with regard to school libraries differs in that the control school library is a resource centre containing mainly non-fiction; whereas the experimental school library contains a good deal of fiction. It is also used less frequently for purposes other than that of library.
5   The schools both have a specialist head of English in charge of English, and teaching at the upper end of the school, whereas in the lower school English is taught by junior-trained class teachers.
6   A similar policy pertains with regard to streaming and setting.

3 Reading Records

'This is my best book. The thing about books like this is that they get your attention and once you've started reading them you just can't stop, and when you've finished reading them you want to read them again and again, but I'm going to read The Starlight Barking you see, look, it "enchants" me like it says here [in the blurb]. It's an adventure!'

'What's an adventure?'

'Well I thought it was where they were always in the middle of things' (conversation with a 6½-year-old about The 101 Dalmatians).

The Reading Record Form

In addition to measuring the effect of an increased supply of books upon children's reading skills, we decided to take the opportunity of monitoring their reading habits for the duration of the experiment. To this end we asked each child to complete a questionnaire (see Appendix I) whenever that child read a non-text book in school. While the main aim of asking the children to keep this record was to enable us to compare the reading habits of pupils in control and experimental schools, it was also believed to be an intrinsically valuable exercise in that it would provide a developmental picture of the children's reading habits and interests.

A detailed account of the design of the questionnaire appears in the 'Annual Proceedings' of the UKRA Conference for 1979, held at the University of Leeds (Ingham, 1980). However, there are a few aspects of the form that I should like to mention at this point before I describe and discuss the findings. First, we thought it important for the children to complete the form as near as possible to the times of borrowing and reading a book, so that there was no question of asking them to recall their reading. Secondly, the recording of actual titles and authors read would facilitate a description of children's reading patterns which would be developed from the reality of the situation. We decided against asking them to tick categories of books which they preferred, e.g. 'adventure stories', 'mysteries', 'historical novels', etc., unlike researchers in a number of previous studies (Jenkinson, 1940; Smith and Harrap, 1957; Butts, 1963; Inglis, 1969; Yarlott and Harpin, 1970–1) on the grounds that many books do not lend themselves to categorization; boys often do not wish to admit to a love of animal stories, for instance; and we wanted to produce actual lists of popular authors and titles which we and our readers could examine ourselves. Thirdly, despite the problems of analysis involved we decided to ask the children what made them choose their book and to allow them a free response to this question rather than suggesting possible reasons to them. While there is inevitably some degree of subjective classification of responses on the part of researchers, this course of action seemed to us to be the lesser of two evils. Stages of development of categorization of responses are mentioned in the UKRA paper (Ingham, 1980), and the final category system appears in Appendix II. Fourthly, a record was kept of the 'type' of each book in terms of fiction, non-fiction, poetry, or jokes/puzzles.

It is impossible to know to what extent the responses to the questionnaire represent an accurate record of the children's reading, but I did keep a regular check by spending on average one day per fortnight in each school, often arriving unexpectedly; I also interviewed all heads, teachers involved in the teaching of English, 'school librarians' and approximately 10 per cent of the children. The returns certainly show a high degree of internal consistency and children seem to have been prepared to record the fact that they did not like a book and did not finish it. They were told at regular intervals by myself and by their teachers that honesty was most important, that their response would not affect the way in which they were treated at school, and that no discriminating person could be expected to like all books. Certainly the proportions are right and the record is likely to be far more accurate than those obtained by the 'one-off' survey approach to children's reading interests (Jenkinson, 1940; Carsley, 1957; Yarlott and Harpin, 1970–1; Whitehead *et al.*, 1977). Another issue is that children in both experimental *and control* schools became more aware of books and authors – probably as a result of completing the questionnaire; and that the attention they received in this way had a positive effect in motivating many pupils in all four schools to read more. Keeping a simple record of children's reading and discussing each child's record with him or her once a term is something that more teachers could profitably do (many already do this); to those who plead lack of time, I would suggest it is a question of priorities and that our research seems to show that, if you are aiming to encourage a love of reading in your pupils, then keeping a simple record of their reading is essential – it shows that you know and care about what they are reading.

Findings and interpretation

If we examine, first of all, the number of Reading Record Forms completed (see Tables 3·1 and 3·2) it is immediately noticeable that in the outer city experimental school only did numbers decrease between the beginning and the end of the experiment. (Admittedly, this is a very crude measure of children's reading habits as it tells us nothing about length of books, difficulty, whether book was finished, etc., and must therefore be considered in the light of other findings.) Number of individual authors and separate titles recorded also decreased in the outer city experimental school (see Tables 3·3 and 3·4).

Although children in both inner city schools recorded a marked increase in reading in the final year of the experiment, it is particularly interesting to note that there was an increase of only sixteen separate titles at the inner city control school and a *decrease* in the number of authors recorded, whereas the number of titles recorded in the inner city experimental school more than doubled and the number of authors recorded almost doubled (see Tables 3·3 and 3·4). The lesson to be learnt from these figures is that if we want children to become familiar with a wide variety of authors and titles we need to make this choice available and accessible. Unless we *do* present children with this kind of variety there is less likelihood that they will find books that they personally feel to be rewarding and less likelihood that they will develop discrimination. Of course, what use is made of a large and varied stock of books is also important, but we will return to that issue later.

Table 3·1   Number of Reading Record Forms completed: outer city schools (matched schools paired)

No. of Reading Record Forms	10+ Exp. Frequency	10+ Cont. Frequency	11+ Exp. Frequency	11+ Cont. Frequency	12+ Exp. Frequency	12+ Cont. Frequency
60–4						
55–9						
50–4						
45–9						
40–4				1		
35–9				1		
30–4	2			3	1	
25–9	2			2	0	
20–4	12		3	1	0	2
15–19	18	1	15	4	1	11
10–14	27	6	22	10	13	24
5–9	12	39	23	26	31	38
0–4	4	37	11	32	24	4
Totals	1095	447	773	666	456	782
n	77	83	74	80	70	79

Table 3·2   Number of Reading Record Forms completed: inner city schools (matche schools paired)

No. of Reading Record Forms	10+ Exp. Frequency	10+ Cont. Frequency	11+ Exp. Frequency	11+ Cont. Frequency	12+ Exp. Frequency	12+ Con Frequency
60–4					1	
55–9					0	
50–4					1	
45–9					0	
40–4					1	
35–9					0	
30–4		1			4	2
25–9	2	0	2		8	
20–4	4	1	6		9	
15–19	6	5	5	1	12	2(
10–14	19	14	13	17	16	2(
5–9	37	30	25	43	19	1(
0–4	26	45	38	25	15	1
Totals	776	590	688	582	1240	125(
n	94	94	89	86	86	8(

Table 3·3   Number of individual titles recorded in each school in each year

1   Outer city schools

	10+ Exp.	10+ Cont.	11+ Exp.	11+ Cont.	12+ Exp.	12+ Con(
No. of titles	554	290	471	322	249	307
No. of returns	1095	447	773	666	456	782
n	77	83	74	80	70	79(

2   Inner city schools

	10+ Exp.	10+ Cont.	11+ Exp.	11+ Cont.	12+ Exp.	12+ Cont(
No. of titles	415	404	479	299	886	412
No. of returns	776	590	688	582	1240	1250
n	94	94	89	86	86	83

Table 3·4   *Number of individual authors recorded in each school in each year*

Outer city schools

	10+		11+		12+	
	Exp.	Cont.	Exp.	Cont.	Exp.	Cont.
. of authors	343	196	314	199	244	272
. of returns	1095	447	773	666	456	782
	77	83	74	80	70	79

Inner city schools

	10+		11+		12+	
	Exp.	Cont.	Exp.	Cont.	Exp.	Cont.
. of authors	274	273	311	157	500	228
. of returns	776	590	688	582	1240	1250
	94	94	89	86	86	83

Table 3·5   *Location, with matched schools paired (percentages)*

Outer city schools

	10+		11+		12+	
ation	Exp.	Cont.	Exp.	Cont.	Exp.	Cont.
olic library	0·4	0·4	0·3	0·9	2·0	4·9
ool library	11·5	3·1	11·9	5·1	11·7	2·6
ss library	86·9	96·0	86·2	91·3	74·8	81·6
ongs to child	0·5	0·4	0·6	1·7	11·0	7·0
ongs to friend	0·1	0·0	0·4	0·2	1·1	0·3
	77	83	74	80	70	79

Inner city schools

	10+		11+		12+	
ation	Exp.	Cont.	Exp.	Cont.	Exp.	Cont.
blic library	0·1	3·9	1·6	11·2	6·4	4·5
ool library	6·2	63·7	16·7	18·0	41·9	1·7
ss library	92·5	20·5	80·5	42·3	38·1	77·4
ongs to child	0·5	9·3	0·7	20·1	9·8	10·9
ongs to friend	0·4	0·8	0·0	4·8	1·4	2·9
response	0·3	1·7	0·4	3·6	2·3	2·7
	49	94	89	86	86	83

The number of children who recorded reading fifteen or more books (a minimum of approximately one book every two weeks of term-time not taken up by other activities like preparing for the carol service or going to camp) decreased drastically in the outer city experimental school only, from thirty-four to two (see Tables 3·1 and 3·2), while it increased in the other three schools: by thirteen in the outer city control school; from fifteen to thirty-six in the inner city experimental school; and from seven to forty-two in the inner city control school. On the other hand, the number of children who completed four or fewer forms increased in the outer city experimental school, from four to twenty-four, but decreased in the other three: from thirty-seven to four in the outer city control school; from twenty-six to fifteen in the inner city experimental school; and from fifty-three to one in the inner city control school. Of course, we must not assume that because children are reading in the class-room they are necessarily enjoying it or benefiting from it; we shall examine the extent of the enjoyment shortly.

The figures suggest that some teachers are keen to have pupils experience books even if the stock is old and limited; and to make the experience available even with totally inadequate resources. Such teachers believe that it is worth while to devote a part of the English timetable to the personal reading development of their pupils, in the belief that it will affect not only their achievement in English, but their achievement across the curriculum and development as people, encouraging in them both self-awareness and awareness of others. The figures also suggest that making available more adequate resources is a *necessary* but not *sufficient* stimulus for developing a love of reading in children.

The low incidence of non-readers in the final year in the control schools could also be indicative of the degree of structure and control over children's reading development in those schools. In each school there were a few more non-readers among the boys than among the girls, but only four fewer readers of fifteen or more books among the boys than among the girls.

Responses to the questions on the Reading Record Form have been analysed for boys and girls together and for the boys and girls separately but, since there is not space to include all the separate results for boys and girls, only some are included in this chapter. The main aim was to look for differences in responses from children in experimental and control schools. Question 1 asked 'Where did you get this book from?' Since no more than a handful of enthusiasts completed forms for books read outside the school, one can safely assume that the figures indicate the places from which books read in school were obtained and that even if the figures are not totally accurate, if some children sometimes forgot to fill in forms (rarely, I believe), at least the proportions are right. We must bear in mind that, for instance, the very small percentage of books borrowed from public libraries (see Tables 3·III, 3·IV and 3·V in Appendix IX), should not be interpreted as a reflection of public library membership (see Table 3·5).

In the outer city pair of schools more of the children's own books are recorded in the final year, in part because avid readers, some of whom were the subjects of case studies, had developed decided preferences by this stage and had exhausted the supply of books that interested them from within the school. Some of the keen readers described discovering a particular author first of all in the class library, tracing other books by that author into the school library and eventually to the public library; then, being impatient about the library obtaining the rest and, in any case, wanting to *own* the set of books, finding ways to buy them. For instance, a girl in the outer city experimental school stated in November of the middle year of the experiment, '. . . I have read all the ones that I liked the idea of . . .'. The increase could also in part be the result of children at 12+ having more pocket-money than at 10+ as well as an increased amount of freedom to visit bookshops and newsagents alone. A greater percentage of children's own books was recorded over the three years in the inner city control school than in any of the other schools, possibly because of the smaller stock of fiction material available in that school than in the others. The fact that approximately one-fifth of the books recorded at 11+ in that school belonged to the children is probably a result of the influence of the teacher who was running the school bookshop at that time and who was also a class teacher with the Book Flood cohort in that year.

In the outer city pair of schools children borrowed more of their books from the class libraries throughout the experiment, although a larger percentage was borrowed from class libraries in the outer city control school where, according to the teacher responsible for the school library at the time of the experiment, very few children used it; also, most of the fiction material was in the class-rooms.

In the inner city experimental school we find a marked decrease in the percentage of books borrowed from the class libraries by the end of the experiment. This is probably because the children were greatly excited by the Book Flood and read voraciously from their books for the first two years of the experiment and, thus, needed to turn to the public library, book ownership and school library in the final year in order to satisfy their literary needs. Certainly the school library is a very active and welcoming place, and is organized by a competent and enthusiastic 'school librarian', who keeps the room manned in breaks and lunch-hours, has a well-organized system of recording and, therefore, feels free to encourage children to borrow and take books home. He is well able to advise on book choice and willing to order on request if money allows; so far this has been possible but that happy situation could have already ceased because of recent cuts in capitation allowance and rising prices of all school requisites including books. Indeed, the Book Flood itself probably encouraged teachers in experimental schools to look with a little less horror at a few book losses per year than did those in the control schools.

In the inner city control school children's school library borrowing decreased when class library borrowing increased. I think this is quite simply a reflection of where the children were at that time in the week that was allocated to the borrowing of books and silent reading. In the first year of the experiment all children were taken each week to the school library, which contains a preponderance of non-fiction books; there were a few fiction books in the school but most of these were probably used in the upper age groups. Since there were more groups of children than there were class-rooms in this school, it was difficult to make available a permanent supply of books anywhere but in the school library, until the final year of the experiment when the English specialist aspired to a class-room in a hut as his English base and, thus, was no longer peripatetic within his own school! Nevertheless, even though he ceased to be seen staggering around like an inexperienced juggler or like a Sahib leading native bearers, he was still afraid to leave books out for other classes using the hut, and felt it necessary to lock the building during breaks and lunch-hours because of possible theft or vandalism (not a reflection on the vast majority of children at that school). In any case, he would have found it difficult to display books in Victorian cupboards (beautiful pieces of furniture) that, for the most part, could only be opened when desks were moved, there being large numbers of children in each class. Thus we come back to availability and accessibility – plus very concrete physical factors!

In Question 2, we asked the children to tell us why they chose the books, the responses being subsequently categorized by the research team. Appendix II contains a detailed breakdown of the final category system, and III gives some examples of children's responses to this question. The majority of the books was chosen because of the perceived content/subject matter, that is, 'what they were about' or because of some aspect of the appearance of the book. Hopefully, in a 'flooded' school, children would develop an awareness of authors; of series; of reliable bases for book choice –

such as reading the blurb and a couple of pages of the book, knowing something of the author, depending upon the recommendations of a reliable friend or teacher, etc., rather than responding to the pictures on the cover or, for example, a title with the word 'adventure' in it. In other words, children surrounded by books might be expected to learn fairly quickly that one cannot always tell a book by its cover. The process of completing the Reading Record Form, particularly when children were asked to record author and reason for choice, could, on its own, have the effect of heightening the children's awareness of reliable criteria on which to base book choice.

Table 3·6   Reasons given for choice of books recorded on the Reading Record Forms (percentages)

Outer city schools

Reason	10+ Exp.	Cont.	11+ Exp.	Cont.	12+ Exp.	Cont.
Read author before	4·9	2·8	2·2	3·4	7·7	6·1
Book in a series	6·3	3·9	5·0	4·6	3·6	3·4
Read some of book	1·1	1·1	2·2	2·6	6·1	12·5
Content of book	32·5	30·2	33·6	23·4	22·9	30·3
Appearance of book	17·8	35·0	25·8	25·3	23·7	18·5
Knowledge of book	14·1	10·8	11·0	4·0	14·8	7·6
Book recommendation	7·1	4·8	7·3	3·0	7·7	8·2
Miscellaneous	2·5	1·1	0·9	0·3	3·6	2·8
Compulsory	0·1	5·9	1·4	26·6	0·2	0·1
Information but no reason	1·1	0·0	0·2	0·3	0·6	3·6
n	77	83	74	80	70	79

Inner city schools

Reason	10+ Exp.	Cont.	11+ Exp.	Cont.	12+ Exp.	Cont.
Read author before	10·8	2·4	6·8	7·1	10·9	5·9
Book in a series	4·3	1·9	4·5	3·3	6·9	2·8
Read some of book	3·8	0·9	9·2	0·8	4·6	3·8
Content of book	30·6	33·5	31·5	21·1	33·2	13·8
Appearance of book	27·9	35·7	22·4	22·3	12·7	28·3
Knowledge of book	10·7	7·6	14·0	9·0	7·7	8·2
Book recommended	6·4	8·2	7·7	6·0	13·8	14·2
Miscellaneous	1·6	3·0	2·6	2·6	2·2	2·0
Compulsory	1·4	1·8	0·3	22·0	2·2	12·6
Information but no reason	0·2	0·7	0·3	0·0	2·7	3·5
No information	2·3	4·2	0·8	5·9	4·0	5·0
n	94	94	89	86	86	83

The figures show a steady decrease in dependence on the appearance of a book as a criterion of choice in the outer city control school – from 35 per cent to 18·5 per cent – but not in the matched experimental school (see Table 3·6). On the other hand, in the inner city pair of schools, appearance of a book continued to be an important criterion for choice in the control school, decreasing by 7·4 per cent only, whereas in the experimental school appearance of a book was mentioned more than twice as often as a reason for book choice in the *first* year of the experiment than in the *final* year. The important variable here is probably teacher knowledge and use of books as an intervening variable between child and book.

More books were read because they were compulsory in the control than in the experimental schools – particularly at 11 +. It is easier to allow children a free choice when a larger stock of books is available. In the final year of the experiment a larger percentage of books in all schools was chosen because they had been recommended to the child, the increase being particularly striking in the inner city schools where all the fourth-year children were taught English exclusively by an English 'specialist' in an English base.

In response to Question 3, children were asked to indicate whether they had taken their books home to read or not (see Table 3·7). It is immediately noticeable that few books were taken home from the outer city control school, although the percentages had doubled by the end of the experiment. According to both class teachers and pupils it was not the policy to encourage children to take class library books home in this school in case they were lost or damaged; books could be taken home at the teacher's discretion, the result usually being that the 'G' stream children, who, in a number of cases had books of their own at home and belonged to the public library, were less likely to be allowed to take books home! However, the motive was good – to make the bookstock of the school available to as many children as possible in school and to try to prevent the supply from being depleted. In *both* control schools, in fact, fewer books were taken home than in the experimental schools – probably partly because of the attraction of the increased supply of brand-new books in the experimental schools and partly because scarce resources are valuable!

Indeed, from a pragmatic, rather than an idealistic, point of view we must consider the difficulties of replacing lost or damaged books in the present financial climate, with cuts in capitation allowance, an increase in the costs of 'essential' commodities like exercise books and an increase in the cost of books. From all four schools in each year, girls took books home more often than did boys in every case but one, that being the final year at the inner city control school.

Table 3·7 Percentages of books recorded on Reading Record Form that were taken home/not taken home

1 Outer city schools

Taken Home?	10+ Exp.	10+ Cont.	11+ Exp.	11+ Cont.	12+ Exp.	12+ Cont.
Yes	61·0	16·1	66·8	13·5	66·0	33·0
No	20·8	73·8	19·7	72·5	19·3	57·5
No response	18·2	10·1	13·6	14·0	14·7	9·5
n	77	83	74	80	70	79

2 Inner city schools

Taken Home?	10+ Exp.	10+ Cont.	11+ Exp.	11+ Cont.	12+ Exp.	12+ Cont.
Yes	57·2	58·5	73·3	48·6	70·0	25·5
No	37·1	30·7	24·3	41·6	27·5	70·1
No response	5·7	10·8	2·5	9·6	2·5	4·4
n	94	94	89	86	86	83

Table 3·8 The extent to which books, recorded on the Reading Record Form, were completed, with matched schools paired (percentages)

1 Outer city schools

Amount read	10+ Exp.	10+ Cont.	11+ Exp.	11+ Cont.	12+ Exp.	12+ Cont.
All of it	61·5	75·8	68·2	69·7	59·2	67·1
Over half	15·0	8·7	14·9	10·7	12·7	12·7
Less than half	11·2	7·2	8·0	11·4	7·5	8·6
A few pages	7·1	4·9	5·2	4·5	5·0	4·5
No response	5·2	3·4	3·8	3·8	15·6	7·2
n	77	83	74	80	70	79

2 Inner city schools

Amount read	10+ Exp.	10+ Cont.	11+ Exp.	11+ Cont.	12+ Exp.	12+ Cont.
All of it	73·7	60·3	76·6	74·4	79·8	73·0
Over half	11·6	15·4	9·3	10·7	12·0	9·9
Less than half	9·3	8·8	8·9	8·2	5·1	7·6
A few pages	5·2	12·7	4·5	3·1	1·3	4·5
No response	0·3	2·7	0·7	3·6	1·9	5·0
n	94	94	89	86	86	83

By means of Question 4, it was attempted to ascertain to what extent books chosen were in fact read (see Table 3·8). About three-quarters of the books chosen were allegedly finished. One would hope that, with a large supply and wide variety of books, along with adequate guidance from teachers, children would gradually become more expert at choosing books that they are likely to want to finish.

In fact, the percentage of books reported completed *decreased* slightly in the outer city experimental school, by 2·3 per cent, and in the outer city control school by 8·7 per cent; however, in the inner city pair of schools, there was a steady, albeit small, increase in the percentage of books allegedly completed – an increase of 6·2 per cent in the experimental school, while in the control school, which began with a smaller percentage of books completed than the matched school, there was an increase of 12·7 per cent. This is not to suggest that children *should* complete books but that educated choice of books can be developed by practice and is less likely to lead to disappointment, thus reinforcing the reading habit. The smallest percentage, and smallest number of books completed, was in the final year at the outer city experimental school, where it may not be a coincidence that children were taught English by class teachers, two of whom were very competent specialists in other subjects and who, on their own admission, had a minimal knowledge of children's literature and would preferably have steered clear of the subject. While ideally we should like all teachers to be conversant with literature for the children they teach, perhaps it is too much to ask that they *should* be so and, in any case, the interests of the children should not suffer while we attempt to convert the teachers, if indeed the proposed cuts in in-service teacher training will allow us to do this. One of these teachers, who must surely represent many others, and to whom I am very grateful for his honesty, admitted that he was totally unable to recommend books to children because of lack of knowledge and interest in the area, and that he felt inadequate when children wanted to discuss the books they had read as he could not make an informed contribution. He believed that the children were well aware of his lack of interest.

It should be added that he and the other fourth-year class teachers in that school were very well able to teach English language, but either needed detailed help and guidance with the literature from a specialist or to have the English divided so that book choice, silent reading, discussions, etc., took place with the English specialist who was available in the school. It should also be added that the teachers lower down the school, who probably viewed themselves more as general class teachers and thus *expected* to teach a wide range of subjects, were usually very well informed and enthusiastic about children's literature. (Unfortunately, the English specialist was acting deputy head for the second half of the experiment because the deputy head had been involved in a car accident.)

In Question 5 we asked the children to indicate their opinion of the chosen books (see Table 3·9). If we combine the percentages for the first two categories, we notice a steady decrease in the percentage of books enjoyed in both of the outer city schools; in the inner city schools, although there was an upsurge of enjoyment in the control school in the middle year of the experiment, it is only in the inner city experimental school that percentage of enjoyment was maintained and even increased slightly, from 61·6 per cent to 66·7 per cent – not a remarkable increase, however. Nevertheless, perhaps with the 12–13 age group, it is an achievement to *maintain* the level of enjoyment of books. The author and titles that were most enjoyed will be discussed in detail later in this chapter.

Table 3·9   Children's expressed opinion of the books recorded on the Reading Record Form, with matched schools paired (percentages)

1   *Outer city schools*

Opinion	10+		11+		12+	
	Exp.	Cont.	Exp.	Cont.	Exp.	Cont.
One of the best	20·7	23·3	20·1	13·7	14·7	11·4
Liked very much	33·9	32·7	30·1	32·3	25·9	30·7
Quite liked	24·5	23·5	28·2	34·7	22·4	30·1
Did not like much	10·9	9·4	12·0	11·7	14·3	14·1
Did not like at all	6·4	6·5	5·8	3·9	7·0	6·8
No response	3·7	4·7	3·8	3·8	15·8	7·0
n	77	83	74	80	70	79

2   *Inner city schools*

Opinion	10+		11+		12+	
	Exp.	Cont.	Exp.	Cont.	Exp.	Cont.
One of the best	18·3	13·6	18·2	18·6	20·4	11·0
Liked very much	43·3	38·3	47·2	45·9	46·3	36·7
Quite liked	22·7	33·9	20·1	26·6	22·3	31·7
Did not like much	11·5	9·5	9·4	4·6	5·7	10·3
Did not like at all	4·0	2·5	3·8	1·7	3·2	3·5
No response	0·3	2·2	1·3	2·6	2·0	6·7
n	94	94	89	86	86	83

Question 6 dealt with the degree of perceived difficulty that a child experienced with a book. Although it is not necessarily disadvantageous for a child to choose a book perceived to be *quite difficult*, we would hope that a decreasing percentage of books chosen by children in the experimental schools would be recorded as *very difficult* (although we should keep in mind the exceptional avid reader who might, perhaps, read *Plague Dogs*, find it *very difficult*, but still get a great deal out of it and be in no way deterred from further excursions into equally difficult literature).

First of all, looking at the data for boys and girls together (see Table 3·10), we find a slight decrease in the percentage of books perceived to be very difficult, and an over-all decrease of 6·1 per cent in those perceived to be quite difficult, in the outer city experimental school, but an overall, albeit very slight, increase in books perceived to be both very difficult and quite difficult (1 per cent) and (1·6 per cent) in the outer city control school. Similarly, in the inner city experimental school, we see a decrease in the percentage of books found very difficult (1·3 per cent) *and* in the percentage found quite difficult (5·6 per cent), but in the inner city control school, while there is a decrease of 0·4 per cent in the books found very difficult, there is an increase of 2·8 per cent in those found quite difficult. However, *all* the differences are slight and the Book Flood does not seem markedly to have affected perceived level of difficulty with books. If we examine the results for boys and girls separately, we find that boys did consistently express a greater level of perceived difficulty than girls, although to a greater extent in the outer city schools than in the inner city.

There is a considerable amount of patience, empathy and knowledge involved in finding books that will appeal to the pre-adolescent boy who is not an avid reader. I think that a 'school librarian' who takes part in many sporting activities with the boys and believes in buying books and periodicals that they request, is likely to have the attention and respect of those boys to whom he recommends books, and that a PE teacher who teaches English and is obviously an enthusiatic reader is an added encouragement, as well as a clear indication that reading is not 'sissy'! Both of these teachers were to be found in the inner city experimental school.

The aim of Question 7 was to try to find out whether children discuss with other people the books they read, and, if so, with whom. What immediately catches the eye is the large percentage of books that were discussed with friends (see Table 3·11) and the large proportion discussed with other members of the family, especially when compared with the small percentage discussed with teachers.

There were fewer books discussed with members of the family in the outer city control school than in the other three schools. Whether this had something to do with the fact that few school books were taken home is difficult to say. It is a staggering thought that approximately one-third of the books recorded in each year in the outer city control school and in the final year in the outer city experimental school, was not discussed with anyone at all. A few teachers in interviews made it clear that they encouraged some semi-formal discussions about books but this tended to be at the lower end of the school or with rather élitist groups of more able children. Often it was felt that the timetable was too tightly packed to accommodate such an indulgence at the upper end of the middle school. Case studies revealed that many children believe that friends are the best authorities on what they are likely to enjoy. One child commented at the end of a Record Form, 'I think advice from friends is quite good as sometimes they can be quite right. It can help you to decide whether you want to read the book.'

Table 3·10   Children's experienced degree of difficulty with the books recorded on the Reading Record Forms, with matched schools paired (percentages)

1   *Outer city schools*

| | 10+ | | 11+ | | 12+ | |
Degree of difficulty	Exp.	Cont.	Exp.	Cont.	Exp.	Cont.
Very difficult	2·8	2·2	2·6	1·4	2·4	3·2
Quite difficult	18·4	17·2	11·6	11·9	12·3	18·8
Not hard, not easy	36·4	35·8	36·6	43·8	32·5	44·5
Easy	28·1	23·7	33·2	28·7	30·0	21·5
Very easy	11·0	16·3	12·3	10·4	7·2	5·0
No response	3·3	4·7	3·6	3·9	15·6	7·0
n	77	83	74	80	70	79

2   *Inner city schools*

| | 10+ | | 11+ | | 12+ | |
Degree of difficulty	Exp.	Cont.	Exp.	Cont.	Exp.	Cont.
Very difficult	2·3	2·2	2·3	2·7	1·0	1·8
Quite difficult	18·0	10·2	17·3	11·5	12·4	13·0
Not hard, not easy	41·8	35·9	51·2	39·0	47·3	33·5
Easy	27·1	30·0	23·4	22·2	28·1	30·1
Very easy	10·6	19·3	4·4	0·2	8·9	14·8
No response	0·3	2·4	1·5	2·6	2·3	6·8
n	94	94	89	86	86	83

Table 3·11   People to whom children talked about the books recorded on the Reading Record Forms, with matched schools paired (percentages)

1   Outer city schools

	10+		11+		12+	
Child talked to:	Exp.	Cont.	Exp.	Cont.	Exp.	Cont.
Class teacher	10·5	16·3	4·3	11·4	4·2	3·6
Other teacher	3·4	1·4	3·2	1·0	1·9	0·2
Friends	29·0	32·2	32·5	41·7	28·2	38·8
Parents	21·8	9·1	21·3	6·9	18·7	10·2
Brothers/sisters	17·8	9·5	18·4	5·9	17·0	10·0
No one	17·4	31·5	20·3	33·9	30·1	34·2
n	77	83	74	80	70	79

2   Inner city schools

	10+		11+		12+	
Child talked to:	Exp.	Cont.	Exp.	Cont.	Exp.	Cont.
Class teacher	5·6	4·0	2·3	8·3	3·4	6·1
Other teacher	1·5	0·9	1·6	3·7	4·3	1·6
Friends	32·1	33·4	34·6	29·9	35·1	37·6
Parents	18·4	19·1	24·1	14·7	18·8	10·8
Brothers/sisters	15·0	20·9	23·2	20·8	18·1	16·7
No one	27·5	21·7	14·2	23·2	20·3	27·1
n	94	94	89	86	86	83

Similarly, an avid reader who was interviewed on one of the case studies said of herself and her friend:

> . . . we both take notice of each other. She will say, 'I've read a book by so and so, and it is very good', and she will give me the basic outline of the story and I will say, 'I would like to borrow that book after you; it sounds right good'.

Perhaps one reason, apart from the feeling that there is insufficient time and book discussions are not a top priority, for the apparent small scale of discussion of books between teacher and pupil, is that some teachers have not achieved what one teacher so aptly described as 'crossing the bridge'. She said, '. . . the bridge is the teacher reading what the children read and chose for themselves.'

She felt this to be an important mark of respect for, and acceptance of, the child, which is necessary if we expect the pupil to have any respect for our recommendations. Along with Leila Berg,

Peter Dickinson and many others, I believe it is a grave mistake to judge children's literature by adult standards, and perhaps an even more harmful error to reject the child's contribution to a discussion of literature, whatever that child offers, as, in rejecting the contribution, one is rejecting the background and the child's own self; on the other hand, I believe it is equally important to introduce the pupil, through literature, to worlds and ways of looking beyond the immediately familiar, but this will never be achieved unless we have the child's trust.

Question 8 is clearly linked with Question 7 and confirms that a great many books are recommended to friends. Obviously a great many others are given the 'thumbsdown'! The difference between schools is not great, except that it is perhaps worth noting that an increasing percentage of books was recommended to friends in the inner city experimental school, and a decreasing percentage in its matched control school (see Table 3·12).

When asked, in Question 9, whether they would like to read another book by the same author, a fair proportion of the children thought that they would (see Table 3·13) but only in the inner city experimental school was the final percentage greater, by 15 per cent, than it had been at the beginning of the experiment. One could tentatively suggest an increased awareness of author and a development of those skills of selection that lead one to the author whom one will find interesting and enjoyable.

On average, less than a quarter of the books chosen inspired their reader to give additional information about them, although we did occasionally come across some very rude remarks! The only outstanding exception to this is the 40·9 per cent of final comments from the inner city control school; perhaps these children welcomed the opportunity of expressing a personal view about a book. Some quotations from the final comments can be found in Appendix III, but to whet your appetite a little, allow me to quote one or two at this juncture (original spelling and punctuation preserved):

1   From a fourth-year girl:
    'This book has been retold by John Kennett. Why?' (*A Christmas Carol* by Charles Dickens).
2   From a fourth-year boy:
    'I think maybe that once you have read one you have read 'em all' (*Secret Seven Adventure* by Enid Blyton).
3   From a fourth-year girl:
    'We had to read it, it was a class book and the teacher set us a question on it in our exams' (*Animal Farm* by George Orwell).

Table 3·12   Whether child told friends that the book recorded on the Readir Record Form was a good book, with matched schools paired (percentages)

1   Outer city schools

Whether recommended book	10+		11+		12+	
	Exp.	Cont.	Exp.	Cont.	Exp.	Con
Yes	46·8	44·1	48·8	39·0	34·1	38·
No	46·9	50·3	43·9	55·9	46·9	53·
No response	6·2	5·6	7·4	5·1	16·0	7·
n	77	83	74	80	70	79

2   Inner city schools

Whether recommended book	10+		11+		12+	
	Exp.	Cont.	Exp.	Cont.	Exp.	Con
Yes	46·5	53·6	59·0	49·7	58·9	43·
No	52·4	41·9	38·8	45·5	38·8	49·
No response	1·0	4·6	2·2	4·8	2·3	7·
n	94	94	89	86	86	83

Table 3·13   Whether child wanted to read another book by the same author, wi matched schools paired (percentages)

1   Outer city schools

Like to read another book by same author?	10+		11+		12+	
	Exp.	Cont.	Exp.	Cont.	Exp.	Con
Yes	35·0	40·9	32·9	39·2	32·9	33·
No	43·6	38·0	46·6	43·4	41·1	46·
Don't know	15·0	15·9	14·1	12·5	11·0	13·
No response	6·5	5·1	6·5	5·0	16·0	7·
n	77	83	74	80	70	79

2   Inner city schools

Like to read another book by same author?	10+		11+		12+	
	Exp.	Cont.	Exp.	Cont.	Exp.	Con
Yes	41·5	42·9	38·1	50·9	56·5	42·
No	49·6	44·1	51·2	39·9	35·2	42·(
Don't know	7·9	8·8	9·3	5·2	5·7	8·
No response	1·0	4·2	1·5	4·1	2·5	7·
n	94	94	89	86	86	84

4 From a third-year girl:
  'It was not as good as *Bettinas Secret* because I could put this
  down when it was teatime but I read *Bettinas Secret* over tea'
  (*The Family that Came Back* by David B. White).
5 From a third-year boy:
  'The sort of thing it had in it was accountant – insect who is
  good with figures; abundance – a waltz for cakes!' (*Professor
  Branestawm's Dictionary* by Norman Hunter).

There was quite a number of comments on class readers, most of
which were extremely derogatory. I should like to come back to this
point in the chapters on the case studies, when I shall discuss in
more detail remarks made by individual children, but the gist of the
argument seems to be that, if they cannot have both a class reader
and silent reading, they prefer silent reading as they can read a book
of their own choice at their own speed, stopping to savour or
stumble, or rushing ahead as they see fit; that some children find
the book interesting, but far too slow; and that poor readers reading
it aloud badly, is unbearable. Perhaps it would be a better idea, as
children get older and books get longer, to stimulate children to
read in various ways, for example by reading a couple of chapters
aloud to them well, and doing this with many different kinds of
books, thus appealing to a wide variety of tastes; by telling
children about a book and reading extracts; by allowing children to
talk to the class about the books they have read; by reminding
children about serializations of books on television and discussing
them, rather than by ploddingly ploughing through the whole
book analysing it the-while! If one were just to read one of the
poems from *Charlie and the Great Glass Elevator,* or a couple of
definitions from *Professor Branestawm's Dictionary,* or the first two
or three chapters of *Stig of the Dump,* many children would quickly
take off on their own tracks.

During the process of coding up the children's reponses for the
computer, we gave each book a 'type' category, according to
whether it was fiction; non-fiction; poetry and plays; jokes, riddles,
puzzles, etc. We found that the bulk of the reading material chosen
fell into the category of fiction (see Table 3·14) but we have to
consider these findings in the light of what was available in each
school (see Table 3·15).

Most of the books read in the outer city control school were
fiction, which corroborates the finding that the children borrowed
most of their books from the class libraries and that the school's
fiction library was little used. Most of the books classified in Table
3·15 as 'reading schemes' would fall into the category of fiction for

coding-up purposes. Slightly more non-fiction was read in the first two years in the outer city experimental school but not in the final year, probably because some of the non-fiction books had been left behind in the second- and third-year class-rooms as the children moved up the school.

Table 3·14   Type of book, with matched schools paired (percentages)

1   Outer city schools

Type	10+		11+		12+	
	Exp.	Cont.	Exp.	Cont.	Exp.	Cont.
Fiction	79·0	90·8	71·5	96·2	90·8	93·5
Non-fiction	12·4	7·8	18·4	3·3	5·5	6·0
Poetry	3·0	1·3	2·7	0·2	1·1	0·1
Jokes, etc	4·1	0·0	6·9	0·0	1·8	0·1
Missing values	1·5	0·0	0·5	0·0	0·9	0·3
n	77	83	74	80	70	79

2   Inner city schools

Type	10+		11+		12+	
	Exp.	Cont.	Exp.	Cont.	Exp.	Cont.
Fiction	75·3	60·2	74·6	87·3	72·2	98·1
Non-fiction	16·0	25·3	16·0	8·8	20·2	0·6
Poetry	1·7	10·5	3·8	2·4	0·4	1·0
Jokes, etc	6·8	2·9	4·9	0·3	1·5	0·2
Missing values	0·3	1·2	0·7	1·2	0·6	0·1
n	94	94	89	86	86	83

In the inner city school, the figures again reflect what was easily accessible and available, for, in the first year of the experiment, when children were taken regularly to the school library, they were faced with a preponderance of non-fiction books, whereas in the final year the books that were readily available to them were in the fourth-year class-room and were almost exclusively fiction. The rationale behind the large number of non-fiction books in this school was the necessity to build up the school library as a reference and resource centre for the children in the first two years at the school, when what had been a secondary school became a middle school, as they could not afford adequate sets of books for each class separately. They now intend to develop the fiction stock.

In the inner city experimental school the proportions remained fairly steady, as the children moved freely and easily from one book area to another. This ease and freedom with regard to book browsing and borrowing, marked a well-organized structure which, I believe, operates throughout the school and was co-ordinated by the 'school librarian', although operated by a variety of teachers and pupils.

On average, girls read a little more fiction than did boys, who read slightly more non-fiction than did girls, but the differences are not tremendous.

Popular authors and titles

The popular authors and titles in the schools in each year were examined by extracting responses 1 and 2 to Question 5 on the children's opinion of a book and combining them, that is, authors and titles that were described as 'one of the best books I have ever read' or of which the child said 'I liked it very much'. First of all, the number of books rated as popular in this way was set against the total number of books recorded, and expressed as a percentage of that total; this was done for boys and girls together and for boys and girls separately.

In the outer city experimental school the percentage of books rated as popular steadily declined, for boys and girls, both together and separately, as it did also in the outer city control school (see Table 3·16. In the inner city experimental school it is noticeable that a large percentage of the books was enjoyed very much throughout the experiment and that in every case, both for boys and girls together and separately, the percentage of books thus rated increased a little during the course of the experiment, which is interesting in view of the fact that disillusionment with books is often beginning to set in by the last year of middle school, especially for the child who feels alienated from the culture of the school. In the inner city control school, the middle of the experiment is by far the healthiest looking, even though the percentage of popular books was slightly higher for boys at the end of the experiment than it had been at the beginning but not for girls. Perhaps the male English teacher was less familiar with books that he could recommend to modern young ladies; in fact, I think he would be happy to admit as much and would welcome some not too time-consuming ways of finding out about the books available.

There was both a lack of money available for new books and of information about appropriate material for the fourth-year girls, who were turning increasingly to magazines like *Jackie* and *Look-In*. One of the case study girls, who was an avid reader, said that she read magazines at home because they told her about 'what a

Table 3·15   Books available in school and class libraries

A   *Outer city schools*

| | Experimental | | | | Control | | | | |
	School library	%	Class libraries	%	School library	%	%	Class libraries	%
Fiction	1521	49	4013	61	813	(27)	21	3126	5
Non-fiction	1585	51	1729	27	2222	(73)	58	403	
Reading schemes			789	12			21	2284	3
	3106		6531		3035	100	100	5813	

of which approx. 4450 were BF books of which
63·8 per cent were fiction
36·2 per cent non-fiction

B   *Inner city schools*

| | Experimental | | | | Control | | | | |
	School library	%	Class libraries	%	School library	%	Class libraries	%
Fiction	1372	42·5	4026	6¹	297	9	606	13·
Non-fiction	1853	57·5	1950	29	3073	91	974	21·
Reading schemes			649	10			2910	65
	3225		6625		3370		4490	

of which approx. 4450 were BF books of which
63·8 per cent were fiction
36·2 per cent non-fiction

Table 3·16   Number of times books rated at 1 or 2 on Question 5 – opinion – se
against total Reading Record Form returns, and expressed as percentages of th
latter, for each school, each year, for boys and girls together and separately

Outer city experimental school

	Boys and girls 10+	Boys 10+	Girls 10+	Boys and girls 11+	Boys 11+	Girls 11+	Boys and girls 12+	Boys 12+	Girls 12+
Total returns	1095	596	499	773	383	390	456	230	226
No. rated as 1 or 2	598	321	277	388	198	190	185	104	81
% rated as 1 or 2	54·61	53·86	55·51	50·19	51·70	48·72	40·57	45·22	35·84
n	77	39	38	74	39	35	70	38	32

Table 3·16 – continued

Outer city control school

	Boys and girls 10+	Boys 10+	Girls 10+	Boys and girls 11+	Boys 11+	Girls 11+	Boys and girls 12+	Boys 12+	Girls 12+
Total returns	447	241	206	666	328	338	782	421	361
No. rated as 1 or 2	250	135	115	306	147	159	329	165	164
% rated as 1 or 2	55·93	50·02	55·82	45·94	44·82	47·04	42·07	39·19	45·43
n	83	46	37	80	46	34	79	46	33

Inner city experimental school

	Boys and girls 10+	Boys 10+	Girls 10+	Boys and girls 11+	Boys 11+	Girls 11+	Boys and girls 12+	Boys 12+	Girls 12+
Total returns	776	378	398	688	372	316	1240	704	536
No. rated as 1 or 2	478	235	243	450	239	211	827	464	363
% rated as 1 or 2	61·60	62·17	61·05	65·41	64·25	66·77	66·69	65·91	67·12
n	94	51	43	89	49	40	86	48	38

Inner city control school

	Boys and girls 10+	Boys 10+	Girls 10+	Boys and girls 11+	Boys 11+	Girls 11+	Boys and girls 12+	Boys 12+	Girls 12+
Total returns	590	170	420	582	224	358	1250	492	758
No. rated as 1 or 2	306	86	220	375	137	238	597	257	340
% rated as 1 or 2	51·86	50·59	52·38	64·43	61·16	66·48	47·76	52·23	44·85
n	94	39	55	86	37	49	83	35	48

teenager does, growing up and all that . . . they're not romantic, they're problems, like if their mother and dad have split up or something like that'. Neither the girls not the teacher had heard of books like Diana Wynne Jones's *The Ogre Downstairs* or Judy Blume's *It's Not the End of the World*; nor had they heard of Betsy Byars, Mary Rodgers, Paul Zindel, Ursula le Guin, or Beverley Cleary, to name a few of my favourites, all of whom this young lady could have coped with very well.

When we look at the places from which children borrowed the books that they really enjoyed (see Table 3·17) we noticed in the outer city schools a greater spread of places for popular books than we did for all books recorded. The percentage of books belonging to the child was approximately twice as great for favourite books as for all books in the final year of the experiment in both outer city schools. Otherwise, the proportions are very similar to those for all books recorded, with slightly higher percentages of own books as favourites in the inner city schools also.

Table 3·17   Favourite authors: location, with matched schools paired (percentages)

1   Outer city schools

	10+		11+		12+	
Location	Exp.	Cont.	Exp.	Cont.	Exp.	Cont.
Public library	0·5	0·4	0·3	1·3	2·7	7·3
School library	9·9	4·4	13·1	6·9	6·5	2·4
Class library	88·3	94·4	84·0	87·9	66·5	72·6
Belongs to child	0·8	0·8	1·0	2·3	22·7	13·1
Belongs to friend	0·2	0·0	0·8	0·3	0·0	0·6
No response	0·3	0·0	0·8	1·3	1·6	3·9
Total returns	598	250	388	306	185	239

2   Inner city schools

	10+		11+		12+	
Location	Exp.	Cont.	Exp.	Cont.	Exp.	Cont.
Public library	0·2	2·9	2·4	11·2	7·1	6·9
School library	5·6	59·5	16·7	17·6	40·5	1·8
Class library	92·9	20·9	49·8	38·9	36·6	69·2
Belongs to child	0·6	13·4	1·1	23·2	12·1	15·4
Belongs to friend	0·0	1·3	0·0	5·9	1·9	3·9
No response	0·6	2·0	0·0	3·2	1·7	2·9
Total returns	478	306	450	375	827	597

Comparing reasons for choice of favourite books with reasons for choice for all books chosen (see Table 3·18) we do find some differences. In every case the percentage of popular books chosen because the child has read the author before is greater than for all books recorded – not dramatically greater but greater in every case; and in all but two cases, favourite books were more frequently

Table 3·18 *Favourite authors: reasons for book choice, with matched schools paired (percentages)*

1 *Outer city schools*

Reasons for choice	10+		11+		12+	
	Exp.	*Cont.*	*Exp.*	*Cont.*	*Exp.*	*Cont.*
Read author before	5·9	2·9	2·6	4·0	11·9	9·8
Book in a series	7·8	4·6	8·3	4·3	4·3	4·9
Read some of book	1·8	1·0	1·5	1·7	4·8	10·5
Content of book	30·6	31·8	32·5	27·5	21·4	33·4
Appearance of book	15·5	33·4	24·4	24·0	20·0	14·4
Knowledge of book	17·0	12·1	14·0	4·3	21·4	8·5
Book recommended	6·6	3·9	6·1	1·7	9·0	9·2
Miscellaneous	2·6	1·0	0·6	0·0	1·4	1·5
Compulsory	0·0	5·9	1·3	26·9	0·0	0·3
Information but no reason	0·8	0·0	0·0	0·6	0·0	1·0
No information	11·2	2·6	8·5	4·9	5·7	6·4

2 *Inner city schools*

Reasons for choice	10+		11+		12+	
	Exp.	*Cont.*	*Exp.*	*Cont.*	*Exp.*	*Cont.*
Read author before	13·9	2·9	8·3	7·7	12·3	7·7
Book in a series	4·3	2·3	6·0	3·9	9·2	3·9
Read some of book	3·9	0·3	9·6	0·0	4·4	3·4
Content of book	34·3	34·5	31·3	24·4	33·7	14·7
Appearance of book	22·7	36·2	18·5	19·1	11·2	25·6
Knowledge of book	12·0	9·6	15·4	10·4	7·8	12·1
Book recommended	5·2	6·9	7·5	7·5	14·1	15·0
Miscellaneous	1·2	2·3	2·7	2·4	2·0	1·4
Compulsory	1·4	0·6	0·4	20·3	0·7	9·3
Information but no reason	0·2	0·6	0·0	0·0	1·9	3·7
No information	0·7	3·8	0·4	4·3	2·5	3·1

chosen for being part of a series than were all books chosen: both those categories suggest that the child had a fairly good idea of what to expect from the book. In every case but one a smaller percentage of favourite books was chosen because of their appearance than was the case for all books, but differences are not as great as one might expect. In *every* case, a greater percentage of favourite books was chosen because the child already had some knowledge of the book – for example, having seen it on television or because a teacher had read some part of it, a criterion for choice less likely to lead to disappointment than merely going by a book's appearance. (Of course, we must remember here that appearance was often given as one of several reasons so that a child instantly attracted by the cover of the book could also read a few pages before deciding to choose it.) Responses to the other categories show very little difference from those for all books.

If we next examine the differences for choice of favourite authors between matched experimental and control schools, we notice that the appearance of a book steadily decreases in importance as a criterion for book choice in the outer city control school (by 13·4 per cent) but not in the experimental school; in the inner city experimental school the appearance of a favourite book decreases in importance by 11·5 per cent, as it does also in the inner city control school by 10·6 per cent. However, in the outer city experimental school, we find a large percentage of favourite authors chosen because the child had some prior knowledge of the book, especially in the final year when 21·4 per cent of the favourite books were chosen on that basis. There was also a larger percentage of books chosen on the basis of recommendations in the final year at all four schools than there had been in the two preceding years.

The majority of popular books, like the majority of all books chosen, fell into the category of fiction. If we examine the percentage for boys and girls together, we find that the percentages of fiction books that were really enjoyed are almost identical to the percentages for all books recorded; the percentages for the other categories are also very close (see Table 3·19). It is noticeable that, in every case but two, more favourite fiction books were recorded by girls than by boys, but the differences are not great; in *every* case, boys recorded more non-fiction books as favourites than did girls (see Table 3·20). In every case but one, girls recorded enjoying poetry more than did boys, whereas boys seemed to be slightly more attracted to jokes and riddles than did girls, except in the first year in the inner city schools. As far as I know, the children in the outer city control school did not have this type of book available.

One of the chief advantages of keeping a longitudinal record of children's reading is that, as a result, we are able to provide, first, lists of authors and titles most frequently chosen but not necessarily finished or enjoyed, in each school, at 10+, 11+ and 12+; and, secondly, lists of books rated as one of the best ever read or as liked very much, most frequently.

Table 3·19   Favourite authors: type of book, with matched schools paired (percentages)

1   *Outer city schools*

| Type of book | 10+ | | 11+ | | 12+ | |
	Exp.	Cont.	Exp.	Cont.	Exp.	Cont.
Fiction	80·9	90·8	75·3	97·4	91·9	92·7
Non–fiction	12·2	8·0	16·2	2·3	5·4	7·3
Poetry	3·0	1·2	2·1	0·0	0·5	0·0
Jokes, etc.	2·8	0·0	6·4	0·0	2·2	0·0
Missing values	1·0	0·0	0·0	0·3	0·0	0·0
No. of returns	598	250	388	306	185	329

2   *Inner city schools*

| Type of book | 10+ | | 11+ | | 12+ | |
	Exp.	Cont.	Exp.	Cont.	Exp.	Cont.
Fiction	77·8	59·8	76·2	86·4	78·5	97·7
Non–fiction	15·1	25·5	15·6	10·1	20·0	1·0
Poetry	1·5	9·2	3·3	2·1	0·2	1·0
Jokes, etc.	5·2	3·6	4·7	0·5	1·2	0·3
Missing values	0·4	2·0	0·2	0·8	0·1	0·0
No. of returns	478	306	450	375	827	597

In the first year of the experiment at the outer city experimental school, a relatively large number and wide variety of authors and titles was popular with the children. It should be stressed at this point, because of the relatively small number involved, one child could be responsible for the apparent popularity of an author who was highly rated five or more times, but rarely for a title thus rated, and not for an author highly rated fifteen or twenty times when only two books by that author were available. It should be remembered also that we are considering popularity and that over-all enjoyment of the books chosen can be seen from Table 3·16.

Table 3·20   Favourite authors: type of book, for boys and girls separately (percentages)

1   Outer city experimental school

Type of book	Girls 10+	Boys 10+	Girls 11+	Boys 11+	Girls 12+	Boys 12+
Fiction	89·9	73·2	83·2	67·7	97·5	87·5
Non-fiction	4·0	19·3	8·4	23·7	0·0	9·6
Poetry	3·6	2·5	3·7	0·5	1·2	0·0
Jokes, etc.	2·2	3·4	4·7	8·1	1·2	2·9
Missing values	0·4	1·6	0·0	0·0	0·0	0·0

2   Outer city control school

Type of book	Girls 10+	Boys 10+	Girls 11+	Boys 11+	Girls 12+	Boys 12+
Fiction	93·0	88·9	98·1	96·3	89·1	—
Non-fiction	4·3	11·1	1·9	2·7	3·7	10·9
Poetry	2·6	0·0	0·0	0·0	0·0	0·0
Jokes, etc.	0·0	0·0	0·0	0·0	0·0	0·0
Missing values	0·0	0·0	0·0	0·7	0·0	0·0

3   Inner city experimental school

Type of book	Girls 10+	Boys 10+	Girls 11+	Boys 11+	Girls 12+	Boys 12+
Fiction	78·6	77·0	84·8	68·8	81·8	75·9
Non-fiction	13·2	17·0	9·0	21·3	17·1	22·2
Poetry	2·5	0·4	2·4	4·2	0·3	0·2
Jokes, etc.	5·8	4·7	3·8	5·4	0·6	1·7
Missing values	0·0	0·9	0·0	0·4	0·3	0·0

4   Inner city control school

Type of book	Girls 10+	Boys 10+	Girls 11+	Boys 11+	Girls 12+	Boys 12+
Fiction	59·1	61·6	91·6	77·4	97·6	97·7
Non-fiction	22·3	33·7	4·2	20·4	0·6	1·6
Poetry	12·3	1·2	3·4	0·0	1·8	0·0
Jokes, etc.	3·6	3·5	0·0	1·5	0·0	0·8
Missing values	2·7	0·0	0·8	0·7	0·0	0·0

All of these popular authors are represented by books introduced to the school as part of the Book Flood Experiment. Enid Blyton heads the charts eight out of twelve times in a consideration of each school year. Of course, we do not know how the chart would have looked had the publishers donated eighty-nine books by Roald Dahl and eleven by Enid Blyton! Certainly, books by Roald Dahl were highly rated more times than there were copies, which is also true of books by Dodie Smith. Very few of the authors in this list could be termed writers of 'classics' and none of them as writers for a reading scheme. The top three authors were virtually equally appreciated by boys and girls. The boys particularly enjoyed Willard Price, Norman Hunter and Roger Price; whereas the girls showed a greater appreciation of Elizabeth Beresford, E. Nesbit and Laura Ingalls Wilder.

After the first year of the experiment, in this school, the numbers of popular authors and titles (Table 3·II in Appendix V) as well as of books chosen, and total numbers highly rated (Table 3·16) decreased dramatically. In the second year of the experiment (11 +), Alfred Hitchcock (Armada series) replaced Enid Blyton, and was hotly pursued by Mary Norton, whose books were highly rated fourteen times by the girls and, therefore, four times by the boys. It is interesting that titles from her *Borrowers* series are the only two titles that scored more than five. This was probably a case of a girl really enjoying the books and telling others about it, but, of course, the books would have to live up to the friend's recommendation. Sheila McCullagh was highly rated eight times but then sixty-eight copies of her books were introduced. All of the top three highly rated authors at 11 + were given that accolade mainly by girls.

In the final year of the experiment at this school, the number of popular authors was depleted even further; Enid Blyton was back at the top, very closely followed by *Asterix,* a deserved favourite with the boys. We see here the emergence of an author introduced as part of the Book Flood, Von Daniken was highly rated five times by an avid reader who was the subject of a case study, and who took those books to school to read because he had exhausted all the Book Flood books that interested him. No title was highly rated five or more times that year.

There are several possible, and very tentatively offered, explanations for the decrease in books chosen, in books enjoyed, and in popular authors and titles in this school, and not all are negative. The second-year teachers were generally very happy to receive the Book Flood books with several results: many of the books, especially ones aimed at the age group, remained in their class-rooms, as they did subsequently in the third-year class-rooms

(11+), after the Book Flood children had moved on and reorganizing books takes time; the teachers' enthusiasm communicated itself to the children with the result that many of them exhausted the Book Flood books that interested them (or that they were able to cope with) by the middle of their third year; the second-year teachers, because of their enthusiasm, their expectation of teaching a variety of subjects including 'reading' rather than specialist subjects, were able and willing to give more encouragement to, and time for, reading, especially to the less able, than were the fourth-year teachers; they were also willing for some flexibility of book borrowing and also swapping between classes. These suggestions are based on numerous visits to the school as well as discussions with staff and pupils. It seems likely that the drawback as far as reading is concerned of having the class teacher responsible for the teaching of English at the *upper* end of the middle school, is that the teacher is often secondary trained with an interest in a particular subject so that, unless reading (beyond a grasp of the basic mechanics that is) is stressed as a top priority in that school and encouragement given to the teacher to gain some knowledge of children's literature, the children at the upper end of the school (apart from the really well established avid reader) will be at a disadvantage.

In the outer city control school we see a steady, but not great, increase in the numbers of popular authors and titles. (We know from Table 3·16 that the percentage of books enjoyed over all *decreased* during the experiment, although there was an *increase* in actual numbers of books read and a smaller *increase* in the numbers highly rated.) In the first and last years Enid Blyton was the most popular author, but not as outstandingly as in the experimental schools (there were not as many Blytons available in the control schools). In the first year, of the eight popular authors, three are writing for 'reading schemes', or for the first steps in 'real books', and two are classics, i.e. Dickens and the *Kennett Library* (some or all of which could have been abridged versions of books by Dickens).

In the second year of the experiment at this school, the list of eleven popular authors includes six writers of reading schemes or first 'real books'; plus Hitchcock, Blyton, Dixon and Keene, among whose works there are many similarities that I shall discuss later in this chapter; only Roald Dahl remains. However, in the final year of the experiment, only two of the popular authors fall into the reading scheme category; Blyton, Keene and Hitchcock held their places; but we also find Serraillier, Garner, Hunter and Mackay, possibly in part because of the enthusiasm of one of the fourth-year teachers who was fortunate enough to have the 'G' stream for English, a teacher training course that gave him an insight into children's literature, a flair for art and display, and a wife who was a junior school teacher and loved books.

In the inner city experimental school at 10+, we again find Enid Blyton heading the list with an enormous lead. This can be partly accounted for by the fact that one of the second-year teachers, being somewhat taken aback at the preponderance of Blyton donations, became involved in discussion with her class about why there were so many when 'people' said that children should be discouraged from reading them. A case study child described the situation: 'She [the teacher] said that people said that Enid Blyton wasn't a good writer, and she said, "How will we find out?" and we said, that people who read the books would find out so we read nearly all of them.'

They were given about 100 Enid Blyton, including forty-four separate titles, for fewer than 100 children.

It is interesting that eight out of fourteen authors also appear in the 10+ list for the outer city experimental school. Again, *all* of the popular authors are represented by books introduced as part of the Book Flood. Enid Blyton and Norman Hunter were equally popular with boys and girls, but the boys were totally responsible for the popularity of *Asterix*. Enid Blyton's books appear four times in the list of favourite titles for that year. None of the authors is either a reading scheme writer or a writer of classics.

At 11+, Enid Blyton was ousted by Sheila McCullagh – who was presumably read with enjoyment mostly by the less-able readers – and followed by Roald Dahl in third place. Again all are represented by Book Flood books. Only McCullagh is a reading scheme writer; there are no writers of classics, but Dixon and Keene join Blyton yet again. The enjoyment of Roald Dahl looks like a result of the Book Flood, as well as of the excellence of his books, and it is noteworthy that *Charlie and the Chocolate Factory* was the favourite title: many children would recognize it because it has been on television several times.

At 12+, the number of highly rated authors had risen to twenty-seven, with eight of these highly rated ten or more times – a marked contrast with the other experimental school – and yet only three of these authors are not represented by Book Flood books and these three are at the bottom of the list. This time Blyton was closely followed by Anita Jackson, who wrote a series of very gripping and readable books in the Spirals series published by Hutchinson in association with the ILEA, initially aimed at adult literacy classes; and Michael Hardcastle, who was obviously a firm favourite with the boys. It is interesting that the girls particularly enjoyed the non-fiction books, mostly in the Visual Library series published by Macdonald, and the Hardy Boys series; while the boys enjoyed Willard Price, Evan Owen writing for the Checkers series and Anne Oates for the Crown Street Kings. The less-able reader, particularly at 12+ and older, has difficulty – as has the teacher of the less-able reader – in finding books outside the reading schemes without getting stuck with Hitchcock, Keene and Dixon.

At 10+ in the inner city control school Anita Jackson was almost as popular as she was at 12+ in the matched experimental school and beat Enid Blyton, but, again, as in the other control school, there were not many Enid Blytons available, whereas there was an ample supply of books by Anita Jackson. The children enjoyed her books so much that they were staying at the end of lessons to finish reading them. The popularity of the Macdonald books must be attributed in part to the preponderance of non-fiction in the school library where the children spent a good deal of their reading time at 10+. Ian Serraillier was popular in every year at this school, partly because his work was much appreciated by the head of English who made copies available. *All* the popular titles are by Anita Jackson, and girls were largely responsible for her popularity.

At 11+, Blyton shared first place with Serraillier, followed by Charles Dickens (abridged versions) second equal with Anne Oates (reading scheme writer), another incongruous couple. Of the twelve popular authors, four are writers of classics and four are writers for reading schemes, leaving Blyton, Serraillier, Benchley *(Jaws)* and Macdonald (publishers). There were far more classics in this school than in any other, largely because of their availability and the almost complete lack of modern equivalents; and there were more reading scheme writers highly rated in the control than in the experimental schools (although we have already noted that Jackson and McCullagh did well there too). Girls were almost exclusively responsible for the popularity of Enid Blyton.

At 12+ (see Table 3.VIII in Appendix V) Blyton was still top The number of popular authors had increased to twenty-three and twelve of those were highly rated more than ten times. Seven are writers of classics; seven writers of reading schemes. Let us consider those highly rated more than ten times: four are writers of classics – Louisa M. Alcott, Charles Dickens, Captain Marryat and Robert L. Stevenson; four are writers for reading schemes – B. Bird, I. Falk, Anne Oates, G. R. Crosher and the Higginses; leaving Orwell, London and Serraillier – all semi-classics. There is no sign of Dahl, Hunter, Goscinny and Uderzo, nor even Dodie Smith and Laura Ingalls Wilder, pointing to lack of availability again. One wonders what the list for this school would have looked like if such a teacher who could introduce books like *Animal Farm* and *The Silver Sword* as class readers and have them high rated, were to be given a wide variety and large numbers of books, including more recent ones, and were given time to become acquainted with them. It seems that books need to be in the hands of teachers who have themselves experienced the pleasure that can be gained from literature and who believe in communicating that joy to the children for whom they are responsible. Heads should take care that there are one or two like this on their staff if they can possibly do so. It is also preferable if teachers themselves choose and are familiar with the books in their own class-rooms.

It is impossible within the space of this chapter to attempt a detailed analysis of the popular authors. Blyton emerges quite clearly as over-all favourite, although it must be remembered that approximately 100 of her books were donated to each of the experimental schools, and that she was highly rated 251 times altogether in the experimental schools, as opposed to 111 times in the control schools. Certainly far more copies of her books were donated than were those of any other author and that fact in itself would attract the attention of the teachers and children especially as this would probably be one of the few author's names with which the children were familiar, as they would also be with the alliterative *Famous Five* and *Secret Seven* – both series accounting for most of the Blyton books introduced. (I have now carried out an analysis of all the data on Enid Blyton from the Reading Record Forms, i.e. where obtained, level of difficulty, reasons for choice, etc. and intend to make an analysis of the responses made by Asian children, which will be particularly interesting.)

In this experiment, Blyton appears almost as much at 12+ as she did at 10+; it is possible that at 12+ some of her votes were taken by Alfred Hitchcock, Carolyn Keene and Franklin W. Dixon, whose books contain similar ingredients but are aimed at a slightly older age group. All are classed as 'adventures' or 'mysteries'; they can be read with relative ease by children who are not the best of readers; the plots are simple; little prior knowledge of anything is required – we are told all we need to know about Aztecs, film-making or whatever is necessary in the course of the story; emotions and relationships are simple and issues clear-cut; vocabulary is limited; there is a minimum of description and simple conversation is interspersed by 'wow!' and 'whiskers!'; they are all written to a formula with which children rapidly become familiar, so that they know they can expect plenty of excitement and constant action within a secure and predictable framework; characterization is two-dimensional; parents are rarely around and, when they are, trust their offspring implicitly; adults never in fact come into conflict with children, unless of course the adults are 'baddies'.

The following extracts illustrate the simplicity of characterization, as in these books each character usually has one outstanding physical feature and/or character trait: Chet Morton, the *Hardy Boys'* friend, is fat and cowardly; Georgina of the *Famous Five* has short boyish hair and behaves boyishly; the *Hardy Boys*, so far as I can gather, are distinguished solely by their hair colour. Let us look, in more detail, first at Alfred Hitchcock's introduction to 'the three investigators' at the beginning of *The Mystery of the Coughing Dragon* by Nick West (in the Armada series):

> By his own admission, Jupiter Jones is the *leader in residence* and the *brains* of the trio. Pete Crenshaw, the most *athletic member*, assists on missions that call for his kind of contribution. Bob Andrews is in charge of Records and Research. Altogether a lively team (my italics).

Now let us compare this with an abstract from *The Hardy Boys: The Mystery of the Aztec Warrior* by Franklin W. Dixon, also published in the Armada series. Chapter 1 begins:

> Frank and Joe Hardy followed their father into the Law Office of Otis Weaver, a Bayport Lawyer.
>
> 'Hello, Fenton!' said Mr Weaver, getting up to shake hands with *the tall, athletic-looking detective*.
>
> 'Frank, Joe, how are you?'
>
> *Tall, dark-haired Frank* said, 'We're fine and ready to tackle a case, Mr Weaver.'
>
> His brother Joe, *blond, seventeen and a year younger* smiled in anticipation.
>
> The four sat down. 'I have a really mysterious one for you to solve,' *the short, balding lawyer* began . . . (my italics).

Other characters are introduced in a similar way, for instance Chet Morton is introduced on page 22 as '. . . a stout, good natured-looking boy . . .', his physical size and lots of good food being continually reiterated throughout the book (a technique reminiscent of dressing Capulet and Montague in striking distinct colours for fear that a modern audience might lose track of the character's affiliations!)

The similarity to Enid Blyton is obvious. We only need to read the beginning of *The Famous Five*, where the characters are introduced, to find that Julian is '. . . a tall strong boy, with a determined face . . .' and that Georgina '. . . looking more like a boy than a girl, for she wore her hair very short, and it curled close about her head . . .'

This is neither the time nor the place to discuss sex stereotyping in children's books but surely the Hardy Boys' mother is the most passive character ever created, although we must not forget that Nancy Drew is female and acts alone a great deal of the time.

Another common feature is the short chapter with the cliff-hanger at the end, typified by the end of Chapter 2 of *The Mystery of the Coughing Dragon:* 'He raised the gun threateningly.' The short chapter obviously appeals to the less-able reader, as well as accommodating itself to the gap at the end of a lesson, or between tea and a favourite television programme.

An obvious but important similarity between these books is that they all belong to easily recognizable series, as do many of the other favourites, like *Professor Branestawm, The Moomintrolls, Asterix, Paddington* and the *Wombles*. One of the case study children who '. . . absolutely loved Roald Dahl', said, 'I read Roald Dahl *but he didn't have enough* – and I wished he would write that little bit older'.

The love of the series is expressed in a number of the children's reasons for choice and final comments from the Reading Record Forms. A fourth-year (12+) girl wrote of Carolyn Keene's *The Hidden Staircase*, 'I chose this book *because I have read other Nancy Drew stories* and I have enjoyed them, I think that the *Nancy Drew* books have exciting titles.' The same girl wrote of *The Moonstone Castle Mystery*, also by Carolyn Keene:

> I chose this book because I like the Nancy Drew series. The mystery in the book is very good. *The Nancy Drew series are just like Alfred Hitchcock*. The adventures in the story itself are easy to understand and *the words are not very difficult*.

The case study girl, who loved Roald Dahl, wrote of Alfred Hitchcock's *The Mystery of the Flaming Footprints*, 'I chose this book because I have read other books by Alfred Hitchcock which were good stories so I decided to read this book by him' (not actually by him, of course, but by Nick West).

In conversation she said that she had read all the Hitchcock books in school by the end of her third year and many other children made similar remarks about other writers whom they read like collectors; for example, '. . . I am reading all the Sheila McCullagh'; or, of Mary Norton's *The Borrowers Aloft*, '. . . it is the last of the series of borrowers and I have read the other three'; or, of Aidan Chambers's books, 'There are only four books by this author [in school] and I would like to see some more'; and, of Anita Jackson, 'I wish there were more of these books'. One of the teachers in the experiment described how children often checked to see if there were others in a series before they took a book by an unfamiliar author, and how they gradually became aware that an author would write more than one book; indeed, how slowly they became aware that the same author's style might even be similar from one book to another.

Many of us are familiar with the feeling of reluctance to reach the end of an enjoyable book. Likewise, children in the experiment talked of saving up a final chapter until they could savour it in peace and quiet, and described the feeling of disappointment that a favourite author had not written more books. It is also likely that the less-able reader has to invest a great deal of effort in broaching a new author and that, once an enjoyable one that the child can cope with is found, probably recommended by a friend, it seems safe and sensible to the child to stick with that author for a while. I suppose, too, that characters in a series become like real friends to some children.

As Asian girl summed up many of my points very well, when she said that she liked *Nancy Drew, The Hardy Boys* and *Alfred Hitchcock* because she liked mystery and detective stories rather than stories about people in everyday life. She concluded, '. . . books that I like are when the adventure starts straight away, because I have found from a lot of people that they like stories that go straight into the mystery'.

The other side of the coin was expressed by an Asian boy who said he did not like Biggles because '. . . you had to read about three-quarters of the book before you got into the adventure'.

The children who read Anita Jackson were able to say only *how much* they enjoyed her books but not to give reasons for that enjoyment; presumably they were the less articulate children. The same thing applies to Sheila McCullagh, who writes for a younger age group. I think the appeal of the books is quite simply that they are easily understood and *not boring* – unlike a great many easy readers; nor are they about everyday life – they 'make a change' from the reading schemes where it is assumed that poorer readers come from poor areas which they want to read about. Perhaps they do sometimes for it is important for these children to see their way of life acknowledged as legitimate, indeed as *existing*, by its representation in literature, but we should not therefore assume that they do not want to read anything else at all!

Anita Jackson has the ability to make the transition from everyday speech or thought to the written word a fairly painless process, for the 'sentence' structures are mainly geared to the patterns of speech and thought. She also holds our attention partly because her characters are so totally immoral; the experience of reading *A Game of Life and Death*, for instance, is a bit like reading with self-righteous disapproval a titillating article in the *News of the World*. We can allow ourselves to enjoy thoughts like: 'She loved me and I killed her. That's very funny when you think about it' (of his wife; p. 18); or, 'I didn't want to see him die. There was no need to upset myself' (p. 20), knowing that he will get his 'come uppance' in the end. Enjoyment of evil in literature, so long as it is eventually punished, is a very old tradition, for example the thieves in Chaucer's *Pardoner's Tale*, or Lucifer in Milton's *Paradise Lost*, and probably appeals to something very basic in our natures. Sheila McCullagh uses the sagas and folk tales/fairy tales as a basis for many of her stories, again making a departure from many easy readers.

I feel bound to put my head on the chopping block and say that the difference between Blyton, Hitchcock, Keene and Dixon, on the one hand, and Hunter or Goscinny on the other, probably represents a cultural, not a social, gap. It seems likely that children who can read Hunter and Goscinny with ease and pleasure will have little difficulty with books like *Stig of the Dump* (Clive King), *Charlotte's Webb* (E. B. White), *Mrs Frisby and the Rats of NIMH* (Robert O'Brien), or *The Ogre Downstairs* (Diana Wynne Jones), to name a few of my favourites, because they will feel at home with the language, will trust an author to lead them into a story and be prepared, therefore, on the basis of past experiences, to put an effort into the beginning of a book; whereas a child who has not had the experience of early stories like *The Blah* (Jack Kent), or the David McKee stories, or *There's No Such Thing as a Dragon* (Jack Kent) (to name a few more of my favourites), but goes straight into reading schemes, will find it easier later on to read books that are simply and undemandingly written to a predictable formula – such children may easily come to see reading as purely work, and words as enemies not friends.

It is easy for a teacher to dismiss the *Asterix* books as 'comic strips' in book form, yet they are full of historical references and the enjoyment of words is immediately apparent. For instance, in *Asterix in Britain* the humour depends partly upon differences between people of different nationalities – Greeks, Romans, Britons – in their speech and in their customs. The particular appeal of these books is that they do not *look* learned and they can be read at several levels.

I feel I cannot conclude the chapter without devoting some space to Roald Dahl's books, especially as he made such a brave attempt in this experiment to compete with Enid Blyton, despite the fact that he began with two major handicaps: first, he simply has not written as many books; and secondly, the publishers donated Blyton's and Dahl's books in the ratio of approximately 6:1. In common with many of the writers for remedial readers, and many of the popular writers already mentioned, Dahl's books contain short chapters, plenty of pictures and a lot of action. Short chapters are less daunting than long ones, whether for parents reading a bit at bedtime, for younger able readers, for teachers introducing a story, or for older, less-able readers. Dahl, like Goscinny and Uderzo, manages to bridge the gap between the really popular writer and the most obviously 'cultured' ones. He also has the advantage of writing at several levels beginning with *The Enormous Crocodile* and *The Magic Finger* at the younger end and progressing to *Danny, Champion of the World* – a fact that teachers could take advantage of. The most popular of his books in this experiment were the two *Charlie* books. I think the appeal for this age group lies in the sense of fun that is far from squeamish, for instance, just after a Vermicious Knid has bumped into the Great Glass Elevator, we read:

> 'He'll have a nasty headache after that', said Granpa Joe.
> 'It's not his head, it's his bottom!' said Charlie.
> 'Look Granpa, there's a big lump coming up on the pointed end where he hit! It's going black and blue!' (p. 57)

Another example is the Oompa–Loompas' song about pills (pp. 101–5) in *Charlie and the Great Glass Elevator*. Part of the song goes like this:

> You see, how could young Goldie know,
> For nobody had told her so,
> The Grandmama, her old relation
> Suffered from frightful constipation.
> This meant that every night she'd give
> Herself a powerful laxative,
> And all the medicines she'd bought
> Were naturally of this sort.
> The pink and red and blue and green
> Were all extremely strong and mean.
> But far more fierce and meaner still
> Was Granny's little chocolate pill.
> Its blast effect was quite uncanny.
> It used to shake up even Granny.
> In point of fact she did not dare
> To use them more than twice a year.
> So can you wonder little Goldie
> Began to feel a wee bit mouldy?

This, along with elements like the fates of the other children in *Charlie and the Chocolate Factory*, represents the cautionary tale element that younger children love.

Dahl also mentions other unmentionables like what is there before you are born, or extreme old age in the description of Grandma Georgina whose '. . . tiny face was like a pickled walnut. There were such masses of creases and wrinkles that her mouth and eyes and ears and nose were almost out of sight. Her hair was pure white and her hands, which were resting on top of the blanket, were just little lumps of wrinkly skin.' We're even provided with a picture!

In *Danny, Champion of the World*, the morality and the emotions are much more complex, facilitating a kind of progression that is not possible for a child to make with many authors.

Dahl also introduces the child to language in a warm, friendly and humorous way, so that the informed and sensitive teacher can lead the children on to writers like Betsy Byars or Mary Rodgers with greater ease, after the experience of Dahl's handling of language and his gradual introduction to more subtle and complex morality and emotions. Personally, I would follow *Danny* with something like *Stig of the Dump* or *Freaky Friday/A Billion for Boris* (Mary Rodgers), or *The Ogre Downstairs*, where a child who is still basically at the level of concrete operations can experience how absurd aspects of our world might look to a caveman, or what it would be like to be someone else. After this, writers like Betsy Byars, Judy Blume, Alan Garner, etc., can be introduced, so long as we always remember that our favourites are not bound to be their favourites and that everyone enjoys a bit of regression from time to time. If I enjoy *Winnie the Pooh* – for myself – when I read it to my children it is a little hypocritical if I criticize a 10-year-old for enjoying *Paddington* or *The Wombles*.

I believe that the teacher does owe it to the children to make an attempt to show what language can do for them and what they can do with language, for, through literature, they can both deepen and extend their knowledge and experience both of themselves and of other people and places. This extension of knowledge and experience is of course inextricably bound up with language, which is why older, less-able readers are so often dissatisfied with the books with which they are able to cope. The language issue cannot be avoided, as much of the most rewarding literature is *not* written in the style of Anita Jackson. A familiarity with literary language often begins in the home as does a love of words. The written word is an alien form of expression to many school children and often a form with disagreeable associations of failure. This is why we must rejoice if children read and enjoy *any* book or make any set of characters in a series their friends, but we must not let the matter rest there!

4 Case Studies: Reading in School

The case studies

In addition to the testing programme and the reading records, we decided to conduct a number of in-depth case studies with a few children from each school. We believed that these case studies would be enlightening in a number of ways:

1 They would reveal some of the complexities and individual variations that inevitably underlie general trends.

2 Since we realized that there were, necessarily, variables that affect reading ability, reading attitudes, and reading behaviour, for which we had not controlled, such as teacher differences, differences in home background, and personality differences in the children, we felt that case studies would give us insight into some of the ways in which these variables operate and interact.

3 Having interviewed teachers, it also seemed logical to interview the children about reading in school, including how it was taught.

4 It seemed likely that it would be of interest to teachers and, hopefully, parents, to find detailed profiles of individual children at home and at school. Researchers *can* leave themselves open to criticism from practitioners in the teaching profession if they give total credence to statistics and ignore the individual. We thought the case studies would help to provide a *balanced* picture of the effects of the Book Flood.

Sampling

We decided to try to choose, as subjects for our case studies, children who indulged in a great deal of voluntary reading and children who read little or nothing voluntarily. Since we had no intention of carrying out computations on the data collected from these case studies, we were able to combine a variety of sampling procedures. We began by examining the number of Reading Record Form returns for the entire first year of the experiment, since those seemed to be the most concrete expression of an interest in or lack of interest in books that we had available to us. Of course, this data did not reveal the children who read a great deal at home but little in school; we found some of those children with the help of the teachers – they are marked 'TA', for Teacher Addition, on the tables. We included any children of Asian origin who had read a great deal in the sample.

The complexity of the situation was increased by the fact that the case study children steadfastly refused to fall into two neat categories of 'avid' and 'reluctant' readers! This was partly because most of the children who appeared to be reluctant were in fact interested in books but lacked reading ability and/or suitable reading material (I shall therefore call those children who completed few Reading Record Forms 'infrequent' readers); it was also because their reading habits displayed an annoying tendency to change during the course of the experiment! In practice, we were left with four categories of readers within this sub-sample:

A Children who were avid readers throughout the experiment, although some of them clearly preferred to do most of their reading at home.

B Those who read very little throughout the experiment either at home or in school.

C Those who read a lot during the first year of the experiment, usually in school, but who appeared to have lost interest in voluntary reading by the time they left the middle school.

D Those who read very little voluntarily at the beginning of the experiment, but who greatly increased their reading during the following two years, perhaps because their reading ability had improved, or because of the *gradual* impact of the Book Flood on those children, or because of an increased awareness of books brought about by the Reading Record Form, or because of the positive attention accorded them as a result of being the subjects of case studies – probably, in most cases, because of a combination of, and an interaction between, these factors.

Methodology

1 A file was compiled for each child, containing data from the tests and the Reading Record Forms. This file was regularly updated until the end of the experiment.

2 I interviewed teachers, asking them to talk freely about each child; the interviews were taped.

3 Each child kept a detailed diary for a week.

4 Each child kept a list of his/her own books at home.

5 I interviewed (taped) each child individually and privately in

school, both about school and about home. Since these interviews were conducted during the final year of the experiment, the children were able to look back over the three years at any changes in reading-related practices in school, as well as at changes in their own reading habits and interests. I also asked the children to describe their homes, their families and a typical evening and week-end, so that I could build up a picture of the child's life-style. Some children were able, in addition, to talk about their early lives and to envisage the future: whereas others were clearly quite unable to do this. Similarly some of the children were extremely articulate in talking about their favourite books and authors whereas others found it difficult to express what they liked about a book or about reading generally. Wherever possible, I allowed the children to talk freely rather than asking a series of formal questions. I found that by asking general questions like, 'What do you usually do when you get home from school?' or saying, 'Tell me about your family', I was more likely to encourage the child to disclose those areas of life that were most important. I tried asking a large number of set questions in a pilot study and found the responses stilted and, I believe, to a large extent dictated by the questions. Therefore, bearing in mind that I could gather any 'missing' information by other means, it seemed more important to establish a trusting relationship with the children than to work through a series of set questions. I impressed upon them that the most important, and helpful, thing was to be honest, and that none of the information would be fed back to their teachers or parents, except anonymously in the final publication.

6   Subsequently, I visited each home to talk with the parents, usually in the evening and usually for about two hours, again taping the interviews. In each case, the headmaster wrote to the parents initially, or a teacher did so, and I followed up this letter with a phone call or a note sent via the child. In only one case did parents, who were described by teachers as 'totally anti-school' refuse to be interviewed, so that I actually visited 27 homes. At one of those twenty-seven I talked to the mother at some length on the doorstep, making notes as soon as I got back into the car, as it was obvious that she did not wish me to go inside the house. For eight out of the twenty-seven interviews the father was absent and for two the mother was absent, in one case because of shift-work and in the other because she had returned to Pakistan for a holiday, so I interviewed:

seventeen sets of parents (mother and father together)
eight mothers (one was a single parent)
two fathers

Total: twenty-seven interviews

In most cases parents went to a great deal of trouble to be at home together when I visited, and all were willing, even eager, to talk about their children – especially if they could do anything to improve their education. I must also add that I was made very welcome on a personal level too, being shown all around houses, allowed to peer into cupboards, and being offered a variety of tasty and sustaining snacks.

Since there is not the space in this small volume to describe twenty-eight case studies in detail, I shall try to do two things: in this chapter I shall attempt to summarize for each school separately, since different conditions pertained in each one, the information gained with regard to reading in school from these case study children; secondly, in Chapter 5, I shall give detailed descriptions of a smaller number of children who indubitably remained 'avid' or 'infrequent' readers throughout the experiment, attempting to relate their interest or lack of interest in reading to factors in the school, the home and the child's personality, drawing particular attention to any common factors that emerge among these variables for 'avid' or 'infrequent' readers.

Reading in school

The best way to enjoy reading is by yourself in a closed room where no one can read over your shoulder. Most schools put reading (after the tots have learned to) way down the list of priorities. When we are 5 our teachers parade archaic *Janet and John* books in front of us. One of the most boring things is being told to sit down by a teacher and read a book that doesn't interest you at all (a comment on reading by one 12-year-old avid reader).

The outer city experimental school

The sample. Table 4·1 summarizes the results from the testing programme, excluding the attitude measures, and gives the number of reading records completed for the case study children in this school. IQ equals the mean score from Forms A and B of the Cattell Culture Fair Test of 'g'; the Standardized Reading Score is the score on the Edinburgh Reading Test Scale 3, the children having been slightly too old for us to standardize the scores at the time of final post-testing; the self-esteem score is that obtained from the shortened version of the Coopersmith Self-esteem Inventory (Bagley *et al.*, 1979), the lower score indicating higher self-esteem. 'TA' indicates that children were added to the sample on their teacher's recommendation.

Table 4·1 Sample of case study children from outer city experimental school

Child	Sex	Year	IQ	Standardized reading score	Schonell Reading Age	Age at testing	Number of Reading Record Forms	Self-Esteem
1	M	10+	116	130+	15·0	10·3	23	9
		11+		130+	17·7	11·3	24	
		12+			17·3	12·8	37	12
2	M	10+	128	130+	14·7	10·7	19	10
		11+		130+	15·0	11·8	16	
TA		12+			18·1	13·2	12	16
3	M	10+	91	92	10·5	10·3	30	3
		11+		97	12·2	11·4	8	
		12+			14·4	12·8	6	10
4	M	10+	93	89	11·0	10·6	20	5
		11+		96	12·2	11·8	11	
		12+			12·6	13·0	4	8
5	M	10+	82	70	7·0	10·4	3	8
		11+		83	7·8	11·2	4	
		12+			9·6	12·7	6	24
6	F	10+	119	109	13·4	10·9	15	5
		11+		111	15·0	11·9	17	
TA		12+			16·0	13·3	4	8
7	F	10+	116	110	12·2	10·4	21	7
		11+		112	15·0	11·4	10	
		12+			16·5	12·9	4	8
8	F	10+	112	126	13·9	10·7	12	7
		11+		124	17·3	11·7	5	
TA		12+			16·0	13·0	5	14

TA = Added at teachers' suggestion.

The first subject (Child 1) is a boy who remained an avid reader throughout the experiment. He is exceptional in that he completed Reading Record Forms for books read entirely at home; discussions with *all* children in the experiment in half-class groups revealed that only four children in all did this and they are the subjects of case studies. The second subject (Child 2) is a boy who was added on his teacher's recommendation, who also read a great deal throughout the experiment but did quite a lot of his reading at home and did not record it. The third and fourth subjects, both boys, began by reading a good deal during the first year of the experiment, but apparently had lost interest by the time they left the middle school. Child 5 was a boy who read very little throughout the experiment.

Looking at the IQ and reading scores for these five boys, it is interesting to note that the two who scored highest continued to read avidly throughout the experiment, while the boy with the lowest score never read a great deal. However, subjects three and four appear to have been inspired to read a lot as a result of the initial impact of the Book Flood but could not tackle books at an older interest level with any ease. Child 7, a girl, was chosen on the basis of the Reading Record Forms, while subjects 6 and 8 were added as a result of teachers' recommendations. All three girls continued to be avid readers throughout the experiment, but increasingly read at home, partly from preference and partly because of the *decreasing* amount of time available for reading in school.

Findings. Table 4·2 gives a breakdown of the places from which the case study children obtained the books recommended on the Reading Record Forms during the three years of the experiment; it also shows, in brackets, the number of books that the children finished reading, although we should bear in mind that non-fiction books are rarely read from cover to cover, and that *some* rejection of books chosen could be a sign of growing discriminatory powers. It is immediately obvious from this table that most of the books read in school were borrowed from the class library; the other outstanding finding is that, apart from Child 1, who was recording books read at home, and Child 5 who read very little anyway, the numbers recorded by every other subject, including the very keen readers, *decreased* during the course of the experiment, as they did for the general Book Flood population in this school.

Rather than interpreting what the case study children said to any great extent, I shall try wherever possible to let them speak for themselves, even at the risk of the text sometimes looking like a string of quotations. However, it has to be admitted that I cannot let the infrequent readers speak for themselves at all times, as they had far less to say and said it far less articulately than did the avid readers.

I believe that what they said, unsolicited, on a particular subject has just as much claim to being considered objective fact and hard evidence as has a test score that is dependent upon how a child feels on that particular day; we must get away from the objectivity/subjectivity dichotomy, to the idea of approaching a problem from several angles all of which involve an objectivity/subjectivity continuum; indeed not quite objectivity, for total objectivity is out of the question; we are not scientists talking about molecules, but human beings talking about human beings – it would be folly to pretend otherwise.

Table 4·2 Outer city experimental school: places from which case study children obtained books recorded on Reading Record Forms and numbers of books obtained from each location, plus (in brackets) numbers of books completed

Child	Sex	Year	Public library	School library	Class library	Belongs to child	Belongs to sibling	Belongs to a friend	Totals
1	M	10+		2 (1)	21 (21)				23 (22)
		11+			22 (22)	2 (1)			24 (23)
		12+		2 (1)	11 (7)	24 (22)			37 (30)
2	M	10+	1 (1)	1 (0)	16 (11)	1 (1)			19 (13)
		11+	2 (1)		10 (7)	1 (1)		3 (3)	16 (12)
TA		12+	5 (3)	1 (1)	2 (2)	2 (2)		2 (2)	12 (10)
3	M	10+		3 (1)	27 (19)				30 (10)
		11+			8 (2)				8 (2)
		12+		3 (N1)	3 (0)				6 (0)
4	M	10+		2 (2)	18 (14)				20 (16)
		11+		5 (3)	6 (3)				11 (6)
		12+		2 (1)	2 (2)				4 (3)
5	M	10+		1 (0)	1 (1)	1 (1)			3 (2)
		11+			4 (4)				4 (4)
		12+			6 (4)				6 (4)
6	F	10+		1 (1)	14 (11)				15 (12)
		11+		14 (13)	3 (3)				17 (16)
TA		12+			4 (3)				4 (3)
7	F	10+		2 (1)	19 (7)				21 (8)
		11+		7 (7)	3 (1)				10 (8)
		12+		1 (1)	3 (3)				4 (4)
8	F	10+		1 (1)	11 (7)				12 (8)
		11+			5 (3)				5 (3)
TA		12+			3 (1)				3 (1)

TA = Added at teachers' suggestion.

I asked the children individually what they had thought when the new books arrived and whether the books had affected them in any way; in other words, what impact the Book Flood had on them. All agreed that they ceased to be taken down to the school library once a week to choose a book to read and that they began, instead, to borrow books from the class-room and read them there more than once a week, at least during the first year of the experiment when they were in the second year at the middle school. Before the Book Flood there had not been a stock of books in their class-rooms. However, reactions to the arrival of the books ranged from fear and disinterest to delight. Child 1 said that he was 'really glad' when the books arrived as 'I had read all the books in the school library that I was interested in and I was getting a bit bored and when these books came I got really interested.' He was also pleased to have the opportunity of borrowing non-fiction books from the school library. Child 2 reacted in a similar way: 'It was great. There was something else to do. There wasn't a lot of books in the library.' He also was attracted by the prospect of being able to borrow non-fiction books. We should remember that while these two boys had a lot of books at home, their parents would not be able to afford a vast array of non-fiction material. Both boys continued to be avid readers throughout the experiment and it is interesting to note that the three girls, all of whom also continued to read a great deal, had a similar reaction to the arrival of the books. One said that she could remember quite clearly being thrilled and helping to put the books on the shelves. However, the reactions of Child 3 and Child 4, both of whom began by reading a great deal but had tired of reading by the time the experiment finished, were somewhat different. They were initially rather disturbed by and suspicious of this new influx of books: 'I didn't like it at first'; 'I didn't know what they were.' Child 5, who read little throughout the experiment, said he could not remember the books arriving but that he 'liked looking at them'.

All agreed that they liked the idea of having books in the class-room and would not want to go back to borrowing solely from the school library, mainly because of convenience in that books are so much more readily available and accessible in the class-room. They said that it had affected the amount of reading they had been able to do, often for very practical reasons. Child 1 expressed this very articulately, 'Because when you come down to the [school] library every week, you've got *one* book, and when you've got them in the class you can get them whenever you want, not just when you are told to go down to the library.'

One girl described reading during registration and not hearing her name called, and others told me how they had made a habit of reading whenever they finished a piece of work. Those of us who belong to the 'older generation' and had desks with wells, and satchels, need to be reminded of the problems created by the use of tables in class-rooms and the fact that satchels have gone out of fashion. Child 1 also remarked that it was possible to borrow books unofficially from other class-rooms during the first year of the experiment as the second-year class-rooms were all adjacent to one another.

However, reactions to the Book Flood did not remain unchanged for any of these children. All had reservations, not about the principle of having books in the class-room of which they totally approved, but about the number and nature of the books. Child 1, like the rest of the keen readers, wished that there could have been either frequent changes of the stock of books in the class-room or a much larger number and wider variety of books. All five continuously avid readers said that they had gradually exhausted the supply of Book Flood books that were of interest to them. Child 6, for example, said, 'If you had *more* books to choose from you wouldn't want to change, perhaps, because there would be a bigger variety of books. I like the books in the class-room.' And Child 7, 'The books in our class-room are OK but there isn't enough choice.' Child 8 found that, on closer examination, most of the books weren't really her 'type'! The result of this disillusionment was that the avid readers reverted to borrowing their books from a variety of sources, in several cases bringing books from home to read; for example, Child 2 said, 'Mostly I bring books from home to read or from the public library' (fourth year). In fact all the avid readers expressed a preference for reading at home rather than in school. Child 6 offered a detailed description of her reading habits in each year of the experiment, illustrating the move away from the class library:

> I think in the second year I was reading Enid Blyton's from the class. I was really interested in her, but she just keeps to one thing and you know what is going to happen before you start. And in the third year I didn't bother with the class library so much because I found a whole selection of Alfred Hitchcock in the school library which I enjoyed very much. And in the fourth year I'm just finding a few books I like in the class library.

(I'd like to discuss the question of teacher guidance on authors later in this chapter.) Child 7 also 'latched onto' the Hitchcock series, exhausted all those available in the whole school, and then began buying them herself: 'I'd read all the Hitchcock's in school, actually!' From November of the second year of the experiment she was doing most of her reading at home, 'I bought a couple around that time and read them. I think I was reading more at home, more of my own books. I had read all the ones in the class-room that I liked the idea of.'

Children 3 and 4, once they had become accustomed to being surrounded by a lot of books, found many to interest them at a suitable level during the first year of the experiment, but increasingly found that they were having difficulty choosing books that they could cope with; they found plenty of books that attracted them and interested them but found the level of difficulty too great. They felt that there *must* have been suitable books somewhere, if only they had known how to find them. They needed careful guidance with book choice; *but they also needed continued help to improve their reading skills.* Child 3 said, 'I like it at first, but when I start reading my book I get fed up about it and want to do something else. . . I *want* to read.'

In his third year, at 11 +, Child 4 read more than half of *The Prince and the Pauper* by Mark Twain, *Sampson's Circus* by Howard Spring and *The Pool of the Black Witch* by 'B.B.' He said, 'I read a lot harder books in the third year . . . I think I did read a lot in the second year because they were new and now I have gone back to normal.' As far as he knew he had exhausted the supply of books that he could cope with *on his own* without a struggle. Child 3 expressed his difficulty in a similar way, when he said that, in the second year, he had read 'some of the harder ones in the class', but in the third year, 'I used to take my time with them. . . . They were longer books.'

I couldn't really blame these 13-year-old boys for not telling me quite openly that the books were too difficult for them, and I wanted to avoid 'putting words into their mouths'.

There was an interesting social bond between the avid readers in this school; the category included another boy who lived in the neighbourhood but had recently joined the school after leaving an independent school. The three girls had been in the same class throughout the school and two of them were 'best friends'. They discussed books, among other topics of conversation, both in and out of school; they also had a disturbing tendency to discuss one another's reading habits, and reading abilities, when I interviewed them (for instance, Child 6 volunteered the following information about Child 8):

> I think that J. reads a lot more than anybody. She is a very good reader – you can tell by the reading age of the books that she has read as well. She reads mostly all the time, and she writes a lot of things as well. . . . People just don't seem to play with her as much as with other children. She is very quiet and she won't dash around like other children. . . . She is very sensible.

There was no doubt that they read widely, with understanding and enjoyment, as they were so eager to come and talk about the books they had read and were able to discuss them intelligently in depth; they were also anxious to pick my brains about other possible authors and titles and, in fact, did so on many occasions informally when they saw me in school. They were thirsty both for recommendations of new books, and for feedback about the ones they had read; I could easily have made a weekly lesson out of the discussions!

The interviews revealed a complex, but haphazard pattern, of teacher–child/child–child recommendation of books. *All* the case study children agreed that the second-year class teachers, who taught them during the first year of the experiment, had tried hard to encourage them to read, and to guide their choice of books, even if they had not always been totally successful. They made such comments as:

'He told us to go and choose one, but then we had to show him what we had got to see if it was right for us.'

'He wanted you to read the book and then he talked to you about it before you got another one.'

'He was telling us some of the books that were good.'

'I think Mr — encouraged us more than anybody because it was sort of a new project and he wanted it to be a real success.'

None of the children mentioned any of the third- or fourth-year teachers recommending suitable books to them, whereas all mentioned second-year teachers. I must add that one child stated quite categorically, and unprompted, that while the second-year class teachers and the head of English were able to recommend books, it was his opinion that the third- and fourth-year class teachers knew very little about children's books; he added that he greatly enjoyed creative English which he felt that his teacher handled well. Several of the children mentioned recommendations made by the head of English who had taught most of them for short periods, but, although they enjoyed the books that he recommended when he was present to give them help and encouragement, they obviously found his choice of author too difficult to tackle alone and possibly a touch remote and élitist *by their standards*. This is not to say that they should not be taken beyond their immediate level of understanding with a book like *The Owl Service* by Alan Garner but, for reading alone, most of them need a more gradual initiation to works of this kind. A couple of the girls confided in me that they really wanted to read love stories and the supernatural: *The Owl Service* contains elements of both of these but what they really needed for personal private reading were books like Beverley Cleary's *Fifteen,* Penelope Lively's *The Ghost of Thomas Kempe,* Diana Wynne Jones's *The Power of Three* or even Paul Zindel's books, like *Pigman* and *I Never Loved Your Mind.* They also liked Judy Blume and Mary Rodgers. The girls who were avid readers enjoyed Garner very much, however, as a class reader; here one of them describes how she began reading his books for herself, demonstrating remarkable perseverance and maturity of approach:

Mr — would tell us about some books and authors . . . that is what got me started off on Garner . . . in the second year we usually had a reading session when everybody had a book between two and we go through the books and everybody reads a little bit. I liked *The Weirdstone* [*of Brisingamen* by Alan Garner] but I couldn't understand it, and then I think it was last year I got *The Moon of Gomrath* and I tried it and only got halfway through it, *so I thought I'll have another go at it because I might not have understood it properly* and I got it again and I really enjoyed it and that is when I started to get the stories. . . . *He told H. how good they were* and she started to get them.

Child 6 talked to me about the network of book recommendations among the avid readers in the fourth year and in particular about herself and her best friend. She said:

I always talk to H. about the books that I have read . . . we both take notice of each other. She will say, 'I've read a book by so and so, and it is very good,' and she will give me the basic outline of the story, and I will say, 'I'd like to borrow that book after you; it sounds right good.'

She said that they would talk like this, 'at playtimes, or during lessons if we are bored'. She also described discussions of books, particularly about girl/boy relationships or space/the supernatural, in the evenings – '. . . myself, and my brother, and G. we talk about books on an evening'. As one result of these discussions, G. persuaded Child 6 to join Bradford Central Library instead of borrowing from the small local library; the following Saturday she also took her father to join!

All the children told me that there was less time available for reading in school in the fourth year than there had been at the beginning of the experiment. One reason for this was that at least two English lessons per week were taken up with the class reader and at least two were spent in creative writing of a story in chapters, with cover illustrations, etc. In addition there would be grammatical work, spelling, comprehension and so on, leaving little time for choosing books and discussing them, even if the actual reading could be largely done at home. For the three girls and Child 4 the situation was exacerbated by the absence of their usual class teacher for half a term, 'We haven't been reading a lot lately – we haven't had a lot of reading lessons lately. We haven't had any since before Christmas!' (Child 4).

Even after the return of the usual teacher, time was scarce:

We are not reading in class as much – we don't get as much chance, and there is a lot of disturbance in class, and I can't get into a book . . . well, they [the teachers] don't do much with it [the Book Flood] and it's hardly ever used now. Mr — doesn't do too much with it. (Child 7)

This was said with regret.

None of the case study children enjoyed a class reader, and the practice was particularly disliked by avid readers, who welcomed being introduced to a book and liked to *discuss* it, but preferred to do most of the reading on their own. One child (girl avid reader) described the situation, as she saw it, when children took it in turns to read aloud passages from the class reader:

> . . . when you read in the class you have got people who aren't very good readers and they stop and they sort of put commas in the wrong places, and full stops, and you've just got to work it all out, and it takes your mind off it as well.

She liked to be read to by the teachers who read fluently, as did all the children. Child 1, however, made the point that he did not like the idea of a class reader being read from beginning to end by anyone as it took up a lot of time, and you were 'stuck with the book if it didn't appeal to you'. He also said that good readers found a class reader particularly irritating because such slow progress was made. Child 2 felt antagonistic towards having to produce written work on a class reader; he preferred to read and discuss books, and keep written work separate.

Silent reading in class was thought by the children to be virtually impossible because there was so much disturbance around them, and because there was insufficient time, had it been quiet, for them to 'get into' a book.

Child 7 said, 'Reading in class is fine if you can change your books regularly and have plenty of time to read them. I like to read by myself in quiet. If I have a good book, I hate to leave it until I have finished it.'

And Child 1: 'Well a lot of kids don't particularly like reading, or can't be bothered to read, as they sort of whisper and chatter a bit – they just enjoy themselves and disturb you.'

But the most effective description of how difficult it can be for even the keenest reader to read in class, comes from the diary of Child 8, who was describing a typical English lesson:

> Now for my favourite lesson, English, I'm doing a story called *The Time Machine,* and I've done a poem to go with it. . . . I've only written four lines but they look promising. D. and H. are giggling next to me and P. is sending messages to me and J., I can hardly read her writing it's so small, H. is making signs at P. and the rest of the children are quietly acting the fool. . . . Mr —

has got his eye on us, so we're behaving as normal as can be expected, D. and I keep trying to read each other's work, H.'s doing a title page, and P.'s kicking D. under the table. . . . I've only written half a page, so I'd better pull my socks up, but I'm finding work difficult because J. is laughing rather like a hyena and keeps disturbing me. (Not my punctuation!)

From all of this a few points emerge very clearly. The decrease in amount of reading in this school in the middle and final years of the experiment, holds true even for the keenest readers, who found that they had neither sufficient time nor a suitable atmosphere in which to read. A contributory factor to the decrease in amount of reading and in the use of the class-room library, was the third- and fourth-year teachers' inadequacy at recommending books, a particularly serious situation for children like 3 and 4, who had lost their initial enthusiasm. I believe that this inability to recommend books also contributed to the avid readers' belief that they had exhausted the Book Flood books that interested them. Had the teachers been able to choose, and read extracts from, a variety of books these children might have broadened their interests. Possibly, teachers are too ready to assume that they can leave keen readers alone to choose sensibly; possibly also, they are too ready to assume that all children can, and should, be able to read well enough for their needs by the time they reach the top of the middle school, and that it is no part of their job to do anything to remedy the situation if they can't. Certainly children 3, 4 and 5 showed no antagonism towards books; only disappointment when they were not able to tackle books that attracted them.

The outer city control school

The sample. Table 4·3 gives scores on the IQ and reading tests plus self-esteem scores and number of reading records completed for the case study children in this school. This sample differs from the other three because of the preponderance of children who were recommended by the teachers. There were *no* children who recorded having read more than twenty books in the first year of the experiment at this school. The largest number recorded by a boy (Child 9) was eighteen. The teachers were incredulous that he should have been included as a possible avid reader, suggesting that he must have filled the forms in 'for the sake of it' and 'if anything, he's one of the most reluctant readers in the year!' This boy had low scores on the IQ and reading tests and comes from a 'broken home'. When I was administering the self-esteem inventory he agreed with one of the items that he did not care what happened to him, adding that no one wanted him and he wished he were dead. His English teacher wrote of him 'Usually amenable, but fusses terribly. Attention-seeking'. Nevertheless, I decided to include him. I also included two boys whom the teachers agreed were the most avid readers in the year. Both Child 10 and 11 were in the top 'G' stream throughout the school, both had above average scores on IQ and reading tests and both came from supportive homes; the father of one of the boys was a parent–governor and the boy's English class teacher was the teacher representative on the governing body. This child, in particular, was an avid reader but did not appear to be such from the reading records because he read mainly non-fiction, particularly science, so that he did not finish a book, but tended to read in sections from a variety of books. He would usually position himself in a corner of the class-room by the non-fiction books, with his back to the rest of the class, and make notes from three or four science books. Child 12 was agreed to be a poor rather than a reluctant reader.

Table 4·3 Sample of case study children from outer city control school

Child	Sex	Year	IQ	Standardized reading score	Schonell Reading Age	Age at testing	Number of Reading Record Forms	Self-Esteem
9	M	10+	79	89	9·0	10·3	18	19
		11+		88	9·8	11·3	9	
		12+			11·4	12·8	13	36
10	M	10+	122	115	12·8	11·0	1	6
		11+		115	15·3	12·9	2	
		12+			17·7	13·4	8	8
11	M	10+	107	113	11·5	11·9	3	10
		11+		114	12·8	12·2	5	
		12+			14·6	13·6	8	10
12	M	10+	86	71	6·4	10·3	0	10
		11+		70	7·0	11·4	7	
		12+			7·5	12·8	5	26
13	F	10+	103	99	11·0	10·9	7	10
		11+		110	MV★	MV	4	
		12+			14·1	13·4	20	23
14	F	10+	76	89	9·6	10·9	6	10
		11+		83	11·6	12·0	11	
TA		12+			12·3	13·3	6	28

TA = Added at teachers' suggestion.
★MV = Missing value, i.e. child absent for test.

The girls presented a problem in that the range of books recorded was so small, none of the girls being outstandingly avid or reluctant on the basis of the reading records. When I discussed this with the teachers they immediately and unanimously agreed that Child 13 was the most avid reader in the school and that Child 14 was an infrequent one. Of Child 13, her class/English teacher wrote: 'D has a great deal of ability which she portrays particularly in her English creative work. Most of this must be accredited to her reading. An *avid* reader!' However, it is interesting to note that Child 14, whom the teachers labelled a reluctant reader, had a low IQ and a low reading score, and wrote of herself: 'I am a sort of person who reads a lot and keeps reading until I've read every single book at home and every single book in the class-room and anywhere else I can think of.' Again, as in the case of Child 9 the teacher felt that she was saying this because it was a desirable response. Certainly both Child 9 and Child 13 had very low scores on the self-esteem inventory and attention-seeking had to be borne in mind; the test was the way in which they talked about the books which they had read.

Findings. Table 4·4 shows the numbers of Reading Record Forms completed by these children in each year of the experiment, shows how many of the books they claim to have finished, and the places from which they obtained the books.

It is noticeable that none of the books was borrowed from the school library, which corroborated the remarks made by the 'school librarian'. In fact books read in school were almost exclusively from class libraries.

On the subject of reading in class these children had quite a lot to say, revealing in particular the wide discrepancy between amounts of time allowed to the children for reading in school. Child 9, who was in the 'C' stream throughout the school, explained that there was more time allocated to reading in the first year of the experiment than in subsequent years: '. . . we had *longer* in Mr G.'s class to read'. In the middle year of the experiment, there was less time for reading, which was particularly frustrating because they were not allowed to take class library books home to read. When asked why he had not finished his books in his third year, 11+, Child 9 replied that he had not had time to read them in class and had not been allowed to take them home: 'I once asked him [the teacher] and he said I couldn't [take books home] because one of them was a new book, just in case it got ripped.' I asked him whether people usually took books home, and he said: 'No, not in our class. No one does.' In the second year he had been able to finish books in class because they were easier, shorter and more time was allowed for reading. In the final year of the experiment even less time was allowed for reading: 'I think the books are very good in class but we should have longer reading in class.' He described how books could be chosen on a Friday after spellings and how children were allowed to read *at the end* of lessons if they had finished their work. Many of the children in his class rarely finished their work early and so, if they began a new book, would forget what it was about before they had a chance to look at it again. These are some of Child 9's comments about reading in class in the fourth year at 12 + :

'We can choose books on a Friday after spellings, and if you have finished one you fill your form in and get another.'

'. . . you can read it in school after spellings and when you have finished your work [We get] . . . about ten minutes.'

'. . . we only have about five minutes after lessons and then we don't have another until two days '

In any case, this particular child had difficulty in coping with the reading level of books as he went higher up the school and obviously needed considerable help with reading. He was a keen reader in his second year at 10+ but eventually found it less of a chore to *watch* Enid Blyton, *Star Wars* and *Blake's Seven* on television than to try to read them. He expressed his feelings about the level of difficulty of books like this:

[In the second year] . . . I read most of the books with pictures because they tell you about what is happening instead of just reading and getting bored you can look at the pictures.

Nearly every page there is a picture of something and then you get the writing on the other side.

He certainly enjoyed reading and made a determined effort to read quite difficult books, such as *The Moon of Gomrath* and *Carrie's War*. He got less than half-way through both. Had he had more time for reading in school, been allowed to take class library books home, had more *help* with reading from a trained remedial specialist and help with choosing suitable books, he would probably have continued to be a keen reader. Child 14, who had similar difficulties, said, 'I would rather read fiction stories because they are more interesting and the pictures are good'.

The children in the 'G' stream had an entire lesson for reading, '. . . once a week, at least'. Unlike the children in the 'F' and 'C' streams, however, who shared the *same* English teacher in the fourth year, the 'G' stream children had *more* time to read in G4 than they had in G2 or G3. Child 10 said, '. . . we have had *more* time to read. We have two lessons which are half an hour'. They could also change books at other times and read if work was finished early. Of course, the fact that these children got through their English work more quickly than the children in the 'F' and 'C' streams affected the teaching practice with regard to reading considerably. It is also much more difficult to create the right atmosphere for silent reading when children have difficulty with reading and shorter concentration spans. The children in the 'G' stream did not usually take books home to read but they read more quickly than the 'F' and 'C' stream children, had more time for reading, and both more, and more attractive, books to choose from – because they tended to treat them with care so they were less likely to be lost or damaged. Both Child 11 and Child 13 confirmed that, in G4, children had two lessons a week for reading, as well as time when work was finished.

Table 4·4   Outer city control school: places from which case study children obtained books recorded on Reading Record Forms and numbers of books obtained from each location, plus (in brackets) number of books completed

Child	Sex	Year	Public library	School library	Class library	Belongs to child	Belongs to sibling	Belongs to a friend	Totals
9	M	10+			18 (14)				18 (14)
		11+			9 (1)				9 (1)
		12+			13 (8)				13 (8)
10	M	10+			1 (1)				1 (1)
		11+	1 (0)		1 (0)				2 (0)
		12+			6 (6)		2 (2)		8 (8)
11	M	10+			3 (3)				3 (3)
		11+	1 (0)		4 (3)				5 (3)
TA		12+	2 (0) NF		6 (5)				8 (5)
12	M	10+							0 (0)
		11+			7 (6)				7 (6)
		12+			4 (4)	1 (1)			5 (5)
13	F	10+			7 (2)				7 (2)
TA		11+			4 (3)				4 (3)
		12+	4 (4)		15 (12)			1 (1)★	20 (17)
14	F	10+			6 (6)				6 (6)
TA		11+			11 (11)				11 (11)
		12+			6 (6)				6 (6)

NF = Non-fiction – large volumes on cricket.
★ = Borrowed from class teacher – *Mrs Frisby and the Rats of NIMH* by Robert O'Brien.
TA = Added at teachers' suggestion.

The variety of approaches from different teachers is well illustrated by the following comments from Child 13:

> [in G2] . . . we had lessons on reading and sometimes in English when we didn't have much to do she told us to read our books. . . . She let us stay in and read playtime and dinner-times. . . . In the third year I don't think we had a proper lesson not a whole lesson to read in.

In the fourth year, when they had two periods of reading a week, she said, 'I like the lessons when we are all reading alone'.

Most of the case study children were dissatisfied with the supply of books in the class-room. The boys, 10 and 11, who were avid readers of non-fiction mainly, would have liked a larger collection and wider variety of non-fiction books. It is unfortunate that Child 11 never used the school library for it contained most of the school's non-fiction books. He said, 'I do not like the books in the class library. I like factual books and books on sport, but not fiction at all.' He had read, and enjoyed, T. H. White, Alfred Hitchcock, Franklin W. Dixon and R. L. Stevenson, among others, in the second and third year but veered more and more towards non-fiction as he got older. Child 10, who was in any case a more keen reader, usually managed to find books to interest him, partly because he was one of the four or five fourth years who borrowed books from the school library and took them into the class-room and partly because he enjoyed science *fiction* as well as science. Child 12 was virtually unaffected by the problem of book choice as he was being given books from reading schemes most of the time. His English teacher wrote: 'He has had remedial teaching most of his school career.'

Child 13 had the most to say about the supply of books in the class-room. She felt that the books in G4 were attractive to look at, unlike those in G3 which '. . . didn't have covers on – they were just plain backed', but she was disappointed in them because she felt the teacher had a different idea of what constituted a good book than she did. What she really wanted, on her own admission, was a kind of 'escapism'. She wanted to get beyond her immediate environment and sought solace in a world of witches, wizards, ghosts, fairies, dragons and magic generally: 'I would rather read fiction because I just like fairy tale stories. It gives you a release for an hour or two from reality.'

Apart from Child 10, who occasionally took books from the school library to the class-room, mainly reference books, none of the children used the school library, and none took books home from the school library to read. Child 13, who had enjoyed *Smith* by Leon Garfield, tried to find other books by him but gave up, saying '. . . we haven't got any more by him in class'. When I asked her why she didn't look in the school library, she said, 'I haven't tried that; I don't go in.'

The extent to which teachers were able to recommend books to children was as varied as the amount of time that they allocated to silent reading. Once again, the children in the 'G' stream seem to have been fortunate, whereas those in the 'F' or 'C' streams, who probably needed more help with choice of books, actually received less help. Child 9 described his experience in C4: '. . . and if we don't find one in about five minutes sir just gives us one'. This was corroborated by Child 14, who, when I asked her what happened if she couldn't find a book to suit her, said, 'He just says choose one and go and sit down.'

Children occasionally referred to teachers lower down the school who had affected them, for instance Child 13 mentioned, '. . . one of the teachers called Miss —, she said there was one called *Black Jack* that was a good book and I want to try and get that one'. However, the teacher whom *all* the G4 children said had helped them most with choice of books was Mr —, their class teacher in that year, who took them for all their English except creative work, and with whom they had the two lessons of silent reading a week. He obviously knew a great deal about their reading preferences. Child 10 said that this teacher knew he liked reading about science and science fiction and could help him to choose books. The teacher wrote: 'Prefers to read fact books (particularly science books) rather than fiction.' The boy confirmed this, adding '. . . he knows I read a bit about space'. In his diary the boy wrote that, on Sunday, he was reading a book '. . . lent to me by Mr —, the book is a science fiction novel called *Foundation* by Isaac Asimov.' The same teacher knew that Child 11 was a cricket fanatic. He was particularly helpful to Child 13 whose parents read a great deal but not books suitable for her age group. She describes how this teacher accepted that the class library did not contain many books that were to her taste, and how he came to lend her *Mrs Frisby and the Rats of Nimh* by Robert O'Brien:

> . . . I had been looking for a book and I didn't like any of the books in class and I spent a long time looking for a book and he said would I like to try that one because it was a right good book so I read it.

She said he had helped her with reading. 'More than the other teachers did. . . . He takes more interest he always tells people if

they are not reading enough. . . . He tells you if it is a good one
when you get it out.'

Child 13 was outstandingly articulate and had a great deal to say
about reading, including topics that the other children did not
mention, and expanding on topics that other children only touched
on briefly. I shall say more about her home background in Chapter
5 but should like to conclude this particular section by including the
remainder of the contribution she makes to the topic of reading in
school. On the subject of how she goes about choosing books, she
showed a dependence upon the appearance of the book and a
remarkable lack of awareness of authors, surprising in such an avid
reader:

> . . . I look at the covers first and see which one has a nice cover,
> and then I read the passage about it, and if I think it sounds good I
> start to read it. . . . The only author I've ever looked at is the one
> who wrote *Smith* and that. He was the only one I took notice of.

When I asked her whether she had thought of looking for another
book by Robert O'Brien, she replied, 'No, I didn't think of it – I
just thought of it as Mr —'s book and I didn't think there would be
another one as good.'

Of the books in the class-room generally, she said that she would
like more stories that are removed from everyday life because '. . .
it's boring, life'.

The passage that she wrote on the topic of reading is, I think,
worth quoting intact, even though it includes remarks about
reading at home, because it epitomizes the mood of even the avid
reader in the 'G' stream at this particular school. There was a
feeling of longing for a wide variety of books and of people to talk
to about them which pervaded all the interviews:

> I like reading, it is good to do when your bored. It is a pleasing
> pass time. I like fiction because for hours you can escape the
> realitys of ordinary life. Reading has also I think made me a
> Romantic. Whenever I am excited or have just done something
> wrong I tend to have a cry then read. When I was nine and first
> started my middle school I was put off reading by Miss —
> because she used to make you wright about your book when
> you'd finished it. So I would go very slow and not finish my
> book. When I'm reading it doesn't matter if I'm in a room of
> talking people or a quiet room although a quiet room is
> preferable. I seem to shut people out when I'm reading or when
> the television's on at home. Sometimes if I'm restless I can't read
> at all. If I'm really interested in a book I don't put it down until
> I've finished it – I've been encouraged to read a lot at home as my
> mum and dad read every weekend.

Inner city experimental school

The Sample. Table 4·5 gives test results for the case study children in this school, plus numbers of reading records completed each year and self-esteem scores. All of these children except for Child 15 were chosen on the basis of the Reading Record Forms. The teachers more or less insisted that he should be included as an avid reader, as indeed he was, being one of the few avid readers who did not complete Reading Record Forms in the first year of the experiment because, he said, 'I thought it was a waste of time, filling in the forms for the books that I had read. I thought they wouldn't do anything with the forms. I couldn't see why I should record it.' Another reason for failing to record his reading was that he was not reading books from the class library, but was taking his own books to school to read. Child 16, Child 17 and Child 19 remained avid readers throughout the experiment. Child 20 began as an avid

Table 4·5   Sample of case study children from inner city experimental school

Child	Sex	Year	IQ	Standardized reading score	Schonell Reading Age	Age at testing	Number of Reading Record Forms	Self-Esteem
15	M	10+	108	113	11·2	10·6	3	11
		11+		115	12·3	11·7	3	
		12+			14·1	12·1	60	MV
16	M	10+	111	123	14·7	11·1	20	2
		11+		122	15·6	12·2	8	
		12+			19·0	13·5	28	11
17	M	10+	105	89	11·6	10·5	25	9
		11+		100	12·3	11·5	7	
Asian		12+			16·0	12·9	52	4
18	M	10+	99	93	10·9	10·7	0	10
		11+		96	12·5	11·7	8	
		12+			13·1	13·1	10	16
19	F	10+	97	100	11·8	11·1	24	3
		11+		98	12·5	12·9	19	
Asian		12+			12·6	13·5	33	19
20	F	10+	95	90	8·6	11·1	25	4
		11+		87	9·7	12·9	3	4
		12+			11·3	13·6	12	10
21	F	10+	103	91	11·5	10·4	1	6
		11+		96	12·6	11·4	3	
		12+			15·3	12·9	31	0

reader but found the level of difficulty of the books available to her increasingly demanding. Child 21 began as a truly reluctant reader, on her own admission, but improved her reading skills during the course of the experiment and developed a keen interest in books, partly because of the availability of them, partly because of her mother's concern and my attention, and partly because of her greater ability, in fact she became a school librarian for the entire final year of the experiment. *All* the children, except for Child 20, increased the amount of their reading during the course of the experiment, so that once again it is difficult to divide them into clear-cut groups of avid and reluctant readers. Table 4·6 gives details of the origins of the 'Asian' case study children.

Table 4·6   Origins of 'ethnic minority' case study children

Child 17: M	– Father and mother both born in Pakistan.
ICES	Child born in Bradford, England.
Child 19: F	– Father and mother both born in India.
ICES	Child born in Bradford, England.
Child 23: M	– Father and mother both born in Pakistan.
ICCS	Child born in Bradford, England.
Child 24: M	– Father and mother both born in Pakistan.
Reluctant –	Child born in Pakistan.
ICCS	
Child 28: F	– Father and mother both born in Pakistan.
Reluctant –	Child born in Bradford, England.
ICCS	

ICES = Inner city experimental school.
ICCS = Inner city control school.

Findings. Table 4·7 gives a breakdown of the places from which the case study children borrowed their books and indicates whether they finished them or not.

An interesting finding in this sample is that the range IQ scores (see Table 4·5) is small, and that Child 19, an avid reader, scored two points *below* Child 18, an infrequent reader.

Looking at Table 4·7, we find that the bulk of the borrowing was from the class libraries. However, Child 16 is outstanding in that he rarely chose books from the class-room, preferring to read books of his own, or ones that he had borrowed from the school and public libraries. Also the children borrowed less from the class libraries as the experiment progressed and a correspondingly increasing amount from the school library, except in the cases of Child 18 who was an infrequent reader, Child 20 who could not cope with the difficulty, and Child 21 who preferred to read her own books.

Table 4·7   Inner city experimental school: places from which case study children obtained books recorded on Reading Record Forms and number of books obtained from each location, plus (in brackets) number of books completed

Child	Sex	Year	Public library	School library	Class library	Belongs to child	Belongs to sibling	Belongs to a friend	Totals
15	M	10+			3 (2)				3 (2)
		11+		3 (3)					3 (3)
TA		12+	15 (15)	26 (25)		15 (15)	2 (2)	2 (2)	60 (59)
16	M	10+		1 (1)	19 (16)				20 (17)
		11+		1 (1)	7 (6)				8 (7)
		12+	1 (1)	15 (15)	7 (6)	4 (4)	1 (0)		28 (26)
17	M	10+		2 (0)	23 (20)				25 (20)
		11+			7 (6)				7 (6)
Asian*		12+	7 (6)	22† (20)	15 (12)	1 (1)	3 (3)	4 (4)	52 (46)
18	M	10+							0 (0)
		11+			8 (4)				8 (4)
		12+	2 (2)	2 (2)	8 (5)				10 (7)
19	F	10+	1 (1)	1 (1)	22 (22)				24 (24)
		11+	2 (2)	8 (8)	9 (9)				19 (19)
Asian*		12+	11 (10)	13 (12)	7 (6)			2 (2)	33 (30)
20	F	10+			25 (17)				25 (17)
		11+			2 (0)		1 (1)		3 (1)
		12+		1 (1)	4 (3)		7 (7)		12 (11)
21	F	10+			1 (1)				1 (1)
		11+			3 (0)				3 (0)
		12+		2 (2)	4 (3)	20 (20)	5 (5)		21 (29)

* = Origins of Asian case study children are given in Table 4·6.
† = two not finished were non-fiction.
TA = Added at teachers' suggestion.

In the middle year of the experiment even the really avid readers did not read so much as they did in the other two years. Their comments suggest that this was because the class teachers in the children's second year (at 10+: year one of the experiment) and the English 'specialist' in their fourth year (at 12+: year three of the experiment), did more to encourage the children to read and were better able to recommend books in an informed way, than the teachers in the middle year who were specialists in subjects other than English.

It is noticeable that in *every* case books recorded belonging to the children were read from cover to cover, which says something about the advantages of book ownership.

For the most part, by the time I interviewed these children in the final year of the experiment, they had come to take for granted the availability of a large and varied supply of books, as well as the ease with which they could borrow books from almost anywhere in school and take them home. Child 15, who had a great many books at home, did not mention the advent of the Book Flood at all, but did say, 'I think there are too many baby books in the class library . . . there are a few baby books that are even too young for the first year. Fourth years are reading them! Books with two inch words and a picture on every page!' He was a school librarian and, therefore, found it easy and convenient to borrow books from the school library. Child 16, however, had been pleased by the arrival of the extra books. He wrote: 'I was glad when all the books came because it gave us a chance to widen our reading scope.' Similarly, Child 17 was impressed; he told me: 'We had a lot (of books) in the second year, because most of our class-room was filled up and we didn't have enough room in the class.' He described in more detail the impact that the Book Flood had on the children in his class, as well as on the teacher:

> When we got the Book Flood it was new and we thought there must be some good books in it, so we read a lot . . . and when we got them out our teacher told us about them. She went through them and said, 'This is a good one, and this is that book', and she would say, 'I wouldn't get that book', and things like that.

None of the other children mentioned the arrival of the books at all, but equally, apart from Child 15's remark about them being too babyish, none expressed dissatisfaction with the books available.

Child 21 was impressed by the organization of the books in the fourth-year English base: 'The books in the class-room are in order, like all Puffin books, all Armada books are altogether.'

The children in this school, unlike those in the outer city experimental school, continued to have library lessons in the school library, after the arrival of the books, in addition to reading in the class-room. The children's comments illustrated that there was less distinction between school and class libraries at this school than at the other three schools, and that children were not confined to borrowing books from their own class-room, as a uniform system for recording the borrowing of books was in operation throughout the school. For instance, Child 17 told me in the first year of the experiment: '. . . we could borrow books from our own class-room or any other class in the school' and in the third year (middle year of experiment): '. . . we used to get books from the next room, the music room, and that was used as an English room as well. There used to be a lot of books in there.'

They all took books home to read. Child 18 was astounded to be asked whether they took books home, saying, 'We all take books home of course . . . we had little tickets . . . if we borrow a book at school, like at the library, when we have a library lesson, we can take them out home and bring them back next week . . . if you want a book in here now, in the school library, all you've got to do in the dinner time is take it, get a ticket out, and take it home with you . . . you can read it at home'. He said it as though he was talking to a complete imbecile, for asking such a silly question! In fact, immediately after my interview with that particular child I was bombarded with children asking for books to be stamped as it was lunch-time.

Child 15 had extremely strong views to express about the amount of time available for reading in school. He wrote:

> We do not get anywhere near enough time for reading in school, the teachers, some of them, take it for granted that you are a good reader, just because you are old and in the top class. When they find out you're not as good as you should be you get into trouble which is wrong. I was lucky because I was taught by my mother to read, who found out that the [first] school I was at was not helping me at all. These library lessons should be in the timetable. It is a very important thing is reading.
>
> Reading on the whole is very educational and enjoyable *if you are confident enough*.

His point about many older children needing continued help with reading, and wanting to read but lacking the confidence, is, I believe, one that cannot be emphasized too forcibly. We are not sufficiently aware of the fear and trembling with which some children approach the written word. Nevertheless, despite this particular child's castigation of the teachers, the case study children at this school always had a lesson set aside for silent reading in the library or the class-room, and often both, as well as smaller chunks of time at the end of lessons if they finished their work.

These children had varying attitudes towards reading a book with the teacher as a class reader or personal silent reading. Child 15 wrote: 'I enjoy listening to a book being read if it is good. I also like reading my own books . . . I really read at home where I am comfortable, usually in my bedroom or in the front room.' In contrast, Child 16 was quite antagonistic towards the idea of a class reader:

> I don't like reading a book with the teacher because they explain nearly every word and you lose track of the story. In the lessons when we all read [silently] I can never settle down because there are too many distractions. I like reading in a quiet atmosphere.

Apart from interruptions by the teacher, the other reason for his opposition to the idea of a class reader was that he disliked the idea of someone else imposing their choice of book on him: 'I enjoy reading books that I like and what I choose but I don't like when teachers thrust books into your hand and say you should read this. . . . On the whole I enjoy reading my own choice of things.'

Child 17 agreed with Child 15 that his attitude depended upon the teacher's choice of book. It is amusing that Child 18, who had some difficulty with silent reading, but read well aloud and loved the sound of his own voice, being quite skilful in verbal communication, should say: 'I think it's good when the whole class read with the teacher and you get picked to read.' Child 19, however, agreed entirely with Child 16:

> If we read the book with the teacher she explains things to you so you forget what she's read. I think you read more with your own reading book, because you can follow it and imagine deep inside you the characters; also when you are reading a book by yourself you can imagine a person there which is you.

Those children did not dislike the idea of a class reader *per se* – what they objected to was constantly having the story interrupted so they were unable to lose themselves in it, and the fear that it could be one lesson a week for a whole term given over to a story that did not interest them. On this point, Child 20 wrote: 'I like reading very much as long as I can read what I want to read', and Child 21:

> I don't really like reading a book with the whole class and the teacher because I sometimes don't like the book we're reading. I like it when we read our own books in the library because you like the book you're reading.

Child 20 was obviously influenced by her difficulty with reading and feared the teacher asking her to read aloud: 'I don't like to read a book in a group because I cannot follow it. I do not like to read aloud I get too nervous. I like to read by myself.' Obviously she needed to read aloud but not in front of the entire class. I am not arguing against hearing children read aloud, nor am I against the teacher reading extracts, nor even the first quarter of books that many children do not like at first or never like at all; like new kinds of food they'll never know until they try it, but it is better to introduce them to a varied diet, fully utilizing the time available, than to stuff them with one new dish that they may never get to like.

There is no doubt that they were becoming articulate and beginning to develop a critical faculty! It might also be wise for teachers to keep discussions about extracts for beginnings and ends of sessions, and I'm sure that literature should not be used as a means for teaching grammar correctly; that can be done in other ways. Finally on this point I must quote Child 17 who wrote, with a note of suffering, I feel: 'Our English teacher recommends us books that we don't usually like, for instance she has started reading *The Owl Service* with us which to me and to quite a lot of other people is boring.' It did not prevent him from commending the extent to which the same teacher helped him with his reading, nor did it stop him reading forty-six books completely in the first year of the experiment when she was his English teacher.

While the majority of the children told me about both second-year class teachers and the English specialist, who taught all of them in the fourth year and a few of them in the third year, recommending books to them, none of them talked in this way about the other third-year English teachers. Certainly, all of the second-year class teachers and the English specialist knew a good deal about children's books and were all able to recommend them whereas the third-year teachers, for the most part, did not. Child 17, who described the second-year class teacher going through the selection of books with them (quoted above) added, '. . . she said, "If you get a book, get one that you will read," and every time we read one we had to tell her about it'. During my many visits to the school I found these teachers exceptionally well informed about children's literature. The same child explained that they did not get the same kind of detailed help from the third-year teachers, although no doubt they were encouraging, because, 'One was a sports teacher, one was a maths teacher and Mr — used to be a sort of music teacher. He knew about, the violin and that, but he didn't tell us about books.' Yet, of the English specialist, he said 'Mrs — is a help to us even more than Mrs — [the second-year class teacher] – it makes me read more'. This degree of variance in teacher knowledge of books is reflected in the fact that even the really avid readers read less in school in the middle year of the experiment than they did in the first and final years.

In addition to teacher influence upon their reading, quite a few of the children mentioned peer group influence, making such remarks as, 'I talk to my mates about the books I've read and they talk to me about theirs and we exchange books during the library lesson'; or, 'I usually talk about books with my friend. Sometimes she recommends books to me or my English teacher does.'

These children were remarkably aware of authors and anxious to talk to me about them, usually giving me a list of favourite authors followed by more detailed remarks about one or two of them. This unusual awareness of authors could well be related to the availability of books and the teachers' knowledge. Child 15 liked 'Willard Price, Frank Richards, Anthony Buckeridge, Richmal Crompton, Nicholas Fisk, Jules Verne, Spike Milligan and Ian Fleming'. He particularly enjoyed reading *Run for Your Life* by David Line, which he read twice. Child 16 said he liked 'football fiction, especially Michael Hardcastle, and thrillers', and Child 17 Roald Dahl, Willard Price, Michael Hardcastle, writers of space books like Michael Pollard and writers of football encyclopedias: '. . . I like books with a lot of action in them'. This child was able to talk in some detail about his favourite books, for instance he described one of his favourite Willard Price books:

> An adventure – two bacteriologists go around the world for zoos, to collect animals, and there is a lot of fighting and exciting bits in it, and mystery. . . . I have read most of them and I have read some of them twice.

However, he did not like *Biggles* at all: 'You had to read three-quarters of the book before you got into the adventure.' Child 18 said 'My favourite authors are Ian Fleming, Agatha Christie and Enid Blyton.' Child 19 liked detective stories, and especially Alfred Hitchcock, Carolyn Keene, Franklin W. Dixon and Enid Blyton:

> . . . I like books when the adventure starts straight away. When you read some books they just go on and on about one thing and they don't start straight away, because I found from a lot of people that they liked stories that go straight into the mystery.

Child 20 liked Enid Blyton and Child 21, Enid Blyton, Judith M. Berrisford (horse stories) and Constance Savery.

In addition to their knowledge of authors these children had developed an awareness of the extent of their own reading abilities and the limitations imposed upon book choice by any difficulties that they might have. For instance, Child 15 wrote: 'Five or six years ago I would not read; also I had great difficulty doing it. My mother taught me to read.' The result was that gradually he greatly increased the amount and range of his reading until he could cope with a book like *Plague Dogs* at 13 years old. Child 20 was well aware of her continued difficulty with reading and at the time of the case study had started going to bed half an hour earlier each night to read and try to improve her ability. She was well aware of the extent to which her difficulties limited her choice of books, and expressed her dependence upon illustrations:

> I think pictures should be put more in books so that you can understand more of the story. It gives you more of an idea what they mean in the book. . . . I like Enid Blyton ones. . . . I read a

few last year and three of *My Naughty Little Sister*. . . . But my Mum thought they were too babyish now, so I have stopped reading these. . . . When I was in Miss —'s class (second year) she told me I was reading books which were too young for me.

This girl told me that she usually chose a book by 'the brightness and the colour', that she knew she was a 'slow reader', and that she found it really hard work getting into a book:

> . . . what I find hardest is to get into the book first of all, because I don't like the first chapter – this is a bit boring. When I get into the middle I can't put the book down because I enjoy it all . . . that's why I carry on.

Child 21, also, made a conscious effort to improve her reading but had more success; both girls were greatly encouraged by a parent.

The case study children in this school had developed a degree of sophistication in methods of book choice beyond that of the children in the matched control school, and were able to articulate the thought process involved. Child 17, for instance, described how he came to read, first of all, James Bond books and then books by Willard Price:

> I started reading James Bond books and at first I thought they would be hard because the second-year teacher, we used to see things on television and ·there would be books written about them, and she used to say the books would be much harder than the television series. But I read *Goldfinger* and it was good – I asked my mate who had read it and I said, 'Is it any good?' and he said it was great, so I got it and I liked it. I knew there was a series, so I took my brother's ticket to the library, because he was feeling poorly so I said I would get his books, and I asked for Ian Fleming and I got three. . . . One month ago I got a book, a Willard Price one, and I said to my teacher (fourth-year English specialist), 'Is this any good?' and she said, 'Yes, they are very good, they are a bit like those James Bond ones,' and I said, 'Is there any more James Bond ones?' and she said, 'No, get some other books.' Then she asked me why I liked them and I said because I had watched the film and I knew what was going to come next in the book, so she said, 'That's very good. I will tell somebody at the university about that.'

This is interesting and amusing, but it also illustrates a further point, and that is the degree of encouragement offered by this teacher, without criticism of the child's personal choice.

While most of these children said that they were enjoying both fiction and non-fiction the two extremes were represented by Child 18, who much preferred reading non-fiction because 'I like to find out what happened before I was born, because it's like adding years on to your life, isn't it, when you know what happened before you were born' and by Child 19, who, like one of the female avid readers at the outer city control school, preferred fiction because she could lose herself in the story and identify with a character and felt that, 'If you read, it makes things better. . . . I like to read fiction stories. This is because there is more excitement and goings on in the book. But in non-fiction you can't make it really exciting because it has happened.' This obviously affected her choice of authors like Hitchcock, Keene and Dixon. She described her strategy for choosing a book: 'I pick the authors that I know first. Then I read the introduction bit that tells me if it is good. Sometimes I read the first and second page as well.'

The Asian children were aware of the fact that reading would help them assimilate the English language; their parents inculcated them with this attitude. For instance, Child 17 wrote: 'Reading is good for you, it's good for your education.' He believed, rightly, that his reading had improved during his time at the middle school. He told me he had been awarded two books at that school as prizes for consistent effort. Similarly Child 19 said, 'It helps me to learn a lot of the words for English and that.'

There was not the interchange of ideas and authors among the group of avid readers in this school that there was in the outer city experimental school, but the combination of the availability of a large and varied supply of books, and teachers who were keen and knowledgeable about children's literature, seemed to go hand in hand with an increased awareness, on the part of the children, of books, of authors, of strategies for book choice, of the state of their own reading skills, and of teachers' knowledge or lack of knowledge of children's books.

Inner city control school

The sample. Table 4·8 shows the sample of case study children for the inner city control school, with scores on the Cattell IQ Test, the reading tests, on the Coopersmith Self-Esteem Inventory, and the number of Reading Record Forms completed each year. Details of the Asian children are given in Table 4·6. All but one of the case study children in this sample were chosen on the basis of the Reading Record Forms. In this, as in the other three samples also, we find a predominance of boys at the two extremes of reading a great deal or of reading next to nothing. Child 22 and Child 23 were both avid readers throughout the experiment. Child 24, as it turned out, was never a reluctant reader, but had tremendous difficulty to begin with, but read a lot more when he improved his reading skills. Child 25 was not only reluctant to read but, sadly, also reluctant to live. Child 26, like Child 24, became keener on reading as his skills developed but was greatly handicapped by his background which was extremely discouraging. Child 27 was added on the teacher's recommendation as no girl emerged as really avid on the basis of the reading records. Child 28, like Child 24, developed her reading as her skills developed and her mastery of the English language increased. In fact, both of the Asian children who began by reading very little (Child 24 and Child 28) were really keen readers by the end of the experiment.

Table 4·8   Sample of case study children from inner city control school

Child	Sex	Year	IQ	Standardized reading score	Schonell Reading Age	Age at testing	Number of Reading Record Forms	Self-Esteem
22	M	10+	93	94	13·9	10·8	17	12
		11+		MV	14·8	11·9	4	
		12+			19·0	13·2	26	6
23	M	10+	105	98	11·8	10·6	33	11
		11+		103	13·2	11·6	7	
Asian		12+			15·0	13·0	27	8
24	M	10+	65	77	8·1	10·4	1	6
		11+		84	9·3	11·5	4	
Asian		12+			11·0	12·9	25	MV
25	M	10+	81	80	6·5	10·6	1	MV
		11+		73	7·4	11·6	5	
		12+			14·7	12·9	10	20
26	M	10+	88	89	7·4	10·2	0	10
		11+		70	8·1	11·3	2	
		12+			13·1	12·6	10	20
27	F	10+	92	98	11·4	10·9	5	12
		11+		MV	MV	MV	0	
TA		12+			13·5	13·3	17	32
28	F	10+	93	83	8·5	10·9	1	35
		11+		92	9·7	11·9	12	
Asian		12+			12·3	13·3	35	19

TA = Added at teachers' suggestion.

Findings. Again the range of IQ scores is small, apart from that of Child 24. Of course, we must remember that IQ is not static and it is particularly important to bear this in mind in the case of children who are, at least in part, from a different cultural background, so that the score of fifty-six for Child 24, for instance, is not to be understood as a permanent measure of his ability.

Table 4·9 gives a breakdown of the numbers of books that these children recorded during the three years of the experiment, showing the places from which they obtained their books and, in brackets, the numbers from each location that they claim to have completed. The bulk of the books recorded was from the classrooms and there were consistently more recorded from the classroom in the final year of the experiment than in the other two years. Child 22 was exceptional in that he preferred to take books from home to read. There is very little use of the school library recorded, and it is noticeable that both of the children who recorded taking public library books to school to read were of Asian origin. The middle year was a particularly lean year for reading in school even for the really avid reader, but far more was recorded in the final year than in either of the other two years.

Table 4·9   Inner city control school: places from which case study children obtained books recorded on Reading Record Forms and numbers of books obtained from each location, plus (in brackets) number of books completed

Child	Sex	Year	Public library	School library	Class library	Belongs to child	Belongs to sibling	Belongs to a friend	Totals
22	M	10+				17 (17)			17 (17)
		11+			1 (1)	3 (3)			4 (4)
		12+			3 (3)	23 (21)			26 (24)
23	M	10+	3 (2)	7 (5)	16 (14)	6 (4)		1 (0)	33 (25)
		11+		4 (3)	3 (3)				7 (6)
Asian		12+	8 (8)	1 (1)	18 (14)				27 (23)
24	M	10+		1 (0)					1 (0)
		11+		1 (1)	3 (3)				4 (4)
Asian		12+			25 (23)				25 (23)
25	M	10+			1 (1)				1 (1)
		11+			5 (5)				5 (5)
		12+			10 (10)				10 (10)
26	M	10+							0 (0)
		11+			2 (2)				2 (2)
		12+			10 (3)				10 (3)
27	F	10+		3 (3)		2 (2)			5 (5)
		11+			2 (1)	2 (1)			4 (2)
TA		12+			13 (9)	4 (4)			17 (13)
28	F	10+			1 (0)				1 (0)
		11+	5 (4)	2 (1)	4 (4)			1 (1)	12 (9)
Asian		12+	11 (9)		21 (18)		3 (1)		35 (28)

TA = Added at teachers' suggestion.

The children in this school had far less to say about books and reading than did the children in the matched experimental school, where, as we have just seen, the children had developed strong and often highly critical views. More of the case study children in the control school were unenthusiastic about the books in the class-room – except for the occasional author. Child 22, who usually took books from home to read in school, said, 'The books in the classroom are boring except for one or two . . . they are all children's'. His favourite authors were ones he had discovered for himself, usually via films and television – authors such as William Goldman, James A. Michener, Peter Benchley, Irving Wallace and Thomas Tryon. This is what he wrote about them:

> I like reading and would rather read on my own than with a class. I like William Goldman's novels because they are exciting and contain a lot of violent action. I have read two of his books and they are very fine thrillers. *Marathon Man* was excitingly done. *Magic* was terrific and it shows how good William Goldman is. Peter Benchley is another good author to read. *Jaws* was marvellously written and excitingly described. *The Deep* was another brilliantly written novel. I like reading adult novels. They are more exciting. Books like *Centennial* are excellent and very educating and dramatic. James A. Michener, the author of *Centennial* is brilliant and he can write good stuff and is worth reading. I dislike love stories because they are boring and soppy. Thrillers and crime are my favourites.
>
> I like reading horror stories.

There is tremendous potential for development here; it is a great pity that all children cannot be exposed to a book flood used by well-informed and enthusiastic teachers. Child 23 had an entirely different sort of taste, preferring *The Bobsey Twins* and Jennings, but not finding much to interest him in the class-room. Child 24, however, was very happy with the books available in school, especially in the fourth-year class-room where he found authors at a level that he could cope with. He wrote, 'I think the books are really great in the class-room library. My favourite author is G. R. Crosher. I like fiction books because they are exciting. I like non-fiction as well because you can learn something.'

Child 24, whose reading skills and interest in books developed to some extent in his final year at the middle school, under the careful eye of the English specialist, was particularly hooked on Anne Oates, again an author who wrote at a level that he could cope with and about people and situations with which he could identify. He told me about three of her books that he had read, demonstrating quite clearly, I believe, that with help and encouragement he could have developed quite a keen interest in books:

I read *Baked Beans Again* twice. The woman was in hospital and the boy was always having baked beans. I read *Leather Jacket Boys,* it's really like that, and *Meet Harry King,* about a kid who always wants to do what he wants to do and his dad doesn't let him . . . and *A Real City Kid* about a boy in a large family . . . and another one of those Anne Oates ones about this ghost in this old house.

He went into quite a lot of detail; he had obviously read the books thoroughly, and talked about them with enthusiasm. His Schonell Reading Age had risen to 14·7 when he was 12·9, so it is probable that there was a link between increased ability and increased interest. The boy himself also connected his increased interest with the fact that, 'We seem to read more with Mr — in English in the Fourth Year. . . . He sees me every day.'

While the English specialist was particularly adept at recommending books to boys, even if he did not always have the books to hand, he was the first to admit that he was sometimes at a loss to recommend them to girls. This was borne out by Child 27, who, incidentally, said that she thought the fourth-year class library could be arranged better, as most of the books were shut away in cupboards. She said she enjoyed reading the books that were available at school but that she much preferred to read about '. . . what a teenager does, growing up and all that. . . . I am probably the only one in my class. The other girls read adventure stories, and Caroline likes ghost stories and monsters and things like that.' She was totally unaware, as were the teachers, of books like those by Diana Wynne Jones, some by Ursula Le Guin, Beverley Cleary and authors like Paul Zindel, Mary Rodgers and Judy Blume; instead she turned to magazines like *Look-In,* not because it was easier to read but because it contained articles and stories on the sort of topics that interested her.

Like the case study children in the other three schools few of these children liked reading a class reader with the teacher and for the same reasons: not because they did not like being read to – they did – but because of other children reading slowly, interruptions and the possibility of disliking the choice of books. Child 22, for example, wrote, 'I do not like reading with the teacher because it is slower. Reading a book [silently] in a lesson is a good idea. . . . I would rather read on my own than with a class. . . . I would rather have my own books. I can have a choice.' Similarly, Child 23 wrote:

> I like a lesson when we all read our own reading books. I don't like reading with the class taking it in turns to read because some of them are slow readers. I like reading to myself, *but sometimes I*

like it when the teacher reads to us. . . . I'm always glad when we're allowed to read at school, when the teacher says so.

Less-able children particularly, and some of the very able, love being read to and it is one of the best ways of introducing them to new authors; but it should be kept totally separate from listening to poor readers and from English Language teaching, although hopefully some of that will be achieved in the process. Child 27 wrote of the English specialist, 'I like Mr — reading to us because he tells us the correct way to say it and what the words mean, something we'd miss if we were reading by ourselves.' Child 21 preferred to read by herself and liked to read at home rather than at school, 'Because I hate being disturbed by other things.' But some children, as we shall see, are constantly disturbed at home and desperately need an atmosphere conducive to reading at school, if they are to read at all.

None of the case study children mentioned their third-year teacher in connection with reading. They all said that they had had more time for reading in their second year than in their third year, and more time, and help, in the fourth year than in either of the other two years. In addition to having a lesson set aside for silent reading in the fourth year, these children read a class reader with the teacher each term, and were able to read at other times when work was completed: '. . . he gave us some work to do and when we have finished it we can read a book until the end of the lesson' (Child 23). Similarly, Child 26 said: '. . . well, if you've finished your work you can read something, like yesterday we read for all of two lessons. . . . I read *The Children of the New Forest, Daredevils* and *Snowdrops* and I was about half-way through a book – what was it called?' When I commented that it must have been a drastically shortened version of *The Children of the New Forest*, he said: 'No, I went half-way through it with Mr — at the beginning of term so I finished it off.'

Some of the children were aware of their difficulties with reading, and the Asian children saw reading as both pleasurable and educational. Child 25, who was described by the headmaster as 'Reluctant to participate in anything. Often in a daydream or a trance. Lacks any self-motivation or interest. . . . Lacks initiative or the will to improve. Complete lack of success and doesn't really care,' wrote (spelling much improved): 'Yes it is difficult to read and then I say Keep it a Secret Because they will make fun of me and then I took no notice of them because they are all Nutters.' One is reminded of the child in the matched experimental school who commented that reading is enjoyable 'if you have the confidence'.

Although Child 28 told me that she had improved her reading so that in the third year she '. . . picked a hard book and in the second year it was easier books', even in the fourth year she still expressed a dependence on illustrations: 'I like ones with pictures showing you what they are doing and all that . . . because if you don't have a picture sometimes you can't understand what they really mean.'

Similarly, Child 24, who was described by the headmaster as 'A real trier, has improved by leaps and bounds as his vocabulary increases', obviously realized the educational value of reading, as well as its pleasurable aspect. He wrote:

> I like reading very much. Sometimes I don't like it. I like reading because it gives you more education, and you can learn something from reading books. I like to read comics because they make me laugh sometimes. My mother and father think reading is good. He say if you can read you might get something out of it and sometimes I get something out of it.

The amount of reading undertaken and enjoyed by the children in the final year at this school, despite the scarcity of books, is very cheering; the English specialist deserves an accolade. He also deserves books and shelving that he will have by now as a result of the fifty-fifty division of Book Flood books. His only weakness was in the area of recommending books to pre-adolescent girls. He had an extremely difficult task in that he had to cater for both first- and second-generation immigrants as well as for English children who were frequently from homes where books were never read. Nevertheless the children, including the apparently 'reluctant' ones, revealed a thirst for knowledge of worlds beyond their own immediate environment, both real and 'fictitious', that would widen their horizons and give them hope. It is a great pity that cuts in expenditure on education means that their thirst is not likely to be quenched.

5 Case Studies: The Homes and the Children

The most important thing we've learned,
So far as children are concerned,
Is never, NEVER, NEVER let
Them near your television set –
Or better still just don't install
The idiotic thing at all. . . .

'All right!' you'll cry. 'All right!' you'll say,
'But if we take the set away,
What shall we do to entertain
Our darling children! Please explain!'
We'll answer thus by asking you,
'What used *the darling ones to do?*
How used *they keep themselves contented*
Before this monster was invented?'
Have you forgotten? Don't you know?
We'll say it very loud and slow:
THEY . . . USED . . . TO . . . READ! They'd READ and
READ,
AND READ and READ, and then proceed
TO READ some more. Great Scott! Gadzooks!
One half their lives was reading books!

(An extract from *Charlie and the Chocolate Factory*,
by Roald Dahl, ch. 27: 'Mike Teavee is Sent by Television'.)

In this chapter I shall describe the similarities in home backgrounds, including upbringing and personalities, among the avid readers as a group, and among the infrequent readers as a group. These children were selected from the total sample of case study children on the basis that they consistently read a great deal or very little. This judgement was arrived at partly as a result of an examination of their Reading Record returns, and, in addition, as a result of talking to the children, their parents and their teachers; when all four yielded the same answer the children became part of the sample. While the reader should bear in mind that the sample is in no way representative, it is interesting to note similarities between my findings and those of, for example, Leila Berg in *Reading and Loving* (1977), Margaret M. Clark in her *Young Fluent Readers* (1976), and Stanley Coopersmith in the *Antecedents of Self-Esteem* (1967), the similarities in the last instance being between children with high self-esteem and the avid readers.

The sample to be considered is shown in Tables 5·1–5·3 where the child numbers in the left-hand column correspond to the numbers given in Chapter 4. The number of consistently infrequent readers is small, partly because of the effect of the Book Flood and

Table 5·1   Avid readers: the sample of boys

Child	School	Year	IQ	Standardized reading score	Schonell Reading Age	Age at testing	Number of Reading Record Forms	Self-esteem
1	Outer	10+	116	130+	15·0	10·3	23	9
	experimental	11+		130+	17·7	11·3	24	
		12+			17·3	12·8	37	12
2	Outer	10+	128	130+	14·7	10·7	19	11
	experimental	11+		130+	15·0	11·8	16	
		12+			18·1	13·2	12	16
10	Outer	10+	122	115	12·8	11·0	1	6
	control	11+		115	15·3	12·9	2	
		12+			17·7	13·4	8	8
15	Inner	10+	108	113	11·2	10·6	3	10
	experimental	11+		115	12·3	11·7	3	
		12+			14·1	12·1	60	MV
16	Inner	10+	111	123	14·7	11·1	20	2
	experimental	11+		122	15·6	12·2	8	
		12+			19·0	13·5	28	10
17 Asian	Inner experimental	10+	105	89	11·6	10·5	25	9
		11+		100	12·3	11·5	7	
		12+			16·0	12·9	52	4
22	Inner	10+	93	94	13·9	10·8	17	12
	control	11+		MV	14·8	11·9	4	
		12+			19·0	13·2	26	6
23 Asian	Inner control	10+	105	98	11·8	10·6	33	11
		11+		103	13·2	11·6	7	
		12+			15·0	13·0	27	6

Table 5·2   Avid readers: the sample of girls

Child	School	Year	IQ	Standardized reading score	Schonell Reading Age	Age at testing	Number of Reading Record Forms	Self-esteem
6	Outer	10+	119	109	13·4	10·9	15	5
	experimental	11+		111	15·0	11·9	17	
		12+			16·0	13·3	4	8
7	Outer	10+	116	110	12·2	10·4	21	7
	experimental	11+		112	15·0	11·4	10	
		12+			16·7	12·9	4	8
8	Outer	10+	112	126	13·9	10·7	12	7
	experimental	11+		124	17·3	11·7	5	
		12+			16·0	13·0	3	14
13	Outer	10+	103	99	11·0	10·9	7	10
	control	11+		110	MV	MV	4	
		12+			14·1	13·4	20	23
19	Inner	10+	97	100	11·8	11·1	24	3
	experimental			98	12·5	12·9	19	
Asian					12·6	13·5	33	19
27	Inner	10+	92	98	11·4	10·9	5	12
	control	11+		MV	MV	MV	4	
		12+			13·5	13·3	17	32

Table 5·3   Infrequent readers: boys and girls

Child	Sex	School	Year	IQ	Standardized reading score	Schonell Reading Age	Age at testing	Number of Reading Record Forms	Self-esteem
5	M	Outer	10+	82	70	7·0	10·4	3	8
		experimental	11+		83	7·8	11·2	4	
			12+			9·6		6	24
12	M	Outer	10+	86	71	6·4	10·3	0	10
		control	11+		70	7·0	11·4	7	
			12+			7·5	12·8	5	26
14	F	Outer	10+	76	89	9·6	10·9	6	10
		control	11+		83	11·6	12·0	11	
			12+			12·3	13·3	6	28
18	M	Inner	10+	99	93	10·9	10·7	0	10
		experimental	11+		96	12·5	11·7	8	
			12+			13·1	13·1	10	16
25	M	Inner	10+	81	80	6·5	10·6	1	MV
		control	11+		73	7·4	11·6	5	
			12+			14·7	12·9	10	20
26	M	Inner	10+	88	89	7·4	10·2	0	10
		control	11+		70	8·1	11·3	2	
			12+			13·1	12·6	10	20

partly, I suspect, because of the attention accorded to all the case study children. I have called the children who read very little *infrequent* rather than *reluctant* readers, because it soon became apparent that they would love to be able to read well. (I realize that this would not *necessarily* apply to a slightly older sample of children.) While the highest IQ scores were gained by the avid readers and the lowest by the infrequent readers, there is *some* overlap, the range for the avid readers being 92 to 128, and the range for the infrequent readers being 76 to 99. Similarly there is some overlap on the Edinburgh Reading Test scores and Schonell Reading Ages. We should not draw the conclusion, from the fact that most of the avid readers gained higher scores on the IQ test than did most infrequent readers, that the infrequent readers simply did not have the innate ability to learn to read fluently. A few of them obviously did, as demonstrated by the overlap of scores with those of the avid readers. Also, we cannot assume that IQ is static and, although there could possibly be some children in this sample who could never read well no matter how much help and encouragement they received, it is perfectly possible that the conditions in the home that helped to make some children avid readers and encouraged the development of their reading skills, simultaneously encouraged the development of their IQs and that the two are mutually supportive. In any case, surely this positive approach is the only possible one for parents and teachers for, while there may well be an in-built, programmed limited to the development of each human being, I doubt whether that limit is frequently reached.

I shall examine briefly the sorts of sociological factors that are often assumed to be contributory to the development of an interest or lack of interest in books. I make no apology for being brief; brevity is necessitated by, first, the sociological homogeneity of the

Table 5·4   Age on leaving school of parents of avid and infrequent readers

(a) Avid						
	Below 14	*14*	*15*	*16*	*16+*	*Totals*
Father		2	7	2	3	14
Mother	2 (Asians)	1	7	3	1	14
Totals	2	3	14	5	4	28
(b) Infrequent						
	Below 14	*14*	*15*	*16*	*16+*	*Totals*
Father		4	2			6
Mother		3	3			6
Totals		7	5			12

Table 5·5 Further education of parents of avid readers

(a) Mothers

Description of Education	Frequency
None	9 (includes 3 Asians)
College of further education part-time	3
College of further education full-time	1
Teacher training course at college of higher education	1
Total	14

(b) Fathers

Description of Education	Frequency
None	8 (includes 3 Asians)
College of further eduction part-time	4
College of art part-time	1
Polytechnic part-time	1
Total	14

Note: No parents of infrequent readers recorded any further education.

sample and, secondly, by the need to devote more space to the findings from the home visits, which, I believe, will be of great interest to the reader.

Table 5·4 shows that some parents of the avid readers left school at 16 or above, whereas *all* the parents of the infrequent readers left school at 14 or 15. Table 5·5 shows that five mothers and six fathers of avid readers received some kind of further or higher education, whereas *none* of the parents of infrequent readers received any additional education after leaving school.

Table 5·6 Occupations of mothers

(a)   Avid readers

Job description	Frequency	Comment
Housewife	4	{ 2 Asians, 2 previously shorthand typists
Packer	1	
Mill-worker and barmaid	1	Polish
Mill-worker	2	
Child supervisor and cleaner in school	1	p
Cook in children's home	1	p
Full-time student (Dip.H.E.)	1	
School ancillary worker	1	
Secretary	1	
Restaurant supervisor	1	
Total	14	

b) Infrequent readers

Job description	Frequency	Comment
Housewife	2	{ 1 previously packer { 1 unknown
Packer	2	
Mill-worker	1	
Stewardess of working men's club	1	
Total	6	

(b = part-time)

Table 5·7 Occupations of fathers

a) Avid readers

Job description	Frequency	Comment
Skilled engineers	3	1 Asian
Welder	1	
Supervisor in textile factory	1	Asian
Supervisor in asbestos works	1	
Supervisor in textile factor	1	
General manager of small mill	1	
Quality control manager	1	
Retired	1	previously inspector engineer
Stonemason	1	
Shop-keeper	1	Asian
Self-employed painter and decorator	1	
Maintenance painter	1	
Total	14	

b) Infrequent readers

Job description	Frequency	Comment
Unemployed, breeds rabbits	1	previously quarry worker
Scrapyard worker	1	
Dustbinman	1	
Steward at working men's club	1	previously long-distance lorry driver
Mechanic	2	
Total	6	

Tables 5·6 and 5·7 list the occupations of both mothers and fathers of avid and infrequent readers. These tables illustrate well both the homogeneity of the sample and the variety within it. We ought not to be surprised if most of the mothers of 12-year-olds in working-class families go out to work, although many of them, nevertheless, went to great lengths to make sure they would be at home when their children got in from school. It is noteworthy that, among the mothers of the avid readers, we find a full-time student, three women who work close to children, a secretary and a supervisor. The majority of the fathers of avid readers are either skilled workers of some kind, self-employed, or have positions involving responsibility for other workers.

Table 5·8   Number of children in families of avid and infrequent readers

Size of family	Avid frequency	Infrequent frequency
1	2	
2	7	
3	3 (including 1 Asian)	
4		3
5	1 (Asian)	
6		
7		1
8	1 (Asian)	2
Totals	14	6

Table 5·9   Position in the family of avid and infrequent readers

Avid position	Frequency	Infrequent position	Frequency
Eldest of 8	1 (Asian)	5 older, 2 younger	2
Eldest of 5	1 (Asian)	Youngest of 7	1
Eldest of 3	1 (Asian)	Eldest of 4	1
Middle of 3	1	1 older, 2 younger	1
Yougest of 3	1	Youngest of 4	1
Elder of 2	5		
Younger of 2	2		
Only child	2		
Totals	14		6

Table 5·8 shows that all – except two children of Asian origin – of the avid readers belong to families where there are three or fewer children, whereas all the infrequent readers belong to families

Table 5·10   Numbers of books at home, belonging to avid readers and infrequent readers

Number	Avid	Infrequent
More than 100	8	
Between 50 and 100	2	
Between 10 and 50	2 (1 Asian)	
Fewer than 10	2 (2 Asians)	6
Totals	14	6

Table 5·11   Membership of public library by avid and infrequent readers and their mothers and fathers

	Avid			Infrequent		
	Child	Mother	Father	Child	Mother	Father
	8	4	5	1	2	1
Possible totals	14	14	14	6	6	6

where there are four or more children. Table 5·9 gives the position of each child in the family. It is noticeable that ten out of the fourteen avid readers are the first-born or only child in the family, only four being middle, younger or youngest; whereas out of the six infrequent readers, only one was the first-born and there were no only children.

In Table 5·10 we find that all the indigenous avid readers but one, had more than fifty books belonging to them at home (in each case

Table 5·12   Truancy, illnesses or disabilities

(a) Avid readers
One girl was referred to the school Psychological Service because she claimed to have 'claustrophobic tendencies'. Otherwise, there were no known truancies, illnesses or disabilities among these avid readers.

(b) Infrequent readers

	Truancy	Illness	Disability
	3 continual		4 referred to Remedial Service
	1 occasional		for help with reading
	2 reformed; rare		1 referred to School
			Psychological Service in
			addition to above
			1 colour blind
			1 left-handed
Totals	6	0	6

I saw the books); whereas none of the infrequent readers had more than ten of their own books at home. Table 5·11 shows that whereas more than half of the avid readers, and about a third of the mothers and of the fathers, belonged to public libraries, only one child, one father and two mothers of infrequent readers went to public libraries at all, and they only went irregularly.

When I came to look at truancies, illnesses and disabilities (see Table 5·12) among avid readers I found no record of truancy or of serious or prolonged illness, the only disability being a self-reported case of claustrophobia from one of the girls; whereas among the infrequent readers all the children were reported by both teachers and parents to have played truant at some time, although two of them appeared to be totally reformed. There was no record of serious or prolonged illness among these infrequent readers nor any serious physical disability. However, four of them had been referred to the Remedial Service for help with their reading, and one of the four had, in addition, been referred to the School Psychological Service because of general lack of motivation or interest in anything at all.

I make no apology for devoting most of this section to the home interviews, for I agree entirely with Margaret M. Clark (1976, p. 45) writing about the home backgrounds of her 'young fluent readers':

> The lesson from these interviews was a clear one that it is crucial to explore the parents' perceptions of education and the support and experiences they provide *by measures far more sensitive and penetrating than social class, father's occupation or even education of the parents.*

I should like to make it clear that information about these children was collected in a variety of ways and that the information, even when thoroughly unpleasant, almost always tallied. I talked with each child in school about their home backgrounds, I talked with the teachers about the children, and I visited each home. I did not ask the parents a list of questions; they knew I wanted to hear about their child in relation to school generally and reading in particular and that I wanted to relate this to the child's home and personality. Beyond that I simply waited for them to talk, and they did! It was quite apparent that they were almost all deeply interested in and concerned about their children. The strategy of allowing them to talk was very effective as, in fact, they all covered more or less the same ground in different orders and with varying emphases – this latter being an important factor in its own right. Some were naturally more articulate than others but most managed to talk almost unprompted for about one and a half to two hours. The tape recordings of these interviews have been analysed and the topics dealt with categorized under twelve broad headings. Everything that was said, apart from the occasional remark about the dog or the weather, falls into one of these categories. Again, as in the case of the reasons for book choice, the categorization is inevitably subjective, but I shall give exact quotations, rather than my paraphrase, wherever possible. For this reason the section may in parts appear to be a list of quotations. Also, *after* all the initial analysis of the home interview transcripts, I gave each child an *unannounced* questionnaire *in school* dealing with roughly the same areas as those covered by the parents by way of a cross check.

1 Rooms

In answer to the request 'Write what your home is like', I received descriptions as diverse as the following:

(a) There are nine rooms altogether – cellar, front room, back room, kitchen, parents' bedroom, sister's bedroom, bathroom, my bedroom, guests' bedroom. Semi-detached house. Extremely large garden. At front two very large entrance gates. At the back are fields, acres and acres of fields. The house itself is insulated and has radiators all over the house. One in my room, in guests' bedroom, bathroom, parents' bedroom, front and back rooms, and kitchen. My bedroom is quite large, has large window overlooking fields. Armchair, bed, three ordinary chairs, desk, bookcase, two wardrobes and chest of drawers make up the furniture. Plus record player. About six model planes hang from the ceiling. Mum says she likes them only because she doesn't have to dust them. (Child 15)

(b) My home is like a detached house, and we have eight rooms. We have got a living-room, kitchen, backroom, bathroom, mum's bedroom, three boys going in one, and three girls in another. My big sister with her husband and baby. My room I have to share with my sisters because their are eight of us kids. (Child 14)

There is not space to describe every room in detail, only to give typical examples of the sorts of physical conditions in the home encountered by avid and infrequent readers. Eight of the fourteen avid readers had rooms of their own, although one was useless for anything other than sleeping in for it was not only cold but also very damp; four shared with one other child; and the two remaining children, both of Asian origin, each shared with two other siblings of the same sex. However, while a warm, quiet room is obviously useful if a child wants to read, it obviously is not sufficient as two of the infrequent readers had rooms of their own and avid readers often overcame apparently adverse conditions. For instance, Child 19, who shared a room with two younger sisters, preferred to read upstairs and told me, 'If they get annoying I tell them to get out of the bedroom!' She assured me that they did as she asked because she is the eldest. The girl whose bedroom was cold and damp, Child 27, habitually read in the living-room with the television on; some did this from choice but she did not. Her mother, talking about the girl's books, said:

> She hasn't got them all together, you know, because we have them in different boxes. Because we haven't got cupboards in this house; we had cupboards in the others, like 'glory' cupboards I used to call them. We haven't things like that here [actually a flat] so a lot of them have to be put in boxes. Even our clothes in our wardrobes go damp, don't they?

The girl added that she could not read in her bedroom because '. . . the bedroom is cold, and if the [paraffin] heater is on and you shuffle about it is a bit dangerous'.

Another avid reader, Child 13, wrote: '. . . my bedroom . . . isn't heated by anything. This doesn't matter to me as I get down into my blankets and put a pair of woollen gloves on.'

However, more typical of the rooms of avid readers is the one described here by a mother of two boys. She and her husband fitted out a small spare room as a study in addition to providing all kinds of facilities in the boys' bedroom:

> We put a desk in [the spare room] and a typewriter; we bought them the desk to do their homework on, and they've got a stereo and a colour television in their bedroom, so they do their viewing and listen to records in there, and if they've got any work to do they go in the spare room where it is quieter. (Child 22)

This was not easily achieved in a small semi-detached house on a trust estate: the arrangement required considerable forethought and sacrifice. Child 16's father built him a work surface and fitted up an angle-poise lamp: 'It is a kind of lamp – it stands on the desk and it shines on my book instead of light that goes all over the room.' He added, 'It's just been decorated; my dad decorated it, he put a desk in so I use it now.' Many of the avid readers had their own television set and record player and/or tape-recorder, yet none lived in palatial homes and none of the families was really well-off. The parents gave a great deal of thought to the needs of the children; for example, Child 8, who lived in a block of flats, had her own room with a large table and a great deal of shelving. Her aunt, who brought her up, said:

> She likes the big table because she can lay out all her books, homework and everything on it. . . . She can go in there and close the door and it is hers entirely. And she will arrange it as she wants. It is hers. She has always had a table in there – before she had a big one she had a small one, and before that she had a desk, a baby's desk. And then she got a blackboard and then she wanted somewhere she could work, spread herself out.

One set of parents was amusingly pushed into providing a light on each side of a pair of beds used by two brothers, one of whom is a really avid reader (Child 2). The mother said:

> We found out that he was going to read in bed whether we wanted him to or not because he got to the stage of the torch, and then he got to the stage he was reading from the staircase light. So we decided if he was going to read, he might as well have the light on and read. Many's the time we go in on an evening, and he's laid there, his book in his hand and he's fast asleep.

All that the parents of the infrequent readers said about rooms was that the child preferred to be downstairs or, more usually, 'playing out', and that they had difficulty fitting everyone in.

2 Personality, hobbies and interests

'Lastly I come to the cheerful if not surprising finding that the heaviest readers are the people most active in everything. The doers are the readers' (Barbara Tuchman, writer, in *Reading in America 1978*, 1979).

Some teachers expressed the opinion that avid readers tended not to be the sporting type, although they were not sure whether the children who read a great deal did not have much time for sport or whether children who found they were poor at sporting activities turned to reading instead. Certainly some of the avid readers thoroughly detested sport, but some of them loved it, and, equally, some of the infrequent readers enjoyed sport and others did not. However, there were general similarities among the favourite activities of infrequent readers. In particular, the infrequent readers spent a great deal of their spare time playing out. When I asked their parents what those children usually did in their spare time, all but one said that they liked to 'play out'. For example:

> . . . he usually goes out to play until about eight o'clock. With the weather as it is now they've been sliding, sledging, having snowball fights . . . and he is always going round to everyone else's house you know . . . I never see him – he comes in for

meals and then he is off again, you know. . . . He is an outdoor lad. (Child 18)

or:

I come home from work and she's always playing out somewhere. (Child 14)

One infrequent reader (Child 26) is an excellent swimmer with a badge for life-saving, another (Child 18) is in the school football team, cricket team, runs, swims and plays table tennis, but the other four simply 'played out' without any particular purpose, and one (Child 25), according to his mother, had '. . . no interest in anything really, not in sport or television. I can't understand it.'

The sportsmen and sportswomen in this admittedly small sample, were to be found among the avid readers, some of whom seemed to cram a phenomenal amount of activity into their lives. One played football for the school team, another belonged to the Bradford Fencing Club and the Scouts, another was in the school athletics team, yet another described himself as '. . . a person who likes a lot of sports . . .', especially football and cross-country, and a fifth played snooker. However, they had a definite purpose in their physical activity and one boy even ran to W. H. Smith's for books '. . . for training so that I would be in good shape for cross-country running'.

Nevertheless, it must be admitted that the majority of avid readers found far more to interest them indoors than outdoors. Child 1 said:

. . . my Mum always tells me to go outside. When I'm staying in and reading my books and all that, my Mum wants me to go out. . . . But I don't like it because there isn't as much to do outside as inside.

His mother told me:

. . . when we first came here and they used to call for him he'd say, 'Oh, I'm not coming out now; I'm reading a book' or 'I'm not coming out now; there's a real programme on television,' and it would be a documentary. And the other kids just stopped calling for him. . . . He doesn't play out; he's never been interested in sport . . . we say to him sometimes 'Get outside; the sun's shining; get some sunshine on your white skin!'

Another mother said:

In fact, he never plays out. . . . No, he doesn't go out at all. He used to play out when he was younger on bikes and things. No, just put him in with a book, or the typewriter, and he's happy. (Child 22)

Child 10 said: 'I can't stand sport, things like football.' And his mother: 'He doesn't like football – he will go out to play but then he will come back and say, "They've gone to play football", and somehow he is out of it then. And he is on his own. But he has never liked football.'

Whether they have any skill at, or interest in, sports or not, what links the hobbies and interests of the avid readers is, first, a *preference* for indoor activities, a preference of varying strength, and, secondly, a similarity of indoor activities. They all read, watched television, listened to records, several made tape-recordings, several wrote, and most of the boys enjoyed model-making. (Only one infrequent reader was described as having an indoor hobby and that was painting.) For example, Child 15 said he liked, 'Modelling, detective games and games like Cluedo': 'I make models – me and my dad do it together.' He makes extremely complex 'Lego' models and aeroplane models. All but two of the boys showed me models that they had made and painted. I shall deal with writing and television in subsequent sections, but, for these children, reading, creative arts and television seemed to be different facets of the process of finding out and creating, of self-expression. For the infrequent readers television was a background noise; they had not learnt to use and select, to make *it* work for *them*.

As far as personality is concerned, the avid readers were described by both parents and teachers as being mature for their ages. For instance, of Child 2, his teachers said: '. . . serious, mature, too old for his age, although he seems happy with it. He's respected by the other kids as the super brain of his class. He has good relations with his teachers. He's neat, fastidious; good at everything except games.' The boy's father, two and a half years later, when the boy was thirteen, said: 'He doesn't circulate, he just listens and watches and doesn't join in. Yet we've been down to school and seen his teacher and they've told us he's very popular. He mixes all right at school. He's definitely a loner, isn't he? [to mother].'

Another mother said of her son: '. . . he has always seemed to be a bit advanced for his years. . . . He's grown up in a lot of ways . . .' (Child 22). One father and two mothers described a very similar personality trait in their sons, that is, the desire to find out absolutely everything about anything that interests them. The father of Child 2 said:

> He also wants to discuss everything he reads. Even from being right little, he's wanted to know whether it was true and whether it had been proven or whether it was just something he's read about, you know, whereas t'little one, you could tell him t'moon

was made of cheese and because I've told him that would be fact and he'd accept it. Whereas M. goes on and on; he's like a terrier. Whatever he gets his teeth into he worries and worries it until he's finished with it. He gets every last ounce out of it before he'll drop it.

Child 1 was currently 'obsessed' with arms and armaments even though he was a pacifist. The mother of the third, Child 22, said:

He wanted to know how the film [*Jaws*] was made. If there's anything he likes, that he's interested in, he wants to know every detail: how the film was made, everything concerning the shark, where you find them, different species. When he was younger it was dinosaurs and he could tell you everything about them. He had every picture, drawing – well everything!

These children had minds of their own and could be very annoying. A teacher described one avid reader, Child 16, as '. . . the bane of my life. . . . I daren't say anything in case he knows more than I do!' The same child said to me: 'The thing I don't understand about adults is that they make decisions about children without consulting them.' One of the girls, Child 13, wrote: 'I think I don't like school because I hate being told to do something I don't want to do, but I suppose I can learn to like it.' The families all had codes of behaviour that the children were expected to adhere to as we shall see in a later section, but the parents had a good deal of respect for the opinions of their children. The strength of character and questioning personality trait rebounded on me when Child 15 said, of completing the reading records, 'I thought it was a waste of time, filling the forms in for the books that I had read. I thought they wouldn't do anything with the forms. . . . I couldn't see why we should record it.'

3   Amount of attention accorded to the child

Leila Berg (1977), writing about a smaller child, said: '. . . an important thing about Kit, something that has already been fed into the baby's confidence, vitality and intelligence, is that he was wanted . . .' I think that it would be presumptuous to suggest that the children who were infrequent readers were *not* wanted, but what I can say with some confidence is that the children who were avid readers were more consciously and positively wanted. For instance Child 18 was brought up by her aunt and uncle and, far from feeling unwanted by her parents, felt that she must be very special to be taken on in this way. She told me: 'And, besides, my auntie was unable to have a daughter so I was left a lot with my auntie and uncle. . . . They did have a child but it died in birth.' The

aunt told me that previously she and her husband had fostered
children, that they had brought up a child whose parents had split
up, and, eventually, had brought up our avid reader. The aunt told
me:

> J. [husband] and I love children. We don't have any of our own
> but there are always some about. I believe that a home is a home
> and you can't keep saying, 'Don't put your feet on that', and
> 'Don't scratch that'. . . . I think that love is far more important,
> wherever they live, than having a beautiful home that they
> daren't move about in, I really do. . . . You don't need anything
> else do you, except to know that you are being loved? – Well, I
> think that, anyway. And it lasts all their lives. . . . J.'s [Child 8's]
> mother has love . . . but not much time.

Time, in this case, was related to occupation, but it is more usually
related to family size. No doubt it is possible for children in large
families to be given attention – particularly if the family is an
extended one, or to feel, at least, that they are not missing anything
because a large family is the norm, as in the case of our 'Asian' avid
readers, but it is *less likely* that children in large families will receive
as much attention *from adults* as will children in smaller families.
Davie, Butler and Goldstein in *From Birth to Seven* (1972) state that
'. . . the effect upon reading attainment at the age of seven of being
in a one or two child family compared to a five or more child
family . . . is equivalent to a gain in reading age of about twelve
months' but that there is not such a strong association with
arithmetic attainment, which '. . . lends weight to the suggestion
that it is in verbal skills that children from large families are most
disadvantaged'. The authors see this effect as far more than the
simple result of parents having to divide their attention many more
ways than do the parents of one or two children. The claim that,
'Amongst larger families *who are not planned* [my italics] in size . . .
there is likely to be a higher proportion of parents whose attitude is
rather feckless and irresponsible, those who in general do not manage
their affairs very successfully and those who tend to live for the
present . . .' I found supported in this research, but would prefer to
call it a feeling of hopelessness and helplessness rather than feckless-
ness and irresponsibility. They tended to have an external, rather
than internal, locus of control. In fact, the five sets of parents of the
infrequent readers with whom I talked all expressed the feeling that
they simply could not control their 12- and 13-year-old children; in
fact, they often talked as though the children were not really theirs
at all. Child 18's mother, who had four boys, said: '. . . they start
going out and you don't know where they are, or what they are
doing, do you? . . . they go their own way, don't they?' Another

mother (of Child 14) talking about her children playing truant and misusing dinner money, said, 'Well, I can't do anything really you know.' Nevertheless, I think *all* these mothers cared about the children; they did not know how to cope. One mother asked to have three of her eight children taken into care for their own good because she simply could not cope with them herself.

The strain put upon a mother with even four children, especially when the father is away a great deal, was expressed by the mother of Child 18. Her husband was a long-distance lorry driver:

> . . . which entailed him being away from home a lot. I've been more or less left with my four lads on my own for most of the time, if you understand what I mean. My husband has always been away, sometimes for a week at a time if the lorry has been stuck somewhere, and all my married life with all the emergencies that we have had with the children I have always seemed to be on my own. My husband has always seemed to be away somewhere and I have had to cope with them myself, all these things, you know.

Child 14's mother, who had one child a year for eight years, said, not surprisingly, 'It is difficult giving them a lot of attention.' In fact she had difficulty remembering which first schools the children had attended. A mother of seven, who could only find a job packing at a local supermarket in the evenings (5.00 to 9.30 p.m.), said: 'Well, I've seven and I haven't had time to give him individual reading, probably that's it' (Child 25).

Quite a different picture emerged from the conversation with the parents of the avid readers. One mother of two boys with five years between them said that the avid reader, Child 2, the elder boy, had been like 'an only child' before he went to school and that she had deliberately not gone out to work so that she could give him individual attention. She told me:

> We lost our first child. It was such a disappointment that we were so thrilled when we got M. that I did everything I shouldn't do. I picked him up when he was asleep. I *talked to him all the time* because we were thrilled to have him. . . . We didn't do anything because we had to do, you know; we did it because we wanted to do it . . . (my italics).

What she says embodies a set of values which was conveyed to me by *all* the parents of avid readers in one way or another. Those parents were *aware* of the effect they were having on their children, and in some cases even looked to future generations. The father of Child 16 said:

> If a sacrifice has to be made it would *be* made for the child's sake; that's our responsibility . . . and if you don't take *your*

responsibility how can you expect the children when they grow up to look after their children? I think that children follow their parents' footsteps in many ways. They see what their parents do and in years to come if, say, they are married with children, and we go over there and there is something they do that we don't like, she might say that they didn't do that to me – and it stands out, you know.

This really is taking one's responsibilities seriously and appreciating the need to postpone gratification if one has certain values in relation to child-rearing.

The mother of Child 16 said that she would never leave her child alone in the house. She also touched on the problem of time and attention:

> When he was younger I definitely wouldn't go out to work and let him come into an empty house, I don't believe in that. . . . And I think another reason [for A. learning to read before he went to school] is that he is the only one and I have more time, you see. I think if you had a lot of kiddies, four or five, say, you just wouldn't have time – and I think that is why, because I have had more time to bother with him.

One mother, who had had a lot of illness when her child (Child 7 – an avid reader) was small, found herself giving that child a great deal of attention later in order to compensate. She said: 'Well if a child isn't wanted you don't bother with it, do you?'

In the fairly large Asian families from which two of our avid readers came, as well as in the smaller ones, the father played an important part in child-rearing. Child 17 said of his father: '. . . and he likes the company of the children. He jokes with us and plays fighting and things like that.' Finally, the least articulate of the mothers of avid readers (Child 27) whom I did need to question directly once or twice, when asked on what principle she had based the rearing of her children, answered me in one word, 'love'.

4 Discipline and principles of child-rearing

Stanley Coopersmith, in *Antecedents of Self-esteem* (1967), says that the families of children with high self-esteem are families in which the parents provide clear guidelines for their offspring:

> Limits provide the child with an interpretation of acceptable behavior that markedly reduces the range of permissible alternatives *and provides a context that is more concrete and manageable.* . . In addition, families in which limits are set – families that produce creative and assertive children are also families that accept and respect their children. (author's italic)

The families of the avid readers in my small study accepted and respected their children, who were both creative and assertive; the parents also set clear limits for their children and, like the parents of children with high self-esteem in Coopersmith's study, led creative, active lives themselves, had strong opinions and considerable self-respect. Inevitably, therefore, there were often disagreements. Child 7 said, 'I usually do as I am told, but if I have a strong feeling of what is right, I will say so.' Another, Child 13, wrote, 'I know the rules they give are for my own good even if I do sometimes oppose them. The important thing to my parents is to bring us up good with love. In return they would like us to make a good life for ourselves.'

The parents of the infrequent readers had a larger number of rules that they would have dearly loved to impose upon their children. I think it is worthwhile describing the plight of one particular mother in some detail. Like all the other infrequent readers in this, admittedly, small sample, her child had played truant from time to time. She explained how it happened:

> She might get in with one or two other kiddies and they say they are not going to school today; she is very easily tempted, you know . . . she set off with her dinner money and everything. In fact, I had a bit of bother with her dinner money as well, you know . . . well, I can't do anything really, you know – they are made to stay in and things like that instead of playing out. But with me working, you know –. (Child 14).

She had had far worse problems with the three eldest boys: the eldest went to Borstal when he was 14 and she had asked for the other two to be taken into care when they were 12 and 11 years old. Again she attributed the problem in part to them not going to school and 'getting in with a group'. She said:

> We tried everything at home – keeping them in, sending them to bed . . . you know, all kinds of things. They just didn't seem to want any discipline, you know; you just couldn't drill it into them. They would get out through the bedroom windows, you know – it was awful. So we ended up having to put them into care ourselves. . . . [The eldest] when he was 15 got electrocuted at the power station. He tried to pinch copper wiring. . . . He is lucky to be alive. He touched 33000 volts – he was in —— Hospital for nine weeks. After that we thought we wouldn't have no more bother with him, but –.

The infrequent reader in this family has already been involved in petty theft before the age of 12. This mother was not uncaring: she simply felt helpless. Eventually, she became passive and seemed to stand apart from the children; probably that was the only way she could remain sane. This attitude is typical of, although more extreme than, that of the rest of the parents of the infrequent readers. This same mother described how her 16-year-old *would not* go back into care:

> D., he wouldn't go back. C. [younger] went off, you know, like he always does, but D. Why hadn't he gone back? He missed the train! So he was off the rest of the week and it got to Friday and he still hadn't gone back. But the more he stayed at home, the more we would get into trouble for it – it is we who get the blame and all you get is, 'I don't know', when you asked him why he hadn't gone back, but he is 16, and what can you do?

I do not intend to suggest that infrequent readers are criminals. The example illustrates the impression given by the parents of the infrequent readers that they had *no control* over what happens to themselves and their families. Somehow there was no point in planning anything because one had *no say;* everything was decided by 'them'. Another explained this same feeling on a much smaller scale when she said, 'Well, *we'll just have to wait and see* what happens to him at school' (Child 26).

The parents of the avid readers *believed* they had considerable control over what happened to themselves and their families and *planned* things, within their means, to fit their values and expectations. They tended to have an *internal* locus of control. On the questionnaire given to the children I asked them if their parents had any rules and regulations for them; what these were, if any; whether they considered them not strict enough, fair, or too strict; and what were the most important things to their parents. One avid reader (Child 16) wrote: 'If I do anything wrong I expect to be punished. The most important thing to my parents is that their children are not known as ruffians, hooligans, etc.' Child 17 wrote: 'The most important thing to my parents is the lives of their children and their own lives.' And Child 7: '. . . especially my dad, he wants me to be happy and not get overfaced with homework.' The parents of those avid readers had few problems with their children. One mother said of her daughter, 'She is a very good child. I'm not just saying it because she is my daughter, but I notice things about her.' Another said her son was '. . . a reasonably sensible kid . . .' (Child 1); and another: 'I don't know, but they have always been sensible. I don't know if it's the way I've brought them up – I mean I have always told them right from wrong. But I've never had any trouble with them' (Child 22).

There were certainly heated discussions, but with an underlying respect for the child *as a child*. The child's opinion was listened to and treated with reverence, but the child sometimes had to back down. When this happened the parents felt it important to give a reason for their action, the reason being based upon caring for the child. Child 1's mother said that her methods were:

> . . . talking to them and listening to them basically, and if it came to something they shouldn't be doing I *tell* them they shouldn't be doing it and if they continue to do it, then I punish them. But I always give a reason first. But basically listening to them and talking to them *as though they were human beings.*

Like the children in Coopersmith's study, who were high in self-esteem, these children were able to make responsible decisions *within* the clear limits set by their parents. Child 6's father said: 'There are decisions that we will make for them, but I like them to decide for themselves, so that when they get older they are not leaning on someone else and can take responsibility.' The daughter said: 'If I like something [activity] we usually talk it over and discuss it before they say "Yes" or "No". The decision is between all of us really.' These children seem to know really well what is expected of them, as well as that their parents love, respect and want what is best for them, so that they can feel free to make decisions and take responsibility within the guidelines set by their parents.

5 Early experiences of books and reading

None of the infrequent readers had stories read or told to them when they were small: the parents and the children were in agreement about this. All the avid readers had stories read and/or told to them regularly by parents or grandparents. The parents of the 'Asian' avid readers tended to *tell* stories as they have an oral tradition where stories are concerned. Child 17 explained:

> My mum and dad used to tell us stories of when they were in Pakistan – they used to tell us stories and we used to like it and that's when we started to read books because we thought they would be a bit the same as the stories they told us. Sometimes they were exciting and sometimes they were scaring, so we just started reading books.

An indigenous girl, Child 7, described a similar experience:

> My grandma used to tell me stories, not from a book but from her mind, and she started reading to me – Enid Blyton books – and she went to the shops and bought me a book and then she bought me another and I liked the books, so I started to build up and I got the whole set and I read them all.

Most of the parents of the avid readers actually *read* stories to the children before they could read, and many continued to read to them long after the child could read. They all recalled the experience with pleasure, saying things like: '. . . and then when they got older, and, you know, it got near bed-time, I'd sit down and read to them. I always used to read to them in an afternoon before they had their afternoon nap and then at night-time I used to tell them a story' (Child 16).

Most of the avid readers had books bought for them when they were toddlers. The mother of Child 2 told me:

We've always had books ourselves and his grandparents have always had books and this old neighbour he went across to had books. Then he has a god-mother who's very fond of him, and she always bought him books, you know, the little *Ladybird* ones. He's always had books.

Child 16's mother took the child with her to buy the books: '. . . we used to be in town and we'd say, "We'll buy this and read it when we get home." I used to right enjoy it – as I say, I'm being made redundant for things like that now . . . I enjoyed it as much as them.' These mothers believe it is the norm to buy books for children and read stories to them: '. . . she had these ABC books. I think nearly all mothers go out and buy them, don't they, when they first start reading?' (Child 27). She and another mother, who was also materially poor, thought it necessary to buy books for their children.

Apart from the enjoyment involved in sitting the children on their knees and reading to them, several parents felt the need to prepare their children for reading in school, or to help with reading after the child had started school. Two families talked about this in detail. Child 1 told me that he had learned to read before starting school:

. . . she thought that the more books I read, the more intelligent I would get and the better I would get on at school . . . she's doing the same with my brother (aged 6) and she's telling my dad and my nan how good he is . . . because it worked with us, so it will work with him.

The mother, a very articulate woman, who had been a cleaner at her children's school and was currently doing a teacher-training course, described what she did in detail:

From an early age, I gave them books, books with pictures in, you know, the real baby books: 'A Ball'; 'A Tree', and that sort of thing. And then, occasionally, I'd buy them books with a bit of writing in. I'd read them stories. I used to buy comics a lot. . . I think comics are as good as anything else to get them interested. And I made sure that if they had any money, rather than go out and buy sweets, I'd get them books . . . As soon as they got to the stage of sitting up, I used to give them magazines, mail order catalogues, just to let them feel paper. They used to eat them; it was quite funny. And then picture books – I used to go out and buy them a nice coloured picture book and just give it them rather than a biscuit to keep them quiet. I'd give them a book even sitting in the park. I only stopped reading to them when they started saying, 'You've missed a word', or 'That doesn't say "shock" it says "amazement".'

This boy was one of the most avid readers of all, as was another, Child 15, who had difficulty with reading when he started school and whose mother described to me her very determined efforts to help him. Her methods may sound a little harsh but they were obviously motivated by love and, above all, she *cared*, as her son realized. The boy said that his interest in books '. . . really started when my mother sort of taught me to read. . . . I was at first school then. Every time I got home from school she gave me a few lessons in reading. That's when I started getting interested in reading.' His mother said:

> . . . books have always been available to K. but he wasn't very good at reading at school at all, to be quite honest. . . . He wasn't pushed at school to do it, and K. is the type of child who must be pushed or he won't do it. If he finds it uncomfortable then K. will stop, and it got to the stage where he would come home every evening and I would *make* him sit down and read – *he* would read to *me*, and I would read to *him*. And if he didn't do it I would smack him. It was as simple as that. 'If you don't read, you'll get a belt on the ear.' And within two or three months we found that he enjoyed Enid Blyton in exactly the same way as I did. And the minute he got reading himself then there was no question of me making him sit down and read.

This mother was quite determined that her son should read, partly because she wanted him to experience the pleasure that she found in reading and partly for educational reasons. When he did not read she set out to remedy the situation systematically. I am not recommending the smacking; what is far more important is the caring and the positive approach. Another avid reader, Child 22, did not take much of an interest in books bought for him until he actually mastered the skill for himself, whereupon '. . . he just seemed to develop this interest in books and read and read. He seemed to shoot through one book after another.'

None of the parents or grandparents of the infrequent readers bought them books or took them to book shops when they were toddlers. Neither did the parents of the 'Asian' children who were avid readers, but one father used the public library a great deal and the other two had books bought by an indigenous aunt or uncle by marriage. All but one of the avid readers just described could read either partially or completely before they went to school. One mother said: 'She picked up the words herself. She would say, "What is that word, Mummy?" and I used to tell her. She would remember' (Child 27).

Several of the parents said that they had introduced books to their children along with other beautiful or cultural experiences, as part of showing to the child those aspects of life that they as parents valued and wanted to share with those they loved. The mother of Child 5 told me: 'We go out of our way to make sure he keeps in contact not only with books but with all cultural things, like good music and beautiful furniture.' (The child plays the violin, the mother paints, and both parents collect old books and antique furniture.) An Asian father who introduced his son, Child 23, to history books about his homeland said: 'He had story books and I told him stories. I am interested in history so I tell him. . . . I took him to Lahore to show him the story of the place, you know, Shalimar and other interesting things.'

6   Writing and drawing

A number of avid readers, seven to be precise, were described by themselves and their parents as enjoying writing and several of them enjoyed drawing, whereas the only comments made about writing in conversation with the infrequent readers was that they had difficulty with it. Child 8 described a complex interactive relationship between reading, writing and acting, which I think is of particular interest. She writes poetry, stories, and scripts for plays which she and her friends sometimes tape. She gave an account of how she first became interested in story writing; even in the account fact and fiction become entangled:

> When I was about 5 I remember the first story I wrote – it was called *The Twisted Staircase*. My cousin, my brother and me had all gone to a party and we found this staircase through these trees and it all seemed very mysterious; we imagined there were witches and fairies because we were only very little, and we came to a gate which we daren't go through because we thought there would be giants. So we came back and it was terrible because there were fairies peeping through everywhere. Anyway, when I got home I thought it would be a good story, so I wrote it out – and from then on I started writing little poems and stories! . . . Most of the stories had short bits, sentences, which I got from Enid Blyton books when I was very little. If I was unable to put

some of the ideas into words, I would try and remember how she put them.

I still have in my possession an incomplete story by this child; it is at least fifty pages, incomplete! I also have a set of her poems. She spends a good deal of her time in her room alone or with other children, apparently 'playing' with dolls:

> I like sometimes to play with dolls because that is where I get the ideas for the things I write. If I didn't play with them, I don't think I would be able to write anything. . . . I sort of act it out to see what it would look like and then I write it down. . . . Sometimes me and my friend, when we come home from school, we will act out a piece by ourselves – we don't actually make a play of it; we try to act it out.

She also enjoys drawing, writing letters and teaching younger cousins to read or giving them little comprehension tests. Her uncle described her as being an 'unpaid teacher' to one younger child. The same girl, so her aunt told me, also did a farming project, and unasked wrote an imaginative story based on the project. The aunt said: 'She has style; she would make a good writer of children's books.'

One of the boys who did not tell me directly about writing, put in his diary: 'My friend, Mark, came up to call. We wrote some funny stories and played snooker. Took it in turns at pretending to be a news reader.' This boy also put in his questionnaire: 'Mother writes stories sometimes.' Not all children wrote fiction; Child 1 preferred factual writing. His mother said: '. . . he'll do voluntary projects on arms and armaments and things like that and he'll illustrate them. But he's more technical writing than fiction writing . . . when he was smaller he was more inclined to do pictures of various uniforms and stick labels on them. Now that he's older he'll be a little bit more ambitious.'

Several of the children were interested in the possibility of writing as a career. One boy who expressed this interest thought he might take up journalism and write stories as well. His mother said that he had drawn a lot before he went to school, then she suddenly added:

> He writes – I forgot to tell you that. He writes page after page.' [The father interrupted at this point, saying:] 'You remember *Jaws*? We took him to see that and he wrote about that.' [The mother continued:] 'He's written literally notebooks full. You can see that it is maybe something he's seen on television but he changes all the names and, you know, he's quite good for someone of his age. In fact he's even saying now that he'd like to get on a paper or something like that when he leaves school. . . . I

bought him a typewriter for Christmas, so now he's typing them out' (Child 22).

Child 27, who writes songs and animal stories, told me that she had been influenced by *The Waltons*, a television series in which the eldest boy in the family becomes a writer.

7 Talking and conversation with adults

The 'book baby' is often with an adult who is always encouraging him in conversation. For the child to communicate and learn that communication is a pleasurable experience the adult(s) must have time to listen properly (Berg, 1977).

Most of the avid readers had ample opportunity to converse with adults when they were small. The mother of Child 2 told me that her son had talked not only to her, as she had not gone out to work, but also to his grandmother and to an old gentleman across the road with whom he 'struck up a friendship'. She said that she had deliberately talked to the child before he could talk: 'You don't just start talking when *they* start talking; you start talking to them when they are born, don't you?' She explained why:

I know a lot of people who think it's superior, but I believe you start educating your child from the day they are born and that means talking to them. . . . I really do think they start soaking it up. . . . I talked to him all the time because we were thrilled to have him. . . . I didn't start to talk to him because I thought, 'If I talk to him, it will help him later'; I talked to him because it gave me pleasure.

Another mother said of her son, Child 1, 'He always enjoyed talking to adults when he was little.' She also felt strongly about the need to communicate with a baby:

. . . the only way a baby *can* communicate is through crying, and through experience you learn to recognize different cries as different things and you have to act accordingly. But, if a baby is crying, it is crying for a reason, and whether it is just because it is bored, then you should respond to it. *I've responded to them and their response is to my response to their action in the first place.* . . . I've always talked to them – from the moment I first saw them, even when they were first born, even before feeding them, you talk to them so that they can hear your voice as much as anything. . . . If they said something that vaguely sounded like 'Daddy', I would sort of smile and say, 'Clever boy', or 'Clever girl', and repeat 'Daddy', and the same with other words . . . it was a case of getting them used to sounds, words (my italics).

This mother thought that she was probably emulating her own mother, whom she described like this:

> My mother is a very maternal type of mum and she always kept in contact with us because of that. She was always there when we needed her – all I had to do was go 'Mum' in the middle of the night and she was there, *and she always talked*. I mean she would talk rubbish, or discuss the cost of living and we didn't know what she was talking about, *but it was a comfort hearing my mother's voice. She could make her presence felt by speaking.* [Then of her own children as toddlers:] I didn't realize it then but I found out later that, in comparison with other children, they seemed to find it easier to communicate their ideas to other people.

Several of the parents of the avid readers said that they had never used 'baby talk' to their children. The father of Child 6 said that his daughter started talking early:

> I think it was just the natural thing because we never treated – well, we treated children *as* children – but, also, how can I put it? – not too babyish. Bring them up normal, not as babies. . . . Don't hold anything back, because when the time comes and that child has to find out – if it grows with it, it will find out nice and steadily.

In this case, as in many others, not talking baby talk involved the content as well as the form of the conversations. Similarly, another avid reader, Child 7, was described by her mother as being 'quite forward with talking. My mother lived only a few doors away and I think she talked to her a lot.' The father added:

> The thing I remember is that she never had that baby talk – she started speaking words correctly right from the beginning and whether we did it deliberately or not, we didn't talk baby talk back to her. . . . I think we thought at the time that it was because she was brought up in an environment where people were older. . . . The only way is to discuss openly. H. . . . will tell you, she will ask me just as easily as she will ask her mother. . . . I don't think a child should be shoved aside, you know.

The mother of Child 15 said:

> You can't talk down to children. If you are not prepared to talk to a child as a person . . . but, of course, that also exerts all sorts of standards on the child. There are a lot of things I won't take from K. . . . that I know other mums take from their children. . . . We don't baby him. We are prepared to talk to them on an adult level if they respond.

Apparently these parents treat their children with respect and have high expectations of them in return.

All of the families had times, usually mealtimes, when casual conversation or discussion was a regular possibility. One father said that the family always sat down together for a meal at six o'clock: 'I always ask the pair of them how they've done at school, any problems, what they've had for lunch, all this sort of thing.' Child 1's mother said: 'Up until I started college, they always came home for lunch and there was the "What have you been doing today?" bit. But we always used to talk at lunchtime, and then in the evenings we'd have a snack tea and talk again and then usually at bedtime or when they were in the bath . . .' Child 16's father always looked after his son and daughter in the evenings while his wife was working, when he said he talked to them 'amongst other things'.

. . . I've got the pair of them at night, you see. Sometimes we have a bit of a knockabout – I throw them about the house for half an hour, then throw them in the bath, that sort of thing. [His wife continued:] They have a go at all sorts. I came home from work the other week and they were set to baking and making trifles between them. K. . . . is the type, well he doesn't like me working through the day because we both think you should be there in the morning when they go off to school, and when they come home, so, of course, with money problems, I got a job at night so I leave them with K. . . . We don't leave them with neighbours or anything like that.

One of the infrequent readers, Child 18, was remarkably articulate. His mother told me: 'You don't have to worry about him talking, you have trouble stopping him.' Sadly, however, the other parents of infrequent readers described a lack of communication or using phrases like 'He's right close', or 'You can't get nowt out of him'. Nor did they usually have family mealtimes, nor even necessarily see a great deal of their children. The mother of Child 14 said: 'Mind you – I don't see her much, I mean, I come home from work and she's always out playing somewhere' (already quoted); and another: 'A very close person is our B.; you can't get nowt out of him . . . never tells us much. We never get a thing out of him' (Child 26).

8 Reading habits of significant others, especially parents and grandmothers

I gathered information about the reading habits of people on whom the case study children might have modelled their behaviour, from the children, the parents, and, occasionally, from grandparents, aunts and uncles, and siblings. It became clear that most of the parents of the avid readers were themselves keen readers, whereas most of the parents of the infrequent readers were not. Child 6, talking about her mother who is Polish told me: '. . . when she was reading the Catherine Cookson book she was reading it all the time, when she was getting the tea and everything'. The mother said:

> I've always been a keen reader, even when I was a child, and my father read quite a bit as well. My mother used to shout at me at three and four o'clock in the morning. . . . There was a time when we were married that I would be having my tea with a book on the table, especially when I had a good book. I just couldn't put it down!

The father also reads a good deal but prefers non-fiction. His sister was present at the home interview as she had just returned from a shopping trip with our avid reader. Apparently the aunt is a very keen reader and works in a library. Child 8, the avid reader who was brought up by her aunt and uncle, said of her aunt: '. . . whenever I see my aunt, and she has got some spare time, she is reading a book', and of her uncle: 'He reads a lot, normally war stories, but he will read practically anything.' The aunt and uncle corroborated what she told me, the aunt saying that she reads every evening and, 'When we go to bed we usually read, you know.' The uncle said, 'I'm not reading all the time but I read something every day.' All these statements were unsolicited and were made on three separate occasions.

Several children told me that although both parents read regularly, their mothers found it easier to make time for reading than did their fathers. Child 2, for instance, said: 'Dad gets books from work and reads them', but added, 'Mum reads more than Dad, especially Catherine Cookson. . . . At night she will sit down and read . . . when we are watching the television she will sit and read. . . . My dad's parents read, my grandma reads the same sort of books that my mum reads.' The boy's parents had a great deal to say about reading. The father told me:

> I know in that period we didn't have a TV I read about three books a week. I enjoy reading, if I pick a book up. If there's something on the TV I like I'll watch it; but if I pick a book up and start it and get into it, I'll sit up till about 3.00 a.m. . . . I *must* finish it and I can't put it down if it's really interesting. My father used to go around buying books all over the place. . . . He used to pay £5 or £6 for a book when wages were 50/-. He had *David Copperfield,* a big red volume about that thick – Dickens, encyclopedias, *The Rise and Fall of the Roman Empire,* Darwin – all that sort of thing. . . . I think reading is the most important thing there is. You can learn only one way and that's to be

receptive, isn't it? So to me it's what you hear, or what you see or read . . . you can learn your maths and all the other subjects if you can read. . . . Unless you can read, you might as well pack up now.

At this point the parents discussed the question of what proportion of knowledge is usually acquired first hand, and what percentage through reading. The father said that he thought that reading, as opposed to first-hand experience, had contributed 75 per cent of his knowledge, whereas the mother said: 'I'd go higher, I'd say 95 per cent.' By 'knowledge' they did not mean factual information acquired from non-fiction books only, for the father said: 'I think fiction broadens the outlook', and the mother had a very sophisticated view of the issue:

> I think fact and fiction are mixed up, especially in historical things. B. [her husband] likes science fiction and I like period things and I think when you are reading you're there in whatever period it is because you're using your own imagination. You're watching something that is a visual thing. You're reading something and you might be here one minute and the next there in King Arthur's time. . . . Do you know I was amazed when I started reading adult books and I found out the story was the same as children's books. . . . I was amazed as I expected it to open up something completely new, and yet it was the same thing in a story whether it is in a nursery rhyme or whether it's in *Star Trek* – it's the same thing but dressed up different; I like it in period dress.

I quote this at length because it is not merely an indication that the mother reads a great deal but also that she reflects upon what she reads, about why people read, and that she makes *connections* that many people would find surprising. Coming from a working-class home with a similar interest in books and reading myself, I do not find it at all surprising. The mother expressed her love of books forcibly when she said: 'I think it's super when you find an author you haven't read before and you realize you've got all those too!'

Very similar attitudes were expressed by the mother of Child 9, who was taking the teacher-training course and who had formerly been a cleaner in her children's school. I possibly need to remind readers at this point that the comments quoted were not replies to direct questions about reading. Here is part of what this mother had to say:

> Well, books are a way of life. You either have books or you don't have books, and I was brought up with my dad, who shoved books under our noses at an early age and said, 'Look at that

beautiful print. When you get bigger you'll be able to read it.'
And I've always got a lot out of reading and I wanted my kids to
get a lot out of reading, which the two of them must do. Not like
other people's kids. . . . I think it's a shame that a lot of them
don't get a chance to. . . . I never knew my grandfather but he
was a great believer in book learning; he always wanted his
children to read.

There is a tremendous feeling here of the value of reading being
passed down from one generation to another. It is as though the
parent experiences so much joy in reading that he or she tries to
make available the same experiences to the child and also causes the
child to seek the experiences that give so much pleasure to a loved
and respected person. Also, it is likely that the child receives a
further reward in terms of the parents' satisfaction and admiration
if that child reads well and shares the parents' excitement about
books.

The same mother tried to explain what it was that reading did for
her:

Well, being able to travel without moving, being able to do
things without being tired; reading about things that you're never
likely to do but while you're reading that book you're doing it,
finding things out – Recently, I've been reading Jean Plaidy and
Georgette Heyer – pure escapism. I used to read, shall we say,
more ambitious things. I used to like science fiction and I've
always loved classics: I think they are fantastic. But as I got older
and I got more tied to the kitchen sink, I wanted to escape the
kitchen sink momentarily . . . and it was good old historical
novels. When R. was small there would be occasions when he'd
say 'Mummy, I want my dinner', and I'd say, 'Wait until
Mummy's finished this chapter' or if he came down in the night,
which children are wont to do, I'd usually have my nose stuck in
a book.

Such a child would be aware at a very early age that reading was an
activity valued highly by a grown-up who was very important to
him.

Although fathers had something to say about reading, it is
interesting to note that mothers said more, as though they saw
introducing a child to books as a similar activity to introducing that
child to a healthy diet, as part of the process of child-rearing, in
which the majority of those mothers played the major rôle for the
first five years of their children's lives.

The mother of Child 15, who taught her child to read when he
was not learning very well at school, described to me her earliest

experiences of reading. In this case she represented the first generation in her family to take an interest in books:

> Something has to come from the child. If a child is interested in reading, he will continue to read. At the age of 7 you have this marvellous experience – I know with me I actually looked at a page and I would understand what Enid Blyton was actually saying after that. . . . In no time at all, I was as aware as the rest of the children in the gang that at the end of the road was a library that contained books and if I wanted to read a book, you didn't sit at home, you went to the library. And when I went to school the possibilities were endless.

This mother believed that there came a point where the intrinsic reward of reading took over from the desire to please the parent.

Certainly the relationship between parents' and children's reading is not a straightforward imitative one, particularly as the children get older. In fact the mother of Child 22 felt quite sure that her son could not have got his interest in books from herself or her husband. Even though she admitted to having read 'a book a day' at times when she was a child, she insisted that '. . . you couldn't say he has taken it from us, because I gave it up and he hasn't seen me read lately'. The father added, 'So, there you are, it's in his own personality.' However, what these parents *did* do was to encourage any activity in which their sons took an interest and to praise them for their achievements. These were the parents who bought a typewriter and admired their son's writing ability. In this family the parents tended to emulate the son's interest in books to some extent but not a great deal. The boy told me: 'My mother and father read sometimes. They borrow books off of me.' Both parents corroborated this. The mother said: 'I read some of S.'s now, but I don't seem to have the time now'; and the father: 'I never read a book – if S. has a book and says it is interesting I might read that a little bit.'

This is a far cry from the situation in the home of Child 15, above, where the mother taught her son to read. The father there said that his work as a quality control manager involved a lot of technical reading and, 'We've never [himself and his wife] a time when we aren't reading or haven't a book on the go. We have eight books from the library about every seven days.' Their son said, 'My father often takes a book to work to read in the lunch-hour. My mother reads even if there's a good programme on – she'll still read a book anyway. They think it's good to have books and classical things around – things like antiques – culture.' These parents, and the mother in particular, were unusual in the extent of their knowledge of children's books.

Even in families where very little money was available there could be found traditions of reading passed down from one generation to the next. The mother of Child 13 told me:

> My mother used to read. Well, it's just like you said, she had five of us and she couldn't afford to go out and buy them for us. The time I can remember when I got one it would be at Christmas or a birthday present, but she used to read. [Then to husband:] Your dad read a lot, didn't he?

Husband: '. . . every day. About a book a day. I read the same sort of stuff my Dad liked – war books, so I had a lot of war books, also science fiction and cowboy stories.' This father, like most of the fathers of the avid readers, whatever their occupations, swapped books with his friends both at work and in the pub. He said, 'They will play hell if you don't fetch them back. It's like a library.' He showed me some of the books borrowed currently from friends in the pub, including beautifully bound volumes of *The Count of Monte Cristo*. His wife added, '. . . it's a topic of conversation some nights, what you have read: "This were good and that were rubbish"'.

The father of Child 16 described his reading habits:

> I always have done. I love reading, you see at work there is always some form of literature going out, magazines, that sort of thing, and if I get home and I have started a good book at work, nothing else exists until I have read that book. Mainly, if I get any given at work, I tend to keep them in my cupboard at work and I generally have one in my pocket. I read at break time and that . . . I usually have a book on me and, if I do get ten minutes, I can read.

This father insisted that *his* parents had not influenced him at all:

> I just got interested, I do get wrapped up in books absolutely. I think anyone who doesn't read, I think they miss such a lot. . . . If I had my time over again I think things would be a lot different. . . . I think I would go for a job reporting or something like that. . . . As I am now I am virtually at a dead end.

It seems that amount of reading and awareness of possibilities often went hand in hand at least in this series of case studies and that it usually took a couple of generations for values to be crystallized, the implications fully understood and translated into operational terms. I shall examine this idea in more detail in subsequent sections.

Child 7, the girl whose mother was ill when she was small, with the result that her father and grandmother looked after her a good deal, felt that she had not been influenced by her parents: 'My mum doesn't read hardly at all – well, she reads magazines more than anything. It's my two grandmas and auntie who read the most, because they have more time, you know. I read more than my parents.'

A different situation pertained in the Asian families; apart from one father who was particularly keen on reading historical books, the parents did not read a great deal apart from religious books in the parents' native language. Child 19 told me, 'My mum and dad don't read [English books]. They only read Punjabi books. But my uncle reads a lot. He used to read in bed and I used to see him and I asked him what books he read and he started me a little bit.' She was also encouraged by the English wife of her uncle. The girl's father stated quite categorically that the girl's, and her siblings', interest in books was nothing to do with parental influence.

A boy with Asian parents, Child 17, already described as being influenced also by an uncle's English wife, painted a graphic picture of his parents' reading habits:

> My mum reads a book, the 'Old Book', in our language and my dad reads another book in Arabic. And I can read Arabic and so can read my brothers and sisters. They keep them in the dining-room where the visitors sit, because that is better than the room where *we* sit, because we have had it decorated, and we keep them there, and we take a lot of care of them . . . on a big bookshelf . . . about seven or eight and they are thick as well. My dad looks at them every night and my mum about three times a week. And when I get home I read one, because it is our religion to read that.

The mother spoke English well, having learnt it from an English woman married to a Pakistani neighbour.

The parents of the infrequent readers said very little about their own reading. Child 18's mother did volunteer: 'Well, in point of fact, to be quite honest with you, I don't like reading.' She was very eloquent and her son was the boy with great verbal skills. Of the other parents of infrequent readers, information gathered from both parents and children revealed that only one pair of parents did read and their son, I believe, would have been a keen reader had he been able to master the skills. The father of Child 26 believed that he needed nothing more than to be able to read a popular newspaper.

9 Television and time and place of reading
At this point the reader might care to re-read the extract from Roald Dahl's poem/cautionary tale quoted at the beginning of this

chapter. A great deal has been written about the relationship between television viewing and reading, including most recently by Whitehead *et al.* (1977) who found 'an adverse relationship between amount of book reading and amount of television viewing', and in *Reading in America 1978,* where Charles B. Weinberg writes:

> What is striking when you contrast book readers to non-book readers is that the book readers seem quite willing to stop and start their book reading. They seem to have less problems with reading during different times of the day, and perhaps one of the clues to the puzzle of how they come to watch so much television is *maybe they watch television at the same time as they are reading a book* (my italics).

Although our sample was far too small for me to be able to generalize, I was able to examine closely and in detail the part played by television in the lives of a few avid readers. Obviously, every individual has a limited amount of time in which to *choose* activities. I wanted to find how this time was used.

In the family where the girl, Child 8, was brought up by the aunt and uncle, the television was *not* on all evening and some evenings it was not on at all. They *used* the television, rather than keeping it on as a background noise. The uncle said, 'We pick and choose what we want; otherwise it's switched off.' The aunt added, 'We would prefer to sit and talk rather than watch television.' Certainly the girl's pattern of life as described by herself and by her 'parents' did not leave a great deal of time for television viewing. When she arrived home from school, so the aunt told me, the girl usually stayed '. . . in her bedroom mainly, after coming in and giving me a kiss. And she gets a book out. It's a book or writing or the dolls.' She said that J. would read 'anytime'. 'In the morning before she has been called up for school she reads.' The child herself said, 'I take my book in the bathroom and find I'm late for school. I read anywhere if I have a book I like. I normally read at night. The other night I woke up and I had nothing else to read, so I picked up this book called *Heidi,* and read it right through to the end before I turned off the light.' This child *alone* among the avid readers did not give the impression that television played an important part in her life.

Child 6 described a much more common situation of either reading in the room where the rest of the family were watching television, or leaving the room in order to concentrate. She told me that the television is on every day of the week, partly for her younger brother to watch children's programmes and later for her parents. She said that one could often concentrate well enough to read with the television on '. . . unless there is something that really irritates me like football. I think it was last week I got the book *All For Love,* and I was really interested in it and it was just after ten o'clock on Saturday, and I went in the kitchen to read it.'

A boy, Child 1, described a similar situation in which, although he only *actively* watched children's television, he spent most of his time in the room with the television on, as his parents had the television on all evening. The boy described an average evening in this way:

> Well usually until around quarter to six I watch telly, children's programmes, and then I start on my homework if I've got any, then I read some of my aircraft or World War II magazines or a book or make a model if I've got one.

His mother's description of her son's average day painted a similar picture:

> Right, average school day, he wakes up in a morning, he usually comes down here either with books or magazines and sits in here while I make the breakfast, reading. Goes in, shovels his breakfast down, comes back in here and does some more reading. Then he goes to school and he has to stay at school for his dinner, comes home from school and does some more reading again 'til it's time for his evening meal. *The television's on all the time* [my italics]. If there's something really interesting, or the comedy shows he enjoys, he'll watch it, but the rest of the time he'll sit with his nose in a book. . . . He just shuts it out [the television]. I think he stays in here partly for warmth and partly for company. Although, if we sat there and shouted, 'Your pants are on fire!' I don't think he'd notice, but we are there in the room with him.

The boy agreed:

> Yes, I can sometimes hear things when I want to and if there is a documentary on and it gets on to something interesting I just put my book down and look at it [the television] and then I just shut it out when I want to.

This ability to shut out the television at will is a skill that many young people today seem to have developed.

Similarly, in Child 2's home, the television is always on all evening. He watched documentaries and political things 'but does not like sport or soap opera'. The father said, 'M. is not keen on sport and there's a lot of sport on TV. That's when I read [the father]. When there's sport on I read. I can ignore it. I can turn off. *He* [the boy] *can turn off* [my italics]. I can come home from work, television on, J.'s mum, my mother, two kids, I can come in here, pick the paper up and ignore it all.' The mother, talking about the boy, said:

> . . . I say he wouldn't know it if World War III was declared if he's interested in what he's reading. When he was younger, he would go upstairs a lot, lay on his bed and read and write a lot, but when he got older he was frightened of missing something. So he prefers to be with us, but he always reads laid down. He'll stretch out on t'bed or t'rug.

To be with their families these children have to learn mental strategies that will allow them to read when the television is on. Even families who do not particularly enjoy many of the programmes offered on television tend to leave it on.

The father of Child 22 said: 'I would say a lot of it is habit, with putting the box on. . . . To my mind there is a lot of rubbish on television. I don't spent a lot of time watching television because I've too much to do. . . . it's just boring most of the time.'

He added that his son was selective in his use of television. This family, like several others where there were avid readers, had two television sets, one being portable. This did not seem to be an indication that they were doubly keen on watching television, but rather that they were aware of the importance of choice and discrimination – they watched particular *programmes* rather than television *per se*.

Child 7's father expressed the reason for having two televisions very well when he said:

> Well that is something else that I have always been a bit firm on. If there is something that they particularly want to see then we watch it, but don't just come in and turn it on automatically, and go on watching it for hours. We have two TV's specifically because I think there are certain programmes on the television which are not suitable for H. and by the same token I don't see why we should stop watching them, likewise, I can't expect H.'s taste to be the same as mine, so there are obviously some programmes that she enjoys and I can't stand so rather than have a conflict we would get another television. This is the reason why we have two televisions, not we're so keen on television, you know.

The child would sometimes read downstairs, but '. . . then if she gets really interested she goes up to her bedroom and we never see her again until the book is finished. Or sometimes she will go to bed early and read, sometimes for about two hours.' She was currently watching, '. . . two things, my mum used to read this when she was little, *Worzel Gummidge* and *The Peppermint Pig*. I really enjoyed *The Owl Service* and when they put it on television, I was thrilled to bits.' Of course, all three were serializations of children's books.

Sometimes, even in a house where everything was organized so that the child can read elsewhere in a warm, comfortable room, the child preferred to be with the rest of the family. Child 15 described the complex relationship that existed in his family with the television:

> When I get home from school I get changed into my ordinary clothes, and have a cup of coffee, watch television – I like *Screen Test*; I don't mind *Blue Peter*, stories like *Jackanory*, *Record Breakers*. Then I practise my violin. After tea if there's a good programme on the telly we watch it. It stays on 'til my father and mother go to bed. Yet my father would say, 'We're not a television family, or something like that.' He would say, 'There's some good things on television but some very bad things you shouldn't watch.' I read in my bedroom before I go to sleep, or in the room with the TV on. If there's a good programme on I would watch the programme *because it can't be repeated again. If I have got my book I can go back to it anytime I want, not like television.* (my italics).

The parents' interview again confirmed this pattern of behaviour. The mother said: 'He loves television and he loves to read too. He watches 'til about five and then I'll say, "Well it's about time you had your violin practice now, K., isn't it?" and, if he has any homework, he'll do it in his bedroom.' The father added: 'He doesn't go upstairs *to read* – if he is reading he'll bring his book down here. He seems to be able to read when people are talking or the TV is on, like his mother.'

The boy with the typewriter, Child 22, shared a second television set with his brother and watching it seemed to be an inspiration for both reading and writing. He watched little television on a Saturday, not liking sport, or Sunday; on these two days he would shop for books, read and write. His mother told me:

> Well he doesn't really watch all that much because he reads a lot. If the *Best Seller* is on he'll watch that; well, even if it's late, I let him watch it because he doesn't watch very much. And he'll go out straightaway to Smiths and order it if it isn't in. I mean, he doesn't like love books and things like that but if there's a *Best Seller* on TV and he enjoys it, he'll buy it.

I've already described how this boy used television scripts as bases for short stories. It seems that *all* the media that are connected with story-telling interested him as they did several other of the avid readers. This particular boy had developed the ability to discriminate as well as utilizing some of the material promoted on television for his writing. He was one of the two or three avid readers who would go to his own room in order to read. The mother said:

> Well, S. seems to like science fiction and horror things; I think he is influenced by what he sees on television. He's been reading all day today [holiday] once he had done his homework. He likes to be on his own as well. *If he's down here he can't read his book while we're watching TV or if anybody is talking he goes upstairs* [my italics]. He's got to be quiet, hasn't he? It has to be something really special on the television for S. to watch it; otherwise he'll read a book.

The father added: 'If he stops off school, if he *has* to have a day off, you never see him. He gets his book and just goes and reads.'

Child 10, who had his own television set upstairs, said, 'I sometimes go upstairs and read or watch another programme that Mum and Dad don't want to watch.' In this case the parents are also discriminating. The mother told me about her son's viewing habits:

> If there is anything on television like *How* or *Tomorrow's World* – anything like that he'll watch, or anything on BBC 2, you know, which I can't understand – he will watch that. I will say, 'You can't understand that', but he says, 'I do'. We stop him watching if there is something violent on, or something we don't want him to watch. We watch some things, but we play records as well.

The father expressed the opinion: 'There's not much on television that is interesting. I mean, last Sunday we watched one programme and then we switched it off.'

A similar pattern occurs over and over again. The avid reader enjoys television but is discriminating and, when necessary, avoids it – whether by switching off mentally or by going into another room. Some other remarks made on the same subject were:

> 'When it gets to about seven or eight o'clock at night she's off upstairs with her books. Our J.'s more for the television. J. will stop up while one o'clock; but D. will go up and read' (Child 13).

> 'She is always reading and writing. She wouldn't be glued to that [television] – although she likes television. But if she were reading or writing, she would switch off from that' (Child 27).

> 'I don't watch it much. I watch films to do with mystery. I read in my bedroom and sometimes I go to my Auntie's and they get all the newspapers and I can read them there; it's quiet and I can read' (Child 19).

Three of the most interesting comments about television were made by Asian children, the first a girl (Child 19), who said, 'Reading is better than television because you have to use your mind and your imagination, but for television there is a picture there and the words being said.' The second, a boy (Child 17), 'I would read more if we didn't have a television, but most I read or play out, *but if I was bored before television was invented and then it got invented then I would watch it a lot because it would be a new thing to me*' (my italics). These avid readers were far from bored, cramming their days with all kinds of activities, albeit mainly indoors. Of course, if they lived in homes where the television was on a lot, they were bound to come into contact with a good deal of television, for, as we have already established, they preferred indoor to outdoor pastimes. They were possibly able to take this situation in their stride because they had been brought up with television and could therefore adopt a take-it-or-leave-it attitude, whereas their parents were probably, like myself, brought up without television and still regard it as something of a miracle.

The infrequent readers watched far less television than the avid readers, even though their parents watched it. The children all much preferred to play out. The mothers told me:

'He only watches a bit before five o'clock, then he plays out until eight or nine' (Child 18).

'He doesn't watch much television, he's not all that interested in television' (Child 26).

'The TV is on while he's having his tea, but R. doesn't like television; he would rather play out' (Child 25).

'He has his tea with the telly on but he doesn't watch it' (Child 12).

Only one infrequent reader mentioned a programme he enjoyed. He said, 'There isn't much good on television, except I'll watch that scarecrow' (Child 5).

10   Libraries and book ownership

Some of the avid readers did not enjoy visiting libraries or borrowing books, as they preferred to buy their own; a few relied almost entirely upon libraries for their supply of reading material; and several children combined the two methods.

The author of *Reading in America 1978* reports a similar finding:

The Gallup survey also asked where books were obtained by readers who read one book or more over the past twelve months.

Libraries were placed third in popularity – behind bookstores and borrowing from friends. Only one in five respondents (21 per cent) said they obtained their books from libraries, while approximately one in three (36–37 per cent) chose each of the other sources.

All but one of the avid readers had belonged to a library at some time. The girl who was brought up by her aunt and uncle (Child 8) was so well known as an avid reader that, as her aunt said, '. . . everybody tends to buy her books. And she buys a lot of books herself. We used to take her to Smith's and she would buy something there.' The uncle interpolated, 'And we bought her a bookcase so she had somewhere to keep them.' 'Yes', continued the aunt, 'with the books she had got she could start a library'. The girl said that she preferred to own rather than to borrow books because, '. . . I like to read them over and over again if they are good. But from the library it is rare you can get the same book twice.' Another avid reader in the same class, Child 6, who did use the public library to some extent, agreed with this point of view. She offered:

> The thing that bothers me is a bit about libraries, right, it is a good thing for getting books from, but when I get a book and I really enjoy the book, I want to buy the book so that I can keep it because I want to go back again and read it when I have thoroughly enjoyed it.

The same girl decided to join the Bradford Central Library during the course of the experiment instead of her small local library – as she felt that she had exhausted the supply of books that interested her. This same opinion was voiced by several other avid readers. This particular girl involved her father in the move. She said: 'I used to get them from Eccleshill [local library], but now I go to the big library in Bradford – in fact, I joined on Saturday.' Nevertheless, all the members of the family *preferred* to own books. The mother told me: 'I can't pass a bookshop. I must admit that it is one of my favourite things. When I go to Leeds I *have* to go to Austicks and Smith's'. The parents took their two children to bookshops from an early age and the girl's aunt who had taken her to a bookshop on the day of the home interview (as mentioned in an earlier section) worked in a library. The father, her brother, said: 'Yes, I think it was the only solution for you – to work in a library and then you could read as much as you wanted during the day.'

Child 1 was another avid reader who preferred to buy his own books rather than borrow them from a public library. When he was small his mother bought him nursery rhymes, fairy stories,

Ladybirds and so on and continued to buy other books until he was old enough to go and buy his own. He told me:

> If I can't afford the bus fare and I can't afford an expensive paperback, like this one was 85p, I go up to Idle or down to Greengates [local shops] where most of the shops have got paperback shelves; but if I've got the bus fare, and I know there is a book up in town that I would like to buy, I go on the bus to W. H. Smith's or another place like that.

He had been to the local public libraries, first in Eccleshill and then in Idle, but gave it up, 'Because it seemed that I had read all the books that were interesting and all the books that weren't interesting just seemed to pile up. And then there were books that I would like to *use* but I couldn't because they were in the reference library.'

The mother entirely corroborated what he said. She agreed, 'He likes the books; he doesn't like the trips to the library. . . . If there's a book he enjoys he likes to read it again and again, not have to read it in a certain time. But he *has* borrowed books he likes and then saved up to buy them.' She felt that a similar thing had happened with the Book Flood class-room library. 'He said, "They've brought a load of new books in", or words to that effect. And he brought quite a lot of books home, particularly for the first six months and then it faded off. He's read the books he wanted to read and the rest were of no interest to him.'

Child 2 liked *both* borrowing *and* buying books. He had been disillusioned with the public library until the librarian decided to allow him into the adult section. His mother said, '. . . the librarian let him into the adult section because it's only a small library and he'd read the children's section. She wouldn't let him at first. He said to me, "She thinks I ought to be reading *Biggles*".' This mother had taken her son to the library when he was in his pushchair. Yet he also enjoyed buying and owning books. He said, 'I've got a stack of books – I've got a bookcase and that is full and I've got books all over the place'. His father agreed: 'M. spends quite a bit on books . . . on Saturday, whilst J.'s looking at jumpers and all that, we go to the second-hand bookshops.' The mother described an interesting little scene.

> One day I came out of the dress shop and M. was negotiating with him [a market stall holder]. It seemed he had four aeroplane books, but they were £2.50 and M.'s idea was maybe if he talked to him he would get them for £1.50. The man's idea was, 'I've got a right good book on tanks I'll throw in for £2'.

The entire family of Child 15 visited public libraries regularly. The parents had taken both children with them to the local public library at Saltaire but at the time of the interview the boy was using Eccleshill library as it was near to school and he found it convenient to go after school ended. His mother said, 'He's always come with us to the library ever since he was a baby. He went from about three to the children's library.' These parents themselves loved to own books both as objects and for love of the contents. I think it is worth quoting the mother at length in order to demonstrate the depth of emotion associated with books. Talking about Rupert Brooke, she said:

> I have always wanted to be able to read and read and read until I knew most of it by heart. It's not just that; for some books that are – your favourite books – you are able to go to them and read them again and again. Not because you don't know exactly the plot – the way the plot is going to work out – but for precisely the same reason you go to a good play to see it again. . . . I prefer an old copy of a book – with that kind of binding – it's lovely to look at, to handle. I like good paper and it is something I'm trying to pass on to K. and I will with E. [younger sister]. E. at the moment has those books that she likes, and she knows they have to be looked after, but, still she reads them, but they are nice books to *have*. It's lovely, isn't it? I've gone through them and said, 'Look at the illustrations in there, E.', and she'll say, 'Yes they're lovely'. But I must admit I like a book to be packaged well too.

The parents said they had not noticed the Book Flood affecting their son at all and they thought that was because he had so many books at home already.

Child 22, who had his own typewriter and enjoyed writing, alone among the avid readers had never been to a public library, although he had obviously had experience of the school library. He said that he preferred to buy his own books, so that 'I can have a choice'. He said he found most of the books at school rather childish and preferred to go into Bradford every Saturday to buy his own. His mother said:

> . . . I think he found the books at school, well not really babyish, but I don't think they were at his level at all . . . even now [at home] he must have a hundred if not more. For his birthday, S. wanted *Roots*, and he wanted the proper *Roots*, not the paperback one, the hardback one . . . well, I come into town every Saturday and take both of them with me and while I'm doing my shopping I leave them in Smith's, and they're in there, and Boots, for about half an hour, and then I usually pick them up and we go way down to the bottom end of town and they go in Smith's again [another branch]. And nearly always S. comes out with a

couple of books . . . if he has any money in his hand at all he nearly always buys a book. . . . Mr — [English teacher] has been telling him things about Shakespeare – he was reading a book only this dinner time. He asked if I had any of my old books on Shakespeare which I haven't, so I can guarantee when we go into town on Saturday he will get one on Shakespeare . . . when they go on their holidays, oh dear, he will buy six or seven books in one day. He spends most of his holiday money that way. A. [brother] will want to go on the golf course and that sort of thing, but S. will hang on to his money for the bookshop.

Even Child 27, who was very badly off materially, preferred to buy books than borrow them and somehow managed to do so, although not extensively. Her mother said, 'I bought them. She's got stacks and stacks of books. A pity we haven't got a library. We generally buy them, don't we?' This was the family that lived in the damp flat.

Child 13, on the other hand, found it almost impossible to buy books as a regular habit. She told me, 'I sometimes buy books but not very often because they cost a lot of money.' She preferred the atmosphere of the public library to that of the bookshop and made a fascinating comment. She said, 'When I'm in town and I'm choosing books – the love books – I get embarrassed but at the library to me it doesn't seem to matter. . . . The people at the library are always polite as well.' However, she rarely buys books, 'Because I can always get them from the library and I think it saves money.' She gets books for her mother from the library too. The mother said: 'She usually brings six home and she reads all six, besides what she reads at school.'

The two Asian boys (17 and 23) bought books sometimes, but the girl, Child 19, was entirely dependent upon the public library. She had been going since she was 9, first to Carlton Bolling then to Eccleshill. She was not taken by her parents and told me how she came to join:

I go nearly every week . . . I was in the class one day and I just picked this book up, and it was really interesting and I thought that if I could get more of these books, I would like reading them. I asked my friend's brother – he went to a library – and I asked him and he showed me where it was. . . . This week I am taking a form in and getting six [books]. In the holidays I go nearly every day.

She did have fairy tales, nursery rhymes and ABC books bought for her when she was smaller, as did her younger siblings, but she had not owned any books since then.

Child 17, an Asian boy, owned a lot of books, especially Enid Blyton and Willard Price. His younger siblings had '. . . picture books and things like that'. He told me a fascinating tale of how he had begun to buy books:

> When I went to school, I used to say to my dad, 'Will you buy me a book?' and he used to say, 'You will only make paper aeroplanes and things like that out of it', and I used to say, 'I won't'. And then my auntie – my dad's best friend, we call her Auntie – he has got an English wife and she used to buy me Christmas presents of *Beano* and things like that, and then when we used to begin to buy books, I used to ask my dad for money and he would give me money, and I would buy books. . . . We weren't buying books before that.

He also goes to the public library with his brothers and has already aimed a younger brother in the direction of Willard Price!

The other Asian boy, Child 23, and his father both buy books and borrow them from the public library. The father went to the public library first and the son said that when he first saw the building, he thought it was someone's house. The father had belonged to the central library for eight or nine years and the boy asked to go: 'The first time he went with me, he asked me to go with him and he brought one card for me to sign because he wanted some books from the library.' The father was also prepared to buy books, but again waited for the son to *ask* rather than offering: 'He asked me to buy a dictionary and I said OK, and we went to Smith's and I bought it. Once he bought some books from school [*Chip Club* Catalogue], and he said he wanted this book and I said OK and paid the money.'

Child 7 sent her father, who worked in the centre of Bradford, to the bookshop. She *had* belonged to a public library when she was younger but stopped going '. . . because they didn't have enough books'. The father said, 'She is still on with Alfred Hitchcock. She bought one on Saturday and she has given me a list to see if I can find any more in Smith's or Boots, because I can get in through the lunch break, you see. She read the last one from cover to cover, the one she bought on Saturday.' The girl herself was not very well satisifed with Bradford bookshops. She said, quite rightly I believe, 'I sometimes go to bookshops but Bradford doesn't have a proper bookshop. W. H. Smith's is perhaps the best. The only trouble is they don't stock enough books.'

I asked the infrequent readers and their parents directly about book ownership and library membership at the end of the interview – if they had not already mentioned it of their own accord. Several of these children conveyed the impression that their parents could not trust them to go into town without getting into some kind of trouble. Child 26 candidly told me, 'No, I don't go into the town because once I was in the town and this policeman told me not to come in for a while.' This boy owns seven or eight books and never goes to a public library. Child 25 told me that he had never had books of his own at home and that, although three of his sisters used the public library, his mother would not allow him to go in case he got into mischief. In fact during the boy's time at the middle school, the mother had bought him a few *Ladybird* books, in an attempt to help him when she realized just how poor his reading was. She told me: 'I gave them away because he can't read them. . . . He thought I was putting him down buying those books' (because the subject matter was too babyish). Child 5 told me that his mother would not allow him to go to the public library and would not let him buy a paperback through the *Chip Club*: 'Well, these little booklets come and then you send off for a book and I took one home, one or two different ones, to see if I could have them, and she said, "No, because we haven't got the money".' Child 12 had no books of his own and never goes to the public library. Among the infrequent readers, one boy only, Child 18, used the public library at all, and that was an occasional use of the mobile library, but even that had been discontinued. The girl among the infrequent readers, Child 14, did have about ten books of her own, mainly *Beano* and *Dandy* annuals, Enid Blyton and 'ghost stories'. She also occasionally visited the local public library at Greengates with her father and the younger children. The father borrowed Westerns for himself and Mills & Boon romances for his wife from the public library.

It seems clear that these children would be more likely to borrow from a mobile library that arrived near their homes when they were playing out than they would be to visit a public library or a bookshop, particularly as their parents would be unlikely to accompany them to either of these places. Also, these children would be more likely to buy a book directly from a school bookshop with their pocket-money, than from a bookshop elsewhere or via a book club – which involved them taking home a leaflet *and asking* for money specifically for books. I think having books *on the spot* (in the classroom) is necessary if these children are to have any chance of borrowing or buying books. Schemes where they can contribute 5p or 10p a week and then choose a book from the school bookshop when they have accumulated enough money might also make book buying less demanding. Such a scheme was operated effectively in the inner city control school.

11   **Freedom of choice of books**

During the case studies of avid readers, some fascinating and, apparently, conflicting findings emerged on the subject of parental attitude towards the child's choice of books. At one end of the continuum were the parents who believed in offering considerable guidance, while at the other end were those who took the attitude that if you let children read what they liked they would eventually learn to discriminate and develop 'good taste'. Sometimes this subject was touched on only by the child, or only by the parents, but in some cases both child and parents talked about it at length.

Child 8 was allowed to read almost anything, the line being drawn at subjects that were considered to be too adult. The aunt told me:

> She has always had a free choice as far as reading is concerned, within reason – I mean we wouldn't allow her to read just anything but she has chosen her own books *and I've noticed that she has progressed from things like Enid Blyton to different types of stories*, and at the moment she is interested in history . . . (my italics).

Often parents allowed their children to read books that were quite adult, provided that the child was prepared to discuss the implications of certain passages with them. Child 2's mother told me her husband had defended her son's choice of books against the criticism of the head of English:

> We were down at the school one day and Mr — who I think is a very good English teacher, said he was a bit worried about the type of his [M.'s] reading. James Bond, Ian Fleming, he thought were too violent. His father took exception to this and said there was nothing more violent than Dickens. He must have been just as shocking in that age, was Dickens as Ian Fleming now.

At this point the father said, 'When it comes to violence, it all boils down to your family.' What interests me here is the parents' defence of their son's freedom to choose, the fact that they found it possible to challenge the opinion of the head of English, and their ability to put a child's reaction to what he reads into the context of his total upbringing. It is quite clear also that they respected both themselves and their son.

Child 1's mother told me that they had made little attempt to influence her children's choice of books since she stopped buying them for them. She explained:

> I don't like his obsession with war and armaments, but it is *his* interest and *his* hobby and I wouldn't stop him. I will admit there are times when I say, 'Not another book about tanks; I can't

stand it!' or he'll say, 'Look at this', and I'll say, 'I don't want to look at a book about tanks'. But, there again, it's *his* life, *his* money, they're *his* books. He gets quite a lot of mature war books, you know, adult novels – but I don't particularly like them.

This mother had strong views and made them clear to her son, but did not attempt to impose them upon him; she made it apparent that she *disapproved* of the boy reading predominantly about war, but that she *approved* of the child. She also realized that the way in which a subject is dealt with can be as important as the subject. She stressed that his interest was 'academic' and added 'R.'s non-violent'. However, to ensure that he understood what could happen in war, she *made* him watch a serious television programme about war. She said:

> . . . it made him sick. I made him watch it, and he didn't like it [Child: No I didn't.]. We made him sit through it just to try and take a bit of the glory out of it. I don't think it's particularly the killing that fascinates him; it's the machinery, the works behind it.

This was a caring attempt to ensure that her son fully grasped the implications of what he was reading so that he could continue armed with information, rather than from a position of ignorance.

Child 22 was given almost complete freedom of choice in buying books and, as already mentioned, progressed in his own time from *Jaws* to *Best Sellers* to Shakespeare. However, there were some mutually understood limits *within* which he was allowed freedom of choice. His mother told me:

> If I saw a book that came out on the television and they said this is terrible; it's got this in, and that in, and the other in, and S. said 'Could I buy that?' Well, I would say, 'I don't think you should buy it, S.' And he would probably say, 'Alright, if you think so'. I've tried to make them a bit responsible.

Underlying this exploration is mutual respect and an already established system of values, which leaves the boy room to develop discrimination by reading widely.

The Asian children were in a situation where their parents were *unable* to advise them about children's books in the English language. Child 17 wrote:

> . . . the majority of my books are *Famous Five* and Willard Price books. I don't like the *Famous Five* books no more because they are boring. . . . I usually read without force. My favourite authors are Roald Dahl, Willard Price, Michael Hardcastle and the writers of space (Michael Pollard) and football encyclopedias.

At the other extreme were mothers who did attempt to influence their children's choice of books much more overtly. One mother, whose son (Child 10) preferred non-fiction to fiction, said:

> . . . I have sort of had to force him to read stories, fiction, because I think he *should* read that sort of thing. I've *made* him get a book and then he reads it in bed until nine or half past. . . . I think it develops their English – I think he is poor on English myself. English in conversation, I mean. Speech. And I think it would help if he would read more fiction than fact.

This mother felt the need to *widen* her son's literary horizons, rather than to restrict them.

The mother with the strongest views on the subject was the one who had taught her son, Child 15, to read. During the interview in school the boy told me that his mother usually went with him to buy books and often suggested what he might buy. He said, 'It's mostly *she* suggests it. If we're shopping, she sorts through some books and if she sees one she thinks is good, she usually buys it for me.' When I asked, 'Does she take notice of what you would like her to buy?' he said, 'No, not really'. He said she would like him to read '. . . authors like Kipling and Charles Dickens. Very old books like that. And Mark Twain.' He did borrow modern children's fiction from the class-room but his mother '. . . thinks some of them are a waste of time – she thinks some of them are trash, but she thinks some of them are quite good'. I asked him why he thought his mother took this attitude. He replied:

> I think she was saying it because *she* read it and she thinks I ought to read it, rather than the sort of trash I bring home. I don't mind, and, anyway, I read the things I want to read as well in my bedroom or when they're out.

He did not resent the fact that his mother recommended books that she thought worth while and he respected her opinion on the classics, but he felt that she was less well informed about modern fiction, which he read in any case. I think her attitude did not deter him from reading avidly for two reasons: first, because he knew she *cared* about him; and secondly, because he had reached the stage where he derived so much intrinsic pleasure from reading, partly *thanks* to his mother's insistence on teaching him to read, that nothing could deter him.

The mother expressed her point of view on two aspects of the subject: first, on books that might be considered too adult in subject matter and, secondly, on books that she considered to be 'trash' from a stylistic point of view:

If he does happen to like some books that are a little bit suspect, I point out the passages to him and we will go through them to find out exactly what it is that is objectionable. All the things which I find objectionable, he may not find it so. He's very taken up with James Bond which I don't approve of but they are there on the shelves – *but I think he's sort of passed them now*, he gets a bit bored with them and he's not read any more.

Here again we are involved in hearing about the very process of developing discrimination. On the subject of what she believed to be 'trash', she said:

Well K. and I had an argument about this last year. He received a book token – it wasn't very much; about £1 – and I said, 'I am going into Smith's. Do you want to see about spending your book token?' 'Oh yes'. And I was beside him. *I* was looking at titles too and I was surprised at the number of titles on the shelves that I could remember reading when I was younger. I was saying, 'Oh look at this; look at this!' You know. 'You'll love this; you'll love this!' 'Yes, yes'. And, in the end, he got a terribly trashy book, a sort of boy and girl romance thing – *terrible it was. It was a nasty book. It was cheaply written* [my italics]. I said, 'K. it's a shame to waste a token on that.' Eventually, later I came across it in his room and he said, 'Oh, it's not any good is that.' So when he got the same token from the same friend this year, he was with us and he got *Plague Dogs* with it.

When I asked the mother whether this had been entirely the boy's decision, she said: 'Well, half and half . . . yes, I *am* prepared to influence him if I think that quite honestly he is going to waste his money. But in the main part he gets what he wants so long as it's not too trashy.'

At first sight this might seem to be a far cry from the attitude of parents who impose few restrictions upon book choice but I *think* this mother's deeper and more detailed involvement was the result of her knowledge of literature, excepting modern children's literature. She shared with other parents a caring attitude towards her son's reading habits.

12 Parental attitudes towards school and education

More was said on the subject of school, and education generally, than on any other subject that was raised during the parental interviews – by parents of both avid and infrequent readers. The attitudes of the two groups of parents were strikingly different. For example, the parents of the avid readers were more knowledgeable than those of the infrequent readers about their children's schools, about the educational system generally, and about the examination system, particularly in relation to their offspring's career prospects. Those parents also felt able to intervene in their children's education and believed that they had a right to do so. They conveyed the opinion that they expected results from their intervention, that they expected their views to be seriously considered, and that they had some *control* over their children's education. The parents of the infrequent readers, on the other hand, cared about their children's schooling but gave the impression that it was not something over which they had any control; they left it to the experts.

All the parents of the avid readers stressed that they would wish their children to do better at school than they had themselves. An Asian boy, Child 17, talking about his father, said, '. . . he says, "Keep trying hard and then you won't have to work like me – look at my nails, you won't have nails like me when you grow up, you will get a better job than me when you grow up".' The other Asian boy, Child 23, said that his father, '. . . wanted to become a scientist but he stopped halfway through, you know, and says, "You must learn your English and you'll be a scientist as well".' *His* father was, but *he* got bored with school and just left to come to England. Child 16's mother said, of her son, 'I'd like him to go as high as he could, actually, we've both said that. . . . I'd encourage him in every way.' The father continued:

> . . . if he went into a job like mine, now then, he is limited. I think he could get a lot further than I have done. He has a lot more scope and he could take a job that he really enjoys. I sit and talk to him and say, 'Now, you can play about at school as much as you want, it's entirely up to you.' But I try to point out that it is *his* future that is at stake, not mine now. Without 'ruling with a rod of iron' as they call it, I try to get him thinking along the right lines for his own benefit. He said it himself, before, that he would like a nice house, and a nice car, and I say, 'The only way you are going to do it is by using this' [pointing to head, i.e. brains]. As I feel now, *I could have done a lot better than what I have done, if I had had the choice or a little bit of encouragement* [my italics]. I said to my dad at that time, 'Oh, I'm going to do this', and he said, 'Oh, you suit yourself', so I suited myself, and I've learnt since that I made a mistake. And I wouldn't like to think that *he* was going to do the same when I could happen help him and put him right. Do you see what I mean?

I did. The attitude of the father's father had been exactly the same as the attitude taken by the parents of *our* infrequent readers. One wonders when and how the change in attitude occurred.

A final example of this viewpoint, as there is not space to quote everything said on the subject, was expressed by one of the avid readers himself, Child 1, who said: (of his mother) 'And she thinks just because she got two "O" levels she wants us to get better.' Of his father he said, '. . . he thinks that he didn't have much of a good education because he was always messing about, so he tells us to do our best at school'.

The parents of the avid readers all had very strong, and often highly critical, opinions about their children's education, probably because they were fairly knowledgeable about the system and were greatly concerned that their children's potential should be fulfilled. They often expressed their views to teachers, headmasters and even the local authority. We have already encountered the father who argued with the head of English about his son's choice of reading material. Another father told me: 'There is just a little problem we have with the headmaster – he won't give in.' He wanted his daughter, Child 6, to be allowed to leave school half an hour early on a Friday so that she could get to her organ lesson, and he did not wish her to attend the particular upper school to which she had been allocated. He had achieved nothing by talking to the head-master, nor by subsequently writing to the local education authority officials. However, he did not intend to give up. He said, 'I will probably go down and see them myself personally, and explain to them . . .' I later discovered that he had done precisely that. He believed very strongly that another school was better as he had discussed the subject with various parents and looked at the type of homework given; he believed that it should be up to them as a family to make the final decision unless someone could 'prove to him that he was wrong'. He had faith in his own judgement. (I do not know the outcome of this disagreement.)

Child 1's mother did not approve of the way in which her younger child was being taught to read at school:

> . . . when he doesn't know the word he says, 'We haven't been taught that word', and it's stupid – he knows all the letters. So I have to take him on one side and say, 'Nobody knows every word. Everybody's got to make the sounds out, then guess.' In fact, really, I didn't want to leave Liversedge because of the education system. We came to Bradford and the kids had to mark time for six months until the school they went to caught up with the school they'd been at. It was a case of, 'We've read that book', and the teachers saying, 'Well, we can't do anything about it; you'll have to read it again'.

She had even stronger views about her son's present school. I quote all these remarks not because I necessarily agree with them but in order to illustrate the strength of the views of these parents as a group, and to show that what must often seem a very annoying habit of critical interference, is basically indicative of a caring attitude and a desire for involvement in their children's education:

> I think it's a disaster. I think the standards are awful. It's nice being told that my kids are geniuses, but *I* don't think my kids *are* geniuses; I just think the standards are too low. . . . He's bored stiff; really he's marking time.

Active encouragement was offered by the parents of avid readers, partly by attending PTA meetings and open days in order to keep themselves well-informed, partly by providing books and places to study as already described, partly by expressing their views to the children, and in some cases by actually teaching their children themselves. The father of Child 16 said:

> If you have a bright child – not even that, if you have a child who is backward you do whatever possible to get that child to the standard you can get it, for the child's sake. . . . It is just as important to a girl as to a man these days.

Child 15's mother said that she and her husband had specifically chosen that school for their son (active intervention), even though it was a long way from home. The father told me: 'We know the headmaster there for one thing, and we agree with his methods . . . we specifically asked for him to go to that school.' The mother particularly encouraged her son in his education, offering active help whenever she thought it necessary, for instance with comprehension. She explained: 'Last year sometime his work fell off a bit, but, eventually, you know the one, *My Last Duchess*, well I read that the first time and I sort of left him with it and we came back to it, because he was having problems with poetry comprehension.' She said that she had felt prompted to give her son encouragement and active help, because:

> I think that remembering my own childhood, my parents were poor and they didn't have a great deal of money and perhaps not a lot of imagination. I got all the *physical* care that they could afford to give me, but, like most children, you sense various other things and, if you've anything about you at all, you can make some sort of effort. But I can also understand that *there are some people who need a sort of hand behind them to push them a little bit further*, to say, 'Look, look, it's there; look, it's there!' And sometimes they can catch the glimmer and once they have got the glimmer then they can follow it! (my italics).

Child 10's mother emphasized that, in her opinion, parents taking an active interest in school would be perceived by the children as indicative of a supporting attitude, and would encourage them. Both parents, like those of the avid readers, regularly attended PTA meetings and the father had eventually been asked by the headmaster to become a parent–governor. He told me how this came about: 'I got talking to him [the head]; we had quite a few discussions, about teaching methods and so on.' The mother said: 'I think *if a child sees that you are interested in what he does at school*, if you show an interest and go, you know, it makes all the difference' (my italics).

These parents, like all the other parents of avid readers, had a definite idea of which upper school they wanted their child to attend.

A father told me how much active help and encouragement his wife had given to their daughter, Child 7. He explained:

Since H. went to the middle school, she [the mother] has been like another school teacher in a way. *Because she realizes the value of it* [my italics] she has spent a great deal of time and I think that is why H.'s ability to read is as good as it is.

The mother told me in what way she could help:

You see she has a spelling test every fortnight and she looks at them and then she gives them to me and I will ask her and she writes them down. . . . I remember that at seven o'clock one morning we were doing the Crusades, and I was asking her questions about the Crusades. I want to encourage H., but not push her to overdo it.

They had just received some information about the upper school to which their daughter had been allocated, and had obviously read it carefully; they were to go and look at the school one evening in the following week. The encouragement offered by the parents of avid readers to their children always included some degree of contact with the school – even if it was not always of an amicable nature.

The avid readers themselves and their parents often had quite clear ideas about career prospects; these thoughts were sometimes linked with past experiences of other members of the family. For instance, the aunt who brought up Child 8 said that she expected the girl to go to university and told me: 'I've got a nephew who is just home from Lancaster University, and Nicholas has had an interview at Oxford . . . when she [the girl] has been off ill, I have said to her that she will have to study because you don't want to fall behind, and you don't want to be the only one who doesn't go to university.'

A mother told me that her son, Child 2, at the age of 11, had been worried about his job prospects: 'I think the situation arose over the TV actually. . . . There was a programme about South Shields, wasn't there, which followed a group and all their expectations?' Child 6's father expected her to become a student at a school of music like her grandmother, who had her 'cap and gown'. When I asked him how he would react if his daughter suddenly decided to leave school when she was 16, he replied:

> I would have to have a really good talk with her and explain to her *that it is not everybody who could do what she has done* [my italics] – I would want to know why; there *must be a reason*, something in the background and I would want to get to the rock bottom of the trouble. I want her to get as far as she can before she gets married and then it is all there for her and she can come back to it later on.

This family, like other families of avid readers, looked far into the future and behaved in such a way as to be as sure as any of us can be of realizing their expectations. The aunt, who was also present at this interview (the father's sister), explained that her children had been to college, and therefore higher education was not alien to them. She told me that one son '. . . took a Farm Management Course and has just taken over his own farm – he is only 25'. The family had reason to believe in the efficacy of education. They also believed in the importance of job satisfaction in terms other than financial reward. The mother said, '. . . you have got to enjoy your work; it's not just the money; you can't just do a job because of the money, you've got to enjoy it'. The aunt added: 'I'm not against those girls in supermarkets but you see them at the checkouts and they look bored to tears.' In the minds of the avid readers and their families there was a clear causal connection between effort on the part of the child (and effective teaching) at school, the acquisition of qualifications, career prospects, future life-style and, to some extent, future happiness. They believed they had some control over the development of this chain of events.

Child 10 wrote in his questionnaire: 'I want to be anything to do with science. I prefer science. *I think I will be able to do it. I will have to work hard at school*' (my italics). His parents said that the boy had discussed the idea with a teacher:

> He was telling us tonight that he had mentioned to Miss —, the science teacher, that he would like to be a science teacher, and *what would he have to do* [my italics]. She said she wouldn't advise him to be a science teacher – something in science, but not a teacher.

The Asian avid readers and their parents were very conscious of the value of education and had faith in its ability to open up career prospects provided one worked very hard. The girl, Child 19, wrote: 'What I like about school is it helps you grow up and you meet more people everyday there. *You also increase your knowledge and stand a better chance of getting a job*' (my italics). Her father said: 'I think it is very good for her to be reading, for her to do school-work. She can make a better life.' The girl wanted to be an author, although she realized she might initially need another job as well; she thought possibly as a policewoman, '. . . but most of all as an author, I think I can do it. I will need a lot of skill, talent and knowledge to write a book.'

The parents of another avid reader, Child 7, spent a great deal of time discussing job possibilities with her. (The reader should bear in mind that these children were 12 or 13 at the *end* of the experiment.) The father told me:

We thought of Marks & Spencer. Well, that is an offshoot of the conversation we were having the other day – not with any motive really, but we were just saying that a firm like Marks & Spencer has so much to offer and H. is the type of person who would appreciate it – the welfare for the employees and all this sort of thing, and if you are clever it doesn't mean to say that you would stop at shop floor level – you can go higher and higher. *We were trying to explain all this to her.*

The father regretted his lack of education, '. . . because I am doing a job now which, if I were better educated, I wouldn't be doing'.

The parents of infrequent readers certainly seemed to care a great deal about their children's schooling and career prospects, but saw very little hope of having any effect upon either. Also, many of them had no faith whatsoever in the system working for them *even if* they 'played the game' and went along with its values. In fact several of the families were very suspicious of authority in any shape or form, and obviously authority embraces the educational system. Child 26's father, for instance, the only one (of those who let me into the house) who did *not* want me to tape-record the interview, greeted me with, 'What's he done?' as he opened the door and, even when I left, he still could not quite accept that I was not a member of the 'opposition'. He believed that his son could still find himself out of work, even if he worked hard at school. He said, 'If you've got a good education and no work and there's nothing to do, then you lose that, lose all the pay and that.' He saw no possibility of an intrinsic pleasure in knowledge. He fully expected his son to work in the local scrapyard like himself and the son told me that he definitely did not want a clerical job, 'Because I wouldn't know what to do, just writing and that.' He wanted to be '. . . a builder or something like that'. The point is that the father saw no good coming of education because he had seen an educated drop-out on the dole. The mother wistfully said that she would like her son to do well but she clearly did not expect him to; she had aspirations but few expectations.

> It would be nice if he did do well at school, but if they don't get 'O' levels they haven't a hope of getting an apprenticeship. But if he got summat what interested him *we wouldn't stop him* . . . L. . . . [his sister] found office work boring and went into t' knitting wool. *We'll just have to wait and see what happens* (my italics).

She is passive, not because of lack of interest, but because of her feelings of inadequacy to help and her lack of hope of success.

Another mother of an infrequent reader, Child 18, expressed a similar attitude more effectively, when she said:

> I would like him to stay on at school. I would have liked them all to have stayed on at school, *and we gave them all the choice – we didn't influence them either way* [my italics]. We said we would like you to stop on but it is your decision, because then, later on, they can't come back and say, 'Well you made me stop on', or 'You made me leave'. Like my eldest son, right up to being 15, he was going to stop on at school, and then, all of a sudden he changed his mind and left. . . . Then he had a right good job, making spectacles. It was a trade. It was a right good job, but all his other mates earned more money, and he had been there years, nearly finished his apprenticeship and he packed it in to go up to GEC driving a crane because it was more money. *We were very upset about it because he had struggled all those years* going through his apprenticeship on a low wage, you see. . . . Another has been through four jobs and he's only 20 (my italics).

Still she was not prepared to push the son who was the subject of the case study, but not because she did not care. These people did not have the self-confidence, nor confidence in their knowledge and experience, nor confidence in the relationships with their children, to attempt to influence them overtly and be prepared to take a certain amount of kicking back from their children for a while, although had a different set of attitudes been learnt at an early age and a good relationship built up, it is likely that the children would have internalized these attitudes in any case.

The mother quoted above did have contact with school but the remainder of the parents of infrequent readers did not. Many said they did not have time and some obviously avoided it like the plague. Child 14's mother rather cagily told me: 'Well, she [her daughter] has played truant a few times but I don't *think* she has been as bad lately you know.' When I asked whether she had ever thought of co-operating with the school in order to curb her children's truancy and thieving, she said, 'I've had letters to go, but I don't get in from work until half past five, anyway.' She thought the teachers knew that her daughter had been in trouble once or twice because, she said, 'I think the social workers get in touch with the teachers and that.'

Most of the infrequent readers told me that their parents *never* talked to them about school. The parents were *aware* of the importance of education but most of them simply did not know enough about it to be able to use it effectively. So much in their lives was difficult, that school could even be seen as a minor problem in some cases. The parents were honest and remarkably trusting and childlike when they spoke to me. If you have problems preventing your children climbing out of the bedroom windows and electrocuting themselves while stealing, then reading progress is not going to be at the top of your list of priorities. The most prevalent feeling that these parents communicated, in this area as in the others, was one of helplessness, a lack of ability to cope with life; there was no feeling of active control, organization, or planning for the future. Child 25's mother rather pathetically explained that her son was absent from school on a Monday because she could not get up:

Unless on a Monday when I don't get up – I'll be truthful here, you know what I mean. I'm shocking on a Monday. *My husband works nights*, you see, and I don't know if it is because I'm relaxed because he's at home that particular night, and I can't get up in the morning. But any excuse, as I say, says he's going to the shop, or his breakfast's a bit late, so he can't go into school.

Child 12's mother was afraid to let me see the inside of the house; and I was told by the school staff that the parents of Child 5 who would not let me visit their home were totally 'anti-school' in every way – even to the extent of never letting their son join in extra-curricular activities or take small amounts of money for things; therefore, he often felt left out. I think this is indicative of fear and ignorance.

One of the most striking aspects of these interviews is the fact that although the parents of the avid readers often began by asking *me* about the Book Flood, there was no suggestion from either the parents or the children that their reading habits had been in any way affected by the Book Flood, although the avid readers had been *pleased* about the arrival of the books. It seems that the teacher in the inner city experimental school was right when she said that it would be the reasonably able readers, but who were not already keen readers because of lack of encouragement at home, who would be more likely to benefit than those who were already habitual readers or those who were totally antagonistic towards reading because of fear/inability. In fact, this was the case in our study where the moderate readers of moderate ability often developed a keen interest at least for the duration of the experiment, whether they were in the 'flooded' schools or not, possibly because of the attention I gave them as the subjects of case studies.

6 Results of the Tests and other Comparisons

The tools for measurement in the Social Sciences are much less perfect and precise than the tools of the natural scientist. We have nothing that can compare with the precision of the ruler, the thermometer, or the numerous laboratory instruments (Ary, D., Jacobs, L.C., and Razawich A., Introduction to Research in Education, *Holt, Rinehart & Winston, USA, 1972).*

1 Results of pre-testing in the schools

In any investigation in which matched groups are used the results are inevitably less dependable if the matching proves faulty in some way. Since our schools were chosen for us by the Chief Adviser we anticipated that the children in each pair of schools would be closely similar in social background and consequently in their performance in the Cattell Culture Fair Test and in the reading tests. It was a considerable disappointment, therefore, to discover that although the schools may have been equal for administrative purposes, the average difference in the Culture Fair Test for one pair was almost 10 points and for the other pair about 5·5 points. An average difference of 2 or 3 points would have been acceptable, and might not have been significant in view of the wide spread of ability between children in any one school; but a difference so great as 10 points, on average, is substantial and is likely to affect all scholastic comparisons not only prior to, but also during, the experiment.

The problem was increased when experimental and control schools were selected by lots before the extent of these differences were known; and it so happened that in each case the school where pupils' performance was superior was chosen to receive additional books.

This has necessarily affected the analyses subsequent to the experiment. Had the schools been initially approximately equal we could have performed several analyses of variance on final scores to determine whether the Book Flood had been effective and what variables interacted during the course of the investigation.

While it is possible, even with poorly matched schools, to perform a four-way analysis of variance on the effects of school location, age, sex and treatment (i.e. receiving a book flood or having no additional books), it is mainly the interactions rather than main effects that are interesting. We needed therefore, in addition, to devise other ways of making comparisons between groups that were initially equal allowing, so far as possible, for the effects of inequalities between the schools (to the informed reader 'statistically controlled for').

Table 6·1 shows that whereas there was little difference between the children in attitudes towards reading or in the NFER AD sentence completion test, the difference between them was greater in both the Schonell Test of reading words and in the Edinburgh Test of reading comprehension. The latter were not so considerable as that in the Culture Fair Test, possibly because, like most tests of achievement, they are more susceptible to the influences of schooling than is a test of non-verbal reasoning.

Table 6·1   Some initial measures (mean quotients or scores and numbers of children)

Test	Outer city Experimental		Control		Inner city Experimental		Control	
	Mean	N	Mean	N	Mean	N	Mean	N
Schonell (reading age)	11·0	73	9·9	78	10·2	90	10·1	83
Edinburgh (reading quotient)	94·3	73	89·8	75	93·1	88	90·8	82
Cattell { A form	96·2	73	86·5	78	93·3	88	89·7	84
Quotient { B form	104·5	73	96·8	78	103·1	88	97·0	84
full scale	100·5	73	91·5	78	98·3	88	93·2	84
NFER AD Test quotient	95·0	70	92·5	78	93·4	89	91·4	84
Teachers' Attitude Assessment	4·5	72	4·9	78	4·4	88	4·5	84
Reading Attitude Scale	7·7	73	7·9	78	7·2	89	7·5	83
Askov Inventory	8·1	73	7·9	78	6·9	90	7·4	83
Sharples–Reid scale	5·6	73	6·1	77	5·4	89	5·2	84

Note: A more detailed table can be found in Appendix VII.

In attempts to cope with initial inequalities between the children in experimental and control schools a number of additional comparisons were introduced. First, pupils in the fourth year in each school in 1978 who had not been involved in the investigation were given the NFER EH2. This enabled us to compare their scores with those of fourth-years in 1979 who had been involved in the investigation since 1976. Second, matched pairs of children were selected from each pair of schools and their final scores in the Edinburgh Test were compared. Third, an analysis of co-variance technique was employed. This is a method which, under given conditions, is well suited to the problems that arise in educational experiments due to difficulty in taking genuinely random or comparable samples. Adjustments are made to the criterion measures on the basis of initial performance, and the adjusted measures (i.e. test scores of fourth-year pupils) are subjected to an analysis of variance.

Each of these methods involves assumptions, and problems of interpretation necessarily follow if the assumptions are not fully complied with. These will be mentioned as results are reported.

In addition another kind of analysis of the test scores has been used: multiple regression analysis. This is outlined at the end of the chapter.

Before proceeding to report on and discuss the various analyses, we will look in more detail at the initial and final test scores. Appendix VII shows numbers of children taking each test, mean test scores and standard deviations for boys and girls separately in each school. Some selected results are considered here.

2 Changes in test scores and ratings

2.1 Children's attitudes to reading
Table 6·2 shows mean ratings given by teachers and scores obtained by the children in the three attitude tests.

Table 6·2   Changes in attitude: ratings and scores

Location		Inner city				Outer city			
Treatment		Experimental		Control		Experimental		Control	
Year		2	4	2	4	2	4	2	4
		(numbers of children range from 34 to 50; see Appendix VII)							
	Sex								
Teacher's ratings	B	4·3	4·1	4·5	3·9	4·2	4·5	4·6	4·5
	G	4·5	4·7	4·6	4·2	4·9	5·3	5·2	4·9
Children's scores									
Bradford Reading									
Attitude	B	6·8	7·1	6·9	7·0	7·2	7·2	7·5	7·3
	G	7·7	7·8	7·9	8·3	8·1	8·4	8·3	8·1
Askov Inventory	B	5·4	6·3	5·9	8·8	6·3	8·0	7·0	8·5
	G	8·9	10·1	8·5	12·3	10·1	10·6	9·1	12·9
Sharples–Reid test	B	5·1	5·1	4·8	5·1	5·1	5·3	5·6	4·9
	G	5·8	5·6	5·6	6·1	6·1	5·8	6·9	5·6

Comparing second- with fourth-year ratings, it is evident that teachers have a tendency to see children's attitudes to reading as rather less favourable in the fourth year than in the second; five of the eight differences are negative. The children's scores, on the other hand, indicate that their attitude may be more favourable in the fourth year than in the second; only five of the twenty-four differences are negative. However, Fisher's exact probability test

for the 2×2 table

3	5
5	19

shows that this difference is certainly not significant, since the probability of such a result is 0·85.

Also, as we noted in Chapter 1, the Askov Test, although reliable, has questionable validity as a test of reading interests. It seems likely that it is even less valid for adolescents than for children since the choice of activities alternative to reading is often for active ones such as children enjoy; social activities or listening to records – which are more likely to appeal to adolescents – are not included in the available choices. In the outer city control schools there are negative changes in both the other tests, between fourth and second years, which suggest that the rise in the Askov Test scores may indicate avoidance of various activities rather than positive preference for reading. Or perhaps, if children do read more, it may be at home and about pop stars or other popular adolescents' interests.

2.2   Ability to read words (Schonell Test)

In Table 6·3 reading ages are shown in the Schonell Test in comparison with chronological age at the time of testing. In the second year, each reading age is lower than the corresponding chronological age in three schools, whereas by the fourth year each reading age is superior to chronological age: as chronological age rises by 2·35 years on average, the Schonell Reading Age rises by 3·63 years on average, i.e. more than half as much again. The change is approximately equally substantial for experimental and control schools. Fisher's exact probability test for this 2×2 table i.e.

6	2
0	8

(six below, two above; none below, eight above) gives the probability of such a difference in independent sample by chance alone as 1 in 286. Since the probability that identical samples will differ so greatly must be less, the change is therefore highly significant.

Table 6·3   Schonell Reading Age and chronological age

Location	Inner city				Outer city			
Treatment	Experimental		Control		Experimental		Control	
Age/School year	2	4	2	4	2	4	2	4
Sex								
M Schonell Reading Age	10·2	13·8	10·0	14·2	10·9	13·8	9·9	13·4
Gain	3·6		4·3		2·9		3·5	
Chronological age	(10·6)	(13·0)	(10·5)	(12·8)	(10·6)	(13·0)	(10·7)	(13·1)
F Schonell Reading Age	10·2	14·0	10·1	14·0	11·2	14·6	9·9	13·4
Gain	3·8		3·9		3·4		3·5	
Chronological age	(10·6)	(13·0)	(10·7)	(13·0)	(10·6)	(13·0)	(10·5)	(12·9)

Note: Numbers of children in each category range from 34 to 50 (see Appendix VII).

A possible explanation of the superiority of the fourth year as compared with the second is that the teaching of reading is very effective in all four schools in so far as it involves word recognition. In addition, part of the increase in scores in the control schools may be due to the tendency mentioned in Chapter 1 for those who do poorly initially to improve their performance on a second occasion, i.e. for a regression towards the mean; there is some suggestion here of a relationship of this kind. In the control schools where initial scores were low, gains in Schonell Reading Age are large, whereas in experimental schools gains are less substantial than in the matched school. This may be the result of a smaller regression effect, if any, since performance in the experimental schools was closer to the population mean of 100, initially.

2.3   Reading comprehension (Edinburgh Test)

Table 6·4 shows mean scores on the Edinburgh Reading Test in the second and fourth years, and gains between these years, in comparison with mean quotients in Cattell's Culture Fair Test obtained in the second year. Although the extension of the Edinburgh Test for use with older groups was available in 1979, in view of the rather low scores of many of these children in 1976, we decided to use the test intended for children aged up to 12 years. This provided sufficient scope for all but a few of the abler children but did not enable us to obtain reading quotients for the fourth year. Consequently, raw scores are used in the table.

Table 6·4   Edinburgh Test raw scores and Cattell Culture Fair Test quotients

Location		Inner city				Outer city			
Treatment		Experimental		Control		Experimental		Control	
Year		2	4	2	4	2	4	2	4
Sex									
M	Edinburgh raw score	60·1	96·6	53·2	92·8	60·3	104·1	55·0	90·8
	Gain	36·5		39·6		43·8		35·8	
	Cattell quotient	(98·9)		(90·6)		(99·1)		(94·0)	
F	Edinburgh raw score	62·7	104·5	56·7	87·4	66·9	107·7	52·6	83·0
	Gain	41·8		30·7		40·8		30·3	
	Cattell quotient	(97·5)		(95·1)		(102·0)		(88·3)	
Totals for both sexes	Edinburgh raw score	61·3	100·1	55·2	89·6	63·5	105·8	54·0	87·5
	Gain	38·8		34·4		42·3		33·5	
	Cattell quotient	(98·3)		(93·2)		(100·5)		(91·5)	

Note: Numbers of children in each category range from 32 to 50 (see Appendix VII).

For this reason, we must be cautious in interpreting gains since we do not know whether it is easier to make larger gains when higher scores are reached or whether gains can be expected to be equal, whatever the initial scores, if equal progress is made.

Assuming the latter, inspection of gains here suggests that a regression towards the mean is operating, if at all, only in the inner city schools. In outer city schools the difference between experimental and control schools increases; in the experimental school the final over-all score is high, while in the control school, where children had the lowest quotients in the Cattell Fair Test, relative performance falls even further. However, in the inner city schools the over-all difference in the Culture Fair Test initially was about 5 points whereas in the outer city schools it was nearly 10.

These differences may be seen either as evidence that children having poor intelligence inevitably do less well relatively in tests of comprehension as they grow older, or as an indication that teachers are less successful in teaching comprehension than in teaching reading skills. There is some evidence from programmes for young disadvantaged children that intelligence quotients, or academic achievement involving reasoning skills, can be raised by suitable experiences. These all involve activities in which the children take part and are usually initiated in talking with mothers, teachers or older children (Black and Solomon, 1968; Gordon, 1972; Lombard, 1973; Bruner, 1980). It is significant too, perhaps, that even university students can gain points of verbal IQ by taking part in an activity that obliges them to think. When science students were asked to describe apparatus to each other, to assist them in writing experimental reports, they not only learned to do this more clearly but incidentally increased their scores in Heim's AH5 verbal intelligence test (Loewenthal and Kostrevski, 1973).

In both cases, whether with young children or students, the exercises were ones that continuously involved them in thinking, often putting thoughts into words and receiving immediate feedback on their success from an adult, in the case of children, or from a fellow student. In schools, children are rarely so intensively involved in thinking things out for themselves. Additional reading may not help greatly, for when children choose their own books the level of comprehension required may increase little, if at all, from one volume to the next unless someone is there to advise them wisely as to choice and, if comprehension required increases rather steeply, to assist them when they need help.

A four-way analysis of variance taking only thirty-two boys and thirty-two girls in each school, using initial and final scores in the Edinburgh Test, shows that there are few significant effects (Table 6·5).

As would be expected, the most highly significant effect is that due to age. The 'treatment' effect, although highly significant, is confounded with ability; thus differences obtained between experimental and control schools may be as much, or more, due to differences in reading ability and intelligence than to the Book Flood. The interaction between treatment and sex can be seen in Table 6·3. In both pairs of schools scores of the girls are higher than those of the boys in experimental schools, whereas in control schools the scores of girls are generally lower than those of the boys. This is more marked in the outer city schools where girls in the control school had a particularly low score in the Cattell Culture Fair Test in their second year at school. Since the scores in year two and year four are those of the same children, they are closer together than in a design where a random selection of children is used. This is allowed for in the analysis of variance by analysing the total sum of squares into between subject effects and within subject effects, the latter involving age. When this is done, the interaction of treatment with age is significant at the ·01 level; the children in experimental schools increase their advantage over those in control schools, especially in the case of the girls. The interaction of age and sex approaches significance at the ·05 level;

the boys in these schools, though inferior to girls in both second and fourth years, have nevertheless made a relatively greater improvement; or perhaps we should say that the girls, especially in the control schools (which were initially poorer), have lagged behind.

Table 6·5   Four-way analysis of variance using Edinburgh Test scores

Effect	S.S.	d.f.	M.S.	F	Proba- bility	Signi- ficance
Between subjects	367437·7	255				
Location	413·3	1	where df = 1	0·3		
Sex	1275·1	1	M.S. = S.S.	0·9		
Treatment	10206·6	1		7·3	<·01	**
Loc./Sex	108·8	1		0·1		
Loc./Treat.	261·6	1		0·2		
Sex/Treat.	7275·2	1		5·2	<·0.5	*
Loc./Sex/Treat.	159·8	1		0·1		
error (between)	347737·3	248	1402·2			
Within subjects	222583·0	256				
Age	186507·8	1		1354·4	<·001	***
Age/Loc.	9·0	1		0·		
Age/Sex	480·5	1		3·5	near ·05	
Age/Treat.	1345·5	1		9·8	<·01	**
Age/Loc./Sex	3·8	1		0·0		
Age/Loc./Treat.	48·8	1		0·4		
Age/Sex/Treat.	0·7	1		0·0		
Age/Loc./Sex/Treat.	37·1	1		0·3		
error (within)	34149·8	248	137			
Total	590020·7	511				

*** For significance at ·001 level, with degrees of freedom one and infinity $F \geqslant 10·0$.

** For significance at ·01 level, with degrees of freedom one and infinity $F \geqslant 6·6$.

* For significance at ·05 level, with degrees of freedom one and infinity $F \geqslant 3·8$.

3 Within schools comparison of fourth-years 1978 (pre-Book Flood) and 1979

In Table 6·6 mean scores are given for children in the schools in their fourth year, figures in brackets representing mean scores on the NFER EH2 when immigrants' scores have been removed. However, the reader should bear in mind that, because of the difficulty of the test, its value is doubtful, particularly at the lower end of the ability range.

Table 6·6   Scores of fourth-years 1978, 1979

Treatment Location	Experimental				Control			
	Outer city		Inner city		Outer city		Inner city	
Sex	Boys	Girls	Boys	Girls	Boys	Girls	Boys	Girls
Number of children	37	32	46	37	43	32	32	46
1978	95·8	96·8	98·8	100·6	94·6	96·2	95·5	95·3
	(97·1)	(97·1)	(100·9)	(101·5)		(96·3)		
Number of children	37	40	41	47	45	45	44	35
1979	95·4	98·6	98·4	100·6	94·0	93·1	93·4	94·5
			(99·8)	(102·5)			(96·9)	(96·5)

Assumptions underlying this comparison are that successive fourth-years in the same school are approximately equal in intelligence, on average, and that their experiences in school have been similar, so leading to similar performance in reading measures. Since the Cattell Culture Fair Test was not administered to the 1978 fourth-years there could conceivably have been some marked difference in intelligence; but it is unlikely to have been considerable, or in the same direction, in all four schools. Teaching of reading could also have been more, or less, effective for children in successive years in a school; but, again, it is improbable that children in all four schools would have had an advantage in one year or the other. If these assumptions are correct – since it is evident from the table of means that there are only very slight differences between them – on the basis of this comparison we must conclude that the Book Flood made no difference to performance in the NFER EH2, although the test would not discriminate effectively except among the most able pupils.

It is appropriate at this point, perhaps, to note a second cause of concern about the choice of schools. When visiting the four schools and in talking with headmasters, we found that they had made every effort to obtain a good supply of books for the children. Although these may not have been in class-rooms, there were several thousand books in each school, reaching a total of about 9000 in one school. An additional 5000 books need not then make a very substantial difference.

4   Comparisons of matched samples in experimental and control schools

There are many ways of matching samples using these test results. It would be possible to match children on one variable only, for example by their Cattell Culture Fair Test score, or their initial score on the Edinburgh Reading Test, prior to comparing their test scores in the fourth year in one of the reading or attitude tests. Here children have been matched twice in four ways simultaneously: first by intelligence test score, initial age, and scores in the Edinburgh Test obtained initially and in the first pre-test and, secondly, by age, intelligence quotient, AD test score and initial Schonell Reading Age. In both instances their final scores on the Edinburgh Test have been compared. These comparisons are essentially scholastic ones, wholly neglecting attitudes to reading.

Using the first method, it proved possible to match twenty-two pairs of boys and eighteen pairs of girls in the outer city schools. Comparison of their final score showed that boys in the experimental schools gained on average 6·7 points higher in the Edinburgh Test in the fourth year than those in the control school. Girls in the experimental school scored only 1·8 points higher on average than their matched pairs. Neither of these differences is significant since the spread of the difference scores is considerable. For inner city schools the corresponding difference for twenty-two pairs of girls is 4·9 points higher for those in the experimental school; but boys in the experimental school scored *less* than their matched pair (twenty-one pairs) by an average of 6·3 points. Again, these differences are not significant.

When matched by the second method, differences were smaller. In inner city schools, differences between twenty-one pairs of boys and thirty pairs of girls in the Edinburgh Test in their fourth year were little above zero on average. For outer city schools where *twenty-four* pairs of boys and *twenty-three* pairs of girls have been matched, differences are positive in favour of experimental schools in both cases, but by only 1·7 on average for the boys and 3·7 on average for the girls; these differences are too small to be significant.

Since the samples were so unequally matched in the first place, taking matched pairs of children in these ways necessarily omits the most able in the experimental schools and the least able in control schools. While the small differences between pairs of children of average ability suggests slight, if any, differences between experimental and control schools, it could be that the effects of having additional new books would be felt most among children at the extremes of ability, although case studies suggest that it was the middle ability band that was most likely to be affected, as the majority of the most able pupils was accustomed to having books at home and the least able, although attracted to the books, first of all needed help with the mechanics of reading. For this reason it is desirable to attempt to take out the effects of initial inequalities in the Cattell Culture Fair Test and the other tests in which experimental and control school children scored very unequally, in order to see whether there is any evidence of effects of the Book Flood in the final adjusted scores.

There are problems in attempting to do this. However, analysis of co-variance is a suitable method for designs such as that of the Book Flood Experiment in which independent variables, like test scores and ages, are used in conjunction with non-metric factors such as sex, school location and treatments. It can easily adjust for differences in age between the samples; but in adjusting for differences in test scores it cannot, of course, allow for continuing differences in treatment of samples such as different methods of organizing and teaching children that may affect their performance throughout the ensuing experiment. Similarly, it can adjust for initial differences in intelligence test scores, but cannot do so for the continuing effects on learning of having higher intelligence. In addition, a number of conditions must be satisfied for the method to be used meaningfully.

5   Analysis of co-variance

The aim in analyses of co-variance is to adjust final scores on the basis of scores in which treatment groups differ initially so that final differences can be attributed to the experimental treatment alone. An assumption, therefore, in making an analysis of co-variance, is that there are no systematic differences between groups during the experiment except that due to the treatment; in this case having many additional books. In other words, if the children's scores in each pair of schools are adjusted so that they begin from an equal base any differences in their fourth-year scores should be due to the Book Flood. Accounts of the schools in Chapter 2 may raise some doubts as to whether this is possible. One school streamed children at first, while others did not, and differences of skill in teaching reading among class and specialist teachers from school to school were evident, but uncontrollable. In addition, it seems possible that although we can remove the initial effect of differences in the Cattell Test of intelligence test, the factors that led to low or high achievement initially might continue to operate and so to affect performance during the experiment also.

For all of these reasons, any significant differences obtained between the adjusted scores of experimental and control samples may be due, in part at least, to uncontrolled differences between the schools. Equally, differences that might have been found had teachers and classes been more exactly matched may have been annulled due to chance differences between the schools.

A second assumption is that the adjusted fourth-year scores have the same mean and variance and are normally distributed. This depends largely on basing the adjustment of these scores on measures in which children initially differed most. All of the distributions of initial measures are, of course, approximately normally distributed.

A third assumption is that the regression of final on initial measures is the same for all treatment populations and that this regression is linear.

In analyses of this kind it is quite usual for final scores to be adjusted for differences between treatment groups in up to three initial measures, say (i)–(iii) in Table 6·7; and it is sometimes asserted that it is rarely worth while to adjust for more than three differences. As the computer can handle adjustments for differences in up to five initial measures it is possible to put this to the test.

In this instance in the first analysis, (1), on the left-hand side of Table 6·7, final scores have been adjusted with respect to variables in which experimental and control schools differed substantially initially even if, as in the Schonell Test, only one pair of schools differed greatly. Although differences in ages are comparatively small, final scores have been adjusted for these too since it is well known, for instance, that children who enter school at different times of year may progress significantly differently.

It will be seen that the effect of these adjustments is different for the two pairs of schools. In the outer city schools no differences remain to be attributed to the Book Flood; in the inner city schools differences in the Schonell and Edinburgh Tests are significant in the fourth year for boys and girls respectively. It makes little difference if the scores of immigrant Asian children (some of whom are fairly new to this country or use little English at home) are excluded.

A second analysis of co-variance, (2), is included on the right-hand side of the table to show the consequence of failing to adjust for a variable in which the outer city schools differed substantially, i.e. the Schonell Test. It might be argued that to allow for differences in the first three, scholastic variables would be sufficient to account for differences in the Schonell Test too. The second analysis shows that this is not the case. If no adjustment is made for the considerable difference in initial scores in the Schonell Test between the experimental and control school, a number of

Table 6·7 Significant results in analyses of co-variance

Significant differences between adjusted fourth-year scores of experimental
and control samples:

(1) Scores adjusted from second-
year measures of:
    (i) age at testing
    (ii) Edinburgh Test raw score
    (iii) Cattell full-scale IQ
    (iv) Schonell Test raw score

(2) Scores adjusted from second-
year measures of:
    (i) age at testing
    (ii) Edinburgh Test raw score
    (iii) Cattell full-scale IQ
    (iv) Reading Attitude Scale
    (v) Askov Inventory

(W) indicates white indigenous population only

Boys in outer city schools

Test	F	Probability	Test	F	Probability
none significant			Edinburgh	6·09	0·016**
			Test	6·50(W)	0·013(W)**
			Number of	14·99	0·001***
			books	14·30(W)	(negative) (W)
			read		

Girls in outer city schools

Test	F	Probability	Test	F	Probability
none significant			Number of	14·00	0·001***
			books	14·74(W)	0·001(W)***
			read		(negative)

Boys in inner city schools

Test	F	Probability	Test	F	Probability
Schonell	3·60	0·062	Schonell	4·79	0·032*
Test raw	3·46(W)	0·068	Test raw	5·09(W)	0·028(W)*
score			score		

Girls in inner city schools

Test	F	Probability	Test	F	Probability
Edinburgh	8·49	0·005**	Edinburgh	6·71	0·012*
Test raw	10·22(W)	0·002**	Test raw	7·58(W)	0·008(W)**
score			score		

* Significant at ·05 level or higher.
**   ,,   ·01 level or higher.
***   ,,   ·001 level or higher.

differences in the fourth year might be attributed to the effect of the
Book Flood. Instead they must be attributed to differences in skill
in reading words initially and – in the case of the negative finding
that number of books read by boys in the experimental school was
very significantly fewer than in the control school – to a difference
in the schools which, perhaps, also accounts for the high initial
score in the Schonell Test at the experimental school. For instance,
teachers there may believe in systematic drilling in reading rather
than allowing children to browse.

The reader may consider that the effect of including the second-
year Schonell Test raw scores among the independent variables

might be clearer if scores in the Reading Attitude Scale and Askov Inventory were not included in the second analysis. When this was attempted, however, the measures of attitude seemed to make only a slight difference, except in the case of boys in outer city schools where significance of differences in the Edinburgh Test was lower when initial attitude scores were not taken into account.

6 Regression analysis

Regression analysis is used in experiments to determine which initial measures may serve to predict final scores. Predictive effects of the independent variables are calculated from the matrix of correlations which includes in this case the criterion measure (fourth-year scores in one of the tests) and scores in initial tests.

A problem arises when several of the initial, predictor, variables are highly correlated. This implies that they are measuring something in common and may, in addition, make some other unique contribution. For example, scores in the Cattell Culture Fair Test and the Edinburgh Test are highly correlated since both measure reasoning, or comprehension, but one is a visual test and the other is verbal; what they measure in common is reasoning ability, while their unique contributions are perceptual and verbal in nature. Consequently, if the regression analysis selects one of those tests because it measures reasoning, it will not select the other unless its unique component is separately predictive of success in the fourth-year test under consideration. Slight differences in a battery of tests can tip the balance as to which test is selected.

Perhaps this instability is not so important here as we are concerned solely with any effect of the Book Flood over and above the effects of reasoning and children's initial perceptual or verbal skills. However, since the Book Flood was introduced in schools when children were relatively good at reasoning there may well be a tendency for it to take a lower place when reasoning tests are selected first than it would have done in a better balanced experiment. Results follow, in Table 6·8, showing levels of significance and the amount of variance that each initial test 'accounts' for.

Study of regression equations based on these analyses shows that for both sexes in outer city schools and for boys in inner city schools, second-year scores most predictive of fourth-year scores in the Edinburgh Test are those in the Edinburgh Test itself, the Cattell Culture Fair Test and the Schonell Test. For girls in inner city schools, their second-year score in the Cattell Test is less important in this prediction.

Also for the first three groups, the best predictor of fourth-year scores in the Schonell Test is their score in this test in the second year. For inner city girls, however, the second-year score in this test is not so good a predictor; a high score in the Sharples–Reid test in the second year is negatively, and age positively, related with score in the fourth year, although their contributions are not large.

As might be expected, since attitudes are less enduring than skills or abilities, there are no good predictors among second-year scores of the fourth-year attitude scores. Conceivably, there may have been clearer patterns emerging if regression equations for experimental and control schools were contrasted, but this seemed unlikely and time did not allow a further analysis.

Table 6·8   Regression analysis

Dependent variable	Subjects	Independent variables (significant predictors only)	F	Sig. level/p
Books read in third year	o.c. Boys	Edinburgh raw score	7·8	0·006
		Book Flood	7·8	0·006
		Age at testing	5·4	0·022
	o.c. Girls	Book Flood	13·3	0·001
		Cattell Culture Fair Test	6·0	0·016
	i.c. Boys	None significant		
	i.c. Girls	None significant		
(1) Edinburgh raw score (year 4)	o.c. boys	Edinburgh raw score (yr 2)	126·8	0·000
		Schonell raw score (yr 2)	15·8	0·000
		Cattell Culture Fair Test	8·0	0·006
		Bradford Reading Att.	5·8	0·019
	o.c. Girls	Edinburgh raw score (yr 2)	139·4	0·000
		Cattell Culture Fair Test	12·4	0·001
		Schonell raw score (yr 2)	9·1	0·004
	i.c. Boys	Schonell raw score (yr 2)	155·6	0·000
		Cattell Culture Fair Test	21·3	0·000
		Edinburgh raw score (yr 2)	6·6	0·012
		Age when tested (yr 2)	3·9	0·051
	i.c. Girls	Edinburgh raw score (yr 2)	117·2	0·000
		Schonell raw score (yr 2)	9·9	0·002
		★Book Flood	8·1	0·006
		Sharples–Reid	4·4	0·038
		Cattell Culture Fair Test	6·3	0·014
(2) Schonell raw score (year 4)	o.c. Boys	Schonell raw score (yr 2)	94·1	0·000
	o.c. Girls	Schonell raw score (yr 2)	35·0	0·000
	i.c. Boys	Schonell raw score (yr 2)	12·0	0·001
		★Book Flood	6·9	0·010
	i.c. Girls	★Book Flood	19·8	0·000
		Age when tested	7·4	0·008

Table 6·8 cont.

Dependent variable	Subjects	Independent variables (significant predictors only)	F	Sig. level/p
(3) Reading Attitude Scale (year 4)	o.c. Boys o.c. Girls	Reading Attitude Scale (yr 2)	15·1	0·000
	i.c. Boys	Reading Attitude Scale (yr 2)	11·1	0·001
		Edinburgh raw score (yr 2)	3·9	0·052
	i.c. Girls	Reading Attitude Scale (yr 2)	6·6	0·012
(4) Askov Inventory (year 4)	o.c. Boys	Askov Inventory (yr 2)	14·2	0·000
		Bradford Reading Att. (yr 2)	9·0	0·004
	o.c. Girls	Askov (yr 2)	8·4	0·005
		★Book Flood	6·5	0·013
	i.c. Boys	Askov (yr 2)	21·2	0·000
		Edinburgh raw score (yr 2)	4·8	0·031
	i.c. Girls	Askov (yr 2)	20·2	0·000
		★Book Flood	4·8	0·031
(5) Sharples–Reid	o.c. Boys o.c. Girls	Edinburgh raw score (yr 2)	9·3	0·003
	i.c. Boys	Askov (yr 2)	14·9	0·000
		Edinburgh raw score (yr 2)	3·8	0·054
	i.c. Girls	Bradford Reading Att.	10·2	0·002
		Askov (yr 2)	4·7	0·033
		Sharples–Reid (yr 2)	5·0	0·028
(6) No. of books read in year 3	o.c. Boys	Edinburgh raw score (yr 2)	7·8	0·006
		Book Flood	7·8	0·006
		Age at time of testing (yr 2)	5·4	0·022
	o.c. Girls	Book Flood	13·3	0·001
		Cattell Culture Fair Test	6·0	0·016
	i.c. Boys	None significant		
	i.c. Girls	None significant		

o.c. = outer city.
i.c. = inner city.
★indicates an area in which the Book Flood appeared to have had a significant effect upon children's reading skills.

7 Conclusions and Recommendations

In this final chapter I shall attempt to draw conclusions and, where appropriate, make recommendations. Although for convenience I shall deal with each chapter separately, there will inevitably be some overlap.

Chapter 1

A common problem faced by researchers in recent years, and most likely *to be faced* in subsequent years, is inadequacy of funds. In our case this limitation affected the research in two ways: first, in that we had to limit ourselves to four schools if research staff were to be able to fulfil their commitments; and, secondly, in that the research had to be completed *within* four years, with the result that the research team had to launch into the testing programme in schools prematurely as there had been inadequate time for preparation, particularly of questionnaires and of attitude measures. Ideally, the first year of the experiment, or an additional first year, would have been allocated to choosing and matching schools, designing test and questionnaire material, selecting tests of reading skills, and carrying out pilot studies; and an *entire* final year, after data collection, would have been devoted to data analysis and writing up, which would have been facilitated by additional staffing, also dependent upon funding.

Chapter 6

Although in the analyses of test data the Book Flood (BF) features eight times among significant factors of success in reading skills in a number of measures in the children's final year of the middle school, we are unable to say *with certainty* that this is due to the Book Flood as such. The success may be attributable instead, or more likely in addition, to differences between the schools that received the Book Flood and those that did not.

Indeed, it may be concluded that *in terms of test results* the effects of the Book Flood seem to be slight or negligible. Although it must be admitted that the test results have not been fully exploited because of pressure to complete the report within a short time, it is unlikely that other significant results would have been found had more time been available for statistical analysis and interpretation.

The most significant result reported in Chapter 6 is that children of both sexes *in all four schools* considerably increased their Schonell Reading Ages. Since the co-variance analyses show that differences between schools initially in Schonell Reading Age contributed significantly to success in reading tests in the final year of the experiment, this is an achievement that is likely to have a favourable effect upon performance during the upper school years. There is a possibility that simply taking part in an experiment of this kind, knowing that the pupils' reading skills are to be tested at intervals, especially bearing in mind the interest in reading displayed by all four headmasters in that they expressed a wish to take part in the experiment, would have the effect of giving both staff and pupils an additional spur to their efforts. Perhaps one of the chief lessons to be learned from this exercise is that we should *do more* to help children read competently in the middle and upper schools, and should *draw attention* to what we are doing in interesting and stimulating ways.

The significant interaction found between sex and treatment may indeed indicate that the Book Flood was more beneficial to girls. However, it could also reflect differences between attitudes in schools and, more likely, *chance* differences between girls, or boys, in pairs of schools.

Had money been available to enlarge the experiment, including another two pairs of schools, it would have been possible to use specified teaching methods in half the experimental and half the control schools to determine whether the way teachers *used books* would influence children's success, either with or without a book flood. Observations suggest that, granted a 'sufficiency' of books, the way in which they are used may be critical for the development of reading habits and interests if not for reading skills, at least as registered by the measures used in this experiment. Indeed, the greatest effect of the Book Flood seems to have been in this area of habits and interests.

Chapter 3

1 The differences between children's reading habits and interests in the four schools were far more striking than the differences in reading skills as measured by the Edinburgh and Schonell Reading Tests. However, comparable with the improvement in Schonell Reading Ages in all four schools noted above, was the fact that teachers, again in *all four* schools, reported an increased *awareness* of book titles, series, authors, the processes involved in choosing books, and other reading-related processes, all of which they attributed to the continual use of the Reading Record Form for the entire three years of the experiment. Many teachers expressed their intention to use a simplified version of the questionnaire after the end of the experiment, as it had the effect of actively involving the child as well as being informative to the teacher, thus facilitating an informed discussion between teacher and child, probably once or twice a term, about the child's reading habits and interests. I cannot over-emphasize the importance of *following up* the record with *discussion* as I believe that one of the reasons for the children's heightened awareness and enthusiasm was the fact that someone was interested in what they read, sufficiently interested to go into school and talk to them about their reading in an informed and involved way.

2 The differences between the kinds of books read in control as opposed to experimental schools substantially reflect the differences in availability; similarly, the differences in amount of reading undertaken in different years in each school substantially reflect the amount of time made available to pupils for personal private reading in school – there is nothing remarkable in these findings. What *is* remarkable is the vast difference between the amounts of reading recorded in the experimental schools *after* the first year of the experiment, given an almost identical supply of books. The differences are, admittedly, differences as recorded on the Reading Record Form, for which no one would wish to claim 100 per cent accuracy, but they are differences freely confirmed by pupils, by teachers, and by my own observation. It must be admitted also that the differences did not affect the children's reading skills as measured on certain reading tests. However, I believe that reading affects people in ways other than those that are measurable by reading tests; that, if the same children *continue* to read a great deal in the upper school, their reading skills could be affected, especially when compared with children who have far fewer books available than did *any* of the children in the four schools involved in the experiment – the most impoverished school had almost 8000 books in school and class libraries; and that their reading skills probably

were affected in ways which our reading tests failed to register, not being sufficiently sensitive to do so.

3   The fact that in the inner city experimental school the children recorded not only an increasing number of books, but also an increasing variety of authors and titles (see Table 7·1), suggests that children are more likely to tackle a wide variety of authors and titles when that choice is readily available and accessible to them; they may, indeed, read as *many* books, as they did in the final year at the inner city control school (1250 recorded as opposed to 1240 in the matched experimental school), but they will not come face to face with the same variety, at least not in school. However, making available the wide choice is obviously a necessary but not a sufficient condition for children to *read* the wide variety of books; this fact is made manifest by the Reading Record Form returns for the outer city experimental school where children reported – on the Reading Record Forms, in group discussions, and during case studies – reading a decreasing number of books, tackling fewer new authors and titles, and having a decreasing amount of time made available for personal private reading in school; simultaneously, they reported lack of access to teachers who were well informed about the books available.

Table 7·1   Increases (+) and decreases (−) in total number of books recorded, in number of individual authors recorded, and in number of separate titles recorded, between the first and final years of the experiment

	Inner city Exp.	Inner city Cont.	Outer city Exp.	Outer city Cont.
No. of returns	+464	+660	−630	+335
No. of authors	+226	−45	−99	+76
No. of titles	+471	+8	−305	+17

Many children, particularly the average and less-able readers, experience difficulty when embarking upon a new author, a fact partly reflected in the addiction to the security provided by a series of books. Children often need reassurance and guidance as they can soon be deterred if they tackle a number of books that are far too difficult or totally unappealing in subject matter or style. They also need the confidence that can come only from success so that care is needed in guiding children to books that stretch them but are not too demanding; also, I believe, they should be allowed to regress from time to time particularly when they experience physical, academic or emotional setbacks. Making available a wide variety of books is not enough; we need to know the children and the books; we also need to *continue to teach the children to read these books*. Many teachers reported less-able readers asking for help with reading after the Book Flood books arrived, as those children presumably saw a future reward for their efforts; we need to make the acquisition of reading skills an attractive proposition. 'Reading on the whole is educational and enjoyable if you are confident enough'! (ibid., Child 15.)

4   One irrefutable fact that emerged from the analysis of the Reading Record Forms was the extent to which children discussed with one another the books they read (see Table 3·11). Children, quite rightly, feel that if a friend who has similar interests and reading ability enjoyed a particular book, then they are quite probable to like it also. Teachers can, and many do, exploit this fact in a variety of ways. For instance, each half-term or term they can put up a 'Top Ten', or 'Top Twenty' chart, marked off like graph paper with a list of books read down the left-hand side; each time that book is highly rated by a pupil, the child fills in a square with red felt-tip. The child can also be encouraged to display the book enjoyed and, *if* he or she would like to do so, to make a few informal remarks about the book to the rest of the class. Children should also be encouraged to discuss books that they did not enjoy and try to verbalize their reasons; above all, they should not be made to feel foolish or inadequate if they do not enjoy a book that the teacher has recommended.

5   Children, in fact, recorded very little discussion with teachers of the books that they had read. To a large extent, this was probably due to a lack of opportunity, but it is worth stressing the importance of exhibiting a certain amount of restraint when recommending books to children. It is all too easy to recommend our own favourite or our own children's favourites and to cast doubt upon the pupils' own choice. Obviously many teachers, including a number already quoted who were involved in the experiment, are well aware of the problems, but, if reading is important to us on a personal level, it is very difficult to avoid conveying our opinion by tone of voice or expression. We need to meet the child *where he/she is* with reading, and then to lead positively with the child's co-operation, rather than totally demolishing what the child offers and attempting to replace it at one fell swoop with our own package deal, however good our intentions.

6   After friends, children talked to members of their family more than to anyone else about books read. However, we noticed that in the outer city control school they did this far less than in the other three schools, probably because far fewer books were taken home

from that school than from the other three. Admittedly, less books were taken home from either of the control schools than from the experimental schools, but, over the three years, the smallest percentage taken home was in the outer city control school. I stress this fact not as a criticism of the schools; the headmasters and teachers were reluctant to deter children from taking books home but, at the same time, felt the need to make as many books as possible available to a maximum number of children. There are two important issues here: one is the need to allow children, particularly when parents are not well off, to take home books – and the concomitant need for money to be made available annually for the replacement of the inevitable lost and damaged books; the other issue is that, being realistic, many children are *not* going to read a great deal at home because circumstances simply do not make reading a viable proposition, so that, if we want them to read, we *have* to make time and create an atmosphere conducive to reading in school. I well remember one – incidentally quite tough – PE teacher who allowed pupils into the class-room during cold winter playtimes and lunch-times so that they could read the Anita Jackson books which they were particularly keen on at that time. The logical conclusion of allowing children to read only when they have finished their work, is to make it possible for those who are already the more able and most likely to have books at home to read in school, and to prevent the least able or deprived.

7   Another factor that emerged quite clearly from the Reading Record Form returns on the 'favourite' authors, was that in every case a greater percentage of 'favourite' books was chosen because the child already had some prior knowledge of the book (see Table 3·18). Naturally, children are less likely to be disappointed by their choice of book if they have a fair idea of what it is they are choosing: often, for instance, they find they can tackle a book a little beyond the usual level of difficulty because they have seen the story serialized on television; or they find that, if the teacher had read aloud the first three or four chapters, thus taking them beyond the stage of 'getting into the story', they are well able to cope with the rest; sometimes they find satisfaction in reading for themselves a book read aloud by a teacher a couple of years previously, or the next in the series if that book was part of one. Teachers can take advantage of these findings in terms of talking about and displaying stories serialized on television; by reading beginnings of books, and/or extracts from books, rather than always entire books, at the same time making available a few paperback copies, six to twelve, rather than a single copy – which could create a frustrating situation; and by making children *aware* of authors and of series, again partly via

discussion and reading and partly via display. It still comes as a surprise to many 11- and 12-year-olds that an author can write more than one book and that there might be some similarity between books by the same author. We must not take for granted any knowledge of the processes involved in intelligent choice of books; the skills need to be taught, not only in theory but also in practice.

If prior knowledge of a book means that a child is less likely to be disappointed in that book, this fact is particularly important to the less-able reader who, as we have already noted above, invests a great deal of energy when tackling a new author. This type of child in particular needs not only continued help with reading, but also continued help with book choice if there is to be any positive reinforcement of the reading habit.

8   I suppose I cannot leave this section without some comment upon the popularity of Enid Blyton and, for the most part, it has to be subjective comment based upon my own observations and experiences. The only objective conclusion we can draw is that more copies of books by Enid Blyton than by any other author were donated to the experimental schools. However, there is no escaping the fact that many, many children love them and many adults who are now avid readers of quite different sorts of books loved Enid Blyton when *they* were children. I *don't* think we should make *hundreds* of her books available in schools – the Book Flood got things out of proportion – but there should be *some*. I don't think we should stop children from reading them; if we make a wide variety and large number of books available, if we teach children to read with comprehension and confidence, if we inform ourselves and the children about the books available, they will read Enid Blyton if they wish to and then go on quite naturally to other things in most cases. We should not make so much fuss about it.

9   Finally, on the subject of authors, some headteachers and teachers seem to have a very 'black and white' attitude towards picture books and non-picture books. While we would not wish children to be permanently dependent upon pictures for interpretation of the text, I can see no harm at all in the semi-dependence on pictures by the less-able reader even up to 15 or 16 years old (or by the adult non-readers for that matter). Also, anyone who has *carefully* read Goscinny and Uderzo's *Asterix* books with their wealth of linguistic and historical information, will realize that there are picture books and picture books! Many teachers react quite violently to the idea of a child reading 'comic strips' in school yet there is far more in terms of puns, satire, information about other languages, countries, customs and history in an *Asterix* book than

in many books containing no pictures at all; they appeal equally to discriminating adults and to children. I think one problem is that teachers feel guilty that they are not really working or doing their job properly if their pupils appear to be just sitting reading picture books, whereas if the teacher is reading aloud from a recognized classic, stopping every few minutes to discuss vocabulary, it seems more like genuine work.

Chapter 2

The findings from the Reading Record Forms, particularly the differences between reading habits in the two experimental schools after the first year of the experiment, point to differences between schools and teachers that have already been outlined in Chapter 2.

1   Something that pupils, teachers and headteachers in all four schools agreed upon, however, was that they would like to see the continued use of class libraries in some shape or form after the end of the experiment. The headmaster of the outer city experimental school, where there had been virtually no class libraries before the experiment, had been the most antagonistic towards them and in favour of centralizing all but remedial readers and reading schemes in the school library, yet he was prepared to admit the advantages of class libraries – despite the administrative difficulties involved – by the end of the experiment.

The Reading Record Form returns show that children borrow books from places where they are easily accessible and available (see Table 3·5), so that in the inner city control school in the first year of the experiment, for instance, children borrowed mainly from the school library, and consequently read more non-fiction because they were taken there once a week and allowed to read; in contrast, in the final year of the experiment, the same children borrowed most of their books from the fourth-year English base and read predominantly fiction (see Table 7·1), because that is what was made available to them. Since availability and accessibility in terms of time as well as location is obviously such an important factor, it follows that having books on hand, as it were, in the class base or English base increases the likelihood of children reading, since a visit to the school library is usually of necessity a more formal, less flexible arrangement. The class library facilitates spare-moment reading, and more closely approximates the situation in the home of the advantaged child than does the weekly or fortnightly visit to the school library. Children can change their books at irregular intervals causing less disruption than if they have to use the school library. Also, reading is more likely to become a habit if it is not

able 7·2   Type of book, boys and girls separately (percentages)

Outer city experimental school

ype of book	Girls 10+	Boys 10+	Girls 11+	Boys 11+	Girls 12+	Boys 12+
iction	89·2	70·5	79·2	63·7	96·0	85·7
lon-fiction	4·0	19·5	10·8	26·1	0·4	10·4
oetry	3·6	2·5	4·1	1·3	2·2	3·0
>kes, etc.	2·8	5·2	5·1	8·6	0·4	0·4
lissing values	0·4	2·3	0·8	0·3	0·9	0·4
	38	39	35	39	42	38

Outer city control school

ype of book	Girls 10+	Boys 10+	Girls 11+	Boys 11+	Girls 12+	Boys 12+
iction	91·7	90·0	97·9	94·5	96·4	91·0
lon-fiction	5·3	10·0	2·1	4·6	3·3	8·3
oetry	2·9	0·0	0·0	0·3	0·3	0·0
>kes, etc.	0·0	0·0	0·0	0·0	0·0	0·2
lissing values	0·0	0·0	0·0	0·6	0·0	0·5
	37	46	34	46	33	46

Inner city experimental school

ype of book	Girls 10+	Boys 10+	Girls 11+	Boys 11+	Girls 12+	Boys 12+
iction	76·4	74·1	83·2	67·2	80·8	74·4
Jon-fiction	14·3	17·7	9·5	21·5	17·4	22·4
oetry	2·8	0·5	3·5	4·0	0·6	0·3
>kes, etc.	6·5	7·1	3·8	5·9	0·7	2·1
lissing values	0·0	0·5	0·0	1·3	0·6	0·2
	43	51	40	49	38	48

Inner city control school

ype of book	Girls 10+	Boys 10+	Girls 11+	Boys 11+	Girls 12+	Boys 12+
iction	59·5	61·8	91·9	79·9	98·2	98·0
Jon-fiction	21·2	35·3	3·1	17·9	0·3	1·0
oetry	14·5	0·6	3·6	0·4	1·6	0·2
>kes, etc.	3·3	1·8	0·0	0·9	0·0	0·6
lissing values	1·4	0·6	1·4	0·9	0·0	0·2
	55	39	49	37	48	35

looked upon as a 'subject', and associated with a single timetabled lesson each week.

The possible disadvantage of the class library, the pitfall to be avoided, is allowing it to become restrictive. While teachers and pupils were unanimous in advocating the continuance of class libraries, many of them felt that the choice soon became limited. This view was expressed less frequently in the inner city experimental school than in the other three, probably because there was a uniform system of borrowing throughout the school and because children, therefore, were able to borrow books from class-rooms other than their own. This also applied in the first year at the outer city experimental school and in both cases was facilitated by the proximity of the class-rooms in one year group. In any case, the possible restrictive nature of the supply can be readily avoided by having a total centralized stock of books from which teachers borrow a certain number, probably half-termly, gearing the non-fiction to specialist subject work and fiction to the range of ability and interests of the children in their class. Obviously, the English rooms at the upper end of the school would have additional stocks of books. There is no reason why children should not have some say as to which books they would like to have available in their class-rooms in the next half-term. It is important, too, I think, that children should be encouraged to see school and class libraries as complementary rather than naturally exclusive, so that a favourite author or topic will naturally be followed up in more depth in the school library, and then the public library. Certainly, though, children who are afraid of the formality of a school library are more likely to make a beginning with book borrowing when books are around them in the class-room, provided that they are given time and encouragement.

2   The greatest differences between school libraries were between the open-plan ones in the outer city schools and the self-contained ones in the inner city schools. While the open-plan libraries were attractive, I feel that they had serious disadvantages in that they were both located near the main door of the building and, therefore, not at all cosy, and near to the PE/assembly hall and dining hall, so that there tended to be a lot of noise; one was also used as an office. These are not criticisms; I am aware of the space problems in these and many other schools, but it seemed to be that the more old-fashioned, self-contained libraries in the inner city schools were quieter, and warmer in winter, than the open-plan ones. However, the open-plan libraries were more likely to contain corners with armchairs, small tables, rugs, plants, fish-tanks, etc., and were *less* likely to be used as class-rooms. What we need to do is to combine

the advantages of the two. If it is humanly possible, the school library should be used as precisely that and nothing else, the only lessons in that room being library lessons, where children either learn to use the library or read the books kept there, taught by a specialist teacher in charge of the school library, by a knowledgeable class teacher or specialist English teacher. The rest of the time, especially if the library is centrally placed, as it was in the two inner city schools, it should be possible for children, individually, to leave lessons and go down to the school library to refer to or borrow a book.

In an ideal world, each school would have a full-time, specialist trained teacher/librarian but, at the least, the teacher in charge of the library should have enthusiasm for and knowledge of children's books; be encouraged to do the course in librarianship for teachers (Certificate in School Library Studies); and headteachers should make every effort to give that teacher time for administrative work, liaising with other staff, library lessons, visits to book suppliers, etc. The teacher responsible for the school library can delegate a good deal of work to responsible pupil librarians who can staff the library on a rota system during breaks and lunch-times; this system worked outstandingly well in the inner city experimental school.

3   One of the chief teacher differences with regard to use of books that I noticed during my visits to the schools was the extent to which they used display and other methods of recommendation. Certainly the teachers who were most successful in encouraging children to read (and obviously this is linked to teacher knowledge of books), were the ones who, in a variety of ways, drew the children's attention to them. For instance, they *organized* the books according to authors, topics, levels of difficulty; they put up ever-changing displays around topics, around authors, around television series or films; they *talked about the* displays, they read beginnings and extracts, and gave résumés in a multitude of ways they made the children *aware* of what was available. They were enthusiastic themselves and communicated their enthusiasm to the children. They were also ready to chat with an individual child about a book on the way to the staff-room at break or in any other spare moment.

4   On the other hand, and this is really the heart of the matter, it is extremely difficult to be enthusiastic about totally unknown books and authors and we have to admit that what we did was to deposit 5000 books in each experimental school without allowing teachers the time to become acquainted with this material. However, having said that, the fact still remains that many teachers involved in the teaching of English know very little about children's literature, particularly *modern* children's literature, partly because they are

unaware of the existence of quite a lot of it and are also unaware of the possible channels for finding out about it. In fact, unless a teacher has recently been to a college where a *good* children's literature course was a mandatory part of the syllabus or has children of his/her own of an appropriate age who regularly demand to be read to, it seems highly unlikely that the teacher will know any other than the books read as a child and certain classics.

The particular problem of the middle school seems to be that it is half primary school and half secondary school. Most of the teachers of the 9 + and 10 + children, having been junior-trained, *expect* to teach reading, to read stories, to diversify, and generally enjoy doing so; whereas most of the teachers of 11 + and 12 + children, being secondary-trained in one or two subject areas, tend to resent having to teach outside those subject areas and, even if they see the importance of *language* across the curriculum, see no reason why they should have to become acquainted with children's and young people's literature – especially if they have no children of their own, and are teaching a full timetable. Therefore it seems to me unrealistic, although ideally desirable, to *expect* them to become thoroughly acquainted with children's books in this way. It should be possible for English in the third and fourth years of the middle school to be taught by an English specialist, either by training or experience, and by one or two other teachers who are perhaps responsible for the school library or remedial English or who, for whatever reason, have a knowledge and love of children's books and who are prepared to keep up to date with them.

Another aspect of this problem is the lack of incentive for specialist English teachers, with a knowledge of literature, to apply for positions in middle schools where there are few scaled posts or promotion prospects.

5   This brings me to the fifth point, which is the number of wonderful children's books available and the increasing difficulty of keeping up to date with them. Teachers have to use all the shorthand methods at their disposal: for instance, many local education authorities now have a booklet put out by teachers from interested schools within the authority containing book reviews; there are journals like *Children's Literature in Education*; there are book exhibitions, which headteachers should make every effort to allow teachers to attend. In addition, the teachers involved in the teaching of children's literature within a school can make themselves responsible for keeping up to date with certain areas of the subject, for example by age and/or ability levels, and keep one another and other teachers informed, either via a news-sheet something like the LEA ones, or via semi-formal seminars where

books are described and then discussed. It was certainly the case in the inner city experimental school, where a *number* of teachers rather than an isolated 'specialist' had an interest in and knowledge of children's books, that informal discussions about books often arose in the staff-room and this sparked off interest in other members of staff.

6 There is also a need for continual in-service training of teachers in the areas of school librarianship, remedial teaching and children's literature. I realize that there are many of these courses available even despite cut-backs, but would advocate *taking them to the teacher* – for instance one afternoon a week – rather than always expecting the teacher to turn out two evenings a week, especially when a qualification is not involved; for example, when they are seeking information in order to become more effective as teachers rather than specifically seeking a qualification that will lead to promotion. As far as pre-service training is concerned a detailed course on literature for the relevant age group should be mandatory for all teachers who are to be involved in teaching the subject and a minor shorter course could be included for those who expect to specialize in another subject with older children – even if it only provided them with a glimpse of the best literature available for the relevant age group and equipped them with the skills for acquiring further information at a later stage.

7 Only one of the four schools was operating a school bookshop when we began the experiment, i.e. the inner city control school; the outer city experimental school started one during the final year of the experiment. The other two schools do not have bookshops at the time of writing. Just as I would advocate the class library as approximating the situation in a book-oriented home, so I would advocate the school bookshop, particularly in areas where parents are frequently unlikely to have the money, the time or the inclination to take children to bookshops. At this point, also, I feel the need to reiterate the scarcity of specialist bookshops in Bradford, although Bradford Libraries organize a children's bookshop in the foyer of the Central Library every Saturday and, recently, a specialized children's bookshop called 'A Child's Place', which also sells some toys, has opened on the outskirts of Bradford. However, it is highly unlikely that children such as those taking part in our study would be taken there. The kind of 'bookshops' to which the majority of children have access are the local newsagent and, occasionally, if they go into town on Saturday with their mothers, either Boots or W. H. Smith; in any case, many children are never taken into town.

The school bookshop, therefore, is crucial to these children, often providing them with the only means to book ownership.

This means that selection of stock, including a ready ear for children's requests, and display of stock, are vital. In addition, it seems to me to be an excellent idea to allow children to save, for example, 10p per week with the teacher who runs the bookshop; that way they can contribute pocket-money 'on the spot' rather than having to ask a harassed parent for money to buy a book. This system operated very successfully in the inner city control school.

Thus the school bookshop can help children become acquainted with the joys of book ownership and, hopefully, encourage them to visit other bookshops, selling either new or second-hand books, when they are older; the class library can help them become aware of the pleasure and convenience of having friendly books around one and, hopefully, encourage them to want books around them in their own homes as adults; and the school library can show them the advantages of the public library with its large and expensive stock of books, including reference books that few people can afford to own. If they are taught to *use* the school library for themselves there is a chance that they will use the public library also and come to find it a less forbidding place than some of them do initially. In all these processes, the teacher is the all-important intermediary between child and facility, taking the role of the parent but with more than thirty children; the teacher, therefore, needs every encouragement and support.

Support inevitably includes financial support. I must emphasize, however inappropriately at this time of cuts in expenditure on education, that most of the recommendations made above in some way do involve *spending money* – for the purchase of new, or replacement books, for display units, for additional class-rooms to be reserved as specialist areas, for teacher training, both pre-service and in-service, and for a reduced staff–pupil ratio if teachers are to give each child sufficient attention and if they are to have time available for the activities described. This would be an investment in our future.

Chapter 4

In this section I shall summarize the main points that emerged from the case studies with regard to *reading in school*.

1   Some of the case study children who were, no doubt, representative of other children in their schools, were stimulated to read at the start of the 'flood', but their interest soon outstripped their reading ability. Such children, as already suggested, need continuous help with the mechanics of reading, in addition to a supply of attractive books. Those members of the teaching profession who do not already do so, might begin to look upon IQ

and reading ability as dynamic processes rather than static inheritances, and aim at constant improvement. This would be facilitated by smaller classes and trained remedial specialists, able to build up the children's confidence, and well supplied with teaching materials in a pleasant room. The ability to give children confidence is vital; the infrequent readers revealed the link between reading failure and attitude towards books; in the upper school fear and distrust becomes antagonism.

2   Case study children were well aware of the wide variety and vast differences in degrees of teacher knowledge of children's books. We should never underestimate the pupils' ability to judge a fellow pupil's or a teacher's strengths and weaknesses. The children's comments confirm the folly of expecting a teacher with no knowledge whatsoever of children's literature to encourage children to read. I think we *can* expect all teachers to have some degree of awareness of *English language,* although schools should have recourse to specialist teachers, but we cannot expect them to be well-versed in children's literature. Perhaps it is no coincidence that more reading was undertaken in the final year at the inner city schools where English at the upper end of the school was taught entirely by specialists (by training and/or experience) who knew the books in the class-room and were able to make recommendations to individual children.

3   In the outer city experimental school children involved in the experiment ceased to be taken to the school library as class groups once the Book Flood arrived, so that unless they made the effort to go themselves, their choice was, effectively, limited rather than extended; whereas in the inner city experimental school both school and class libraries were used by teachers, thus *increasing* the choice of books available.

Case study children in all four schools agreed unanimously that the availability of books in the class-room was convenient but restricting if the supply was not varied. The continued use of the school library in conjuction with class libraries means that children who are stimulated by the books in the class library to explore a particular author or topic further can readily do so in the school library.

4   Most of the case study children, like their classmates, found it difficult to read silently in school and preferred reading on the bed or hearth-rug or in the armchair at home. However, other case study children did not have home conditions that were conducive to this kind of activity and, for them, the silent reading lesson is vital. A few teachers had mastered the skills of creating a quiet but relaxed atmosphere in which children could change books and

pursue personal reading, but, in the main, these were teachers of long-standing who were well respected, and one felt that it had required considerable groundwork before they were able to achieve this. However, I feel it is worth-while groundwork, and that success is facilitated by careful timetabling, probably of a double period, at a peaceful time in the children's week (not just before swimming); by careful room allocation; and by thoughtful organization of class-rooms, possibly involving some long-overdue rethinking about class-room furniture.

Teachers often find it *easier* to hear children read in turn aloud or for themselves to read aloud to the class (both valuable activities) than to have to make the effort to create the silent reading atmosphere. As mentioned before, they also sometimes feel guilty if they are not obviously working and do not have written work to show at the end of a double period. The successful teachers, in this respect, had a deep-seated conviction that what they were doing was worth while.

5   Many of the case study children were averse to the idea of the class reader although they liked the teacher to read aloud to the class. The chief problem seems to be time. Given that limited time is available for reading in school, if a full-length book is read *entirely in school* very little time is left for any other kind of reading. The situation immediately improves if pupils read a considerable portion of the book for themselves at home, but not all will do so, and still the problem is not avoided if many of the children do not like the choice of book.

At 10+, when books like *Charlie and the Chocolate Factory*, for instance, can be read fairly quickly, the problem does not really arise. At 11+ and 12+, however, when suitable books tend to be longer, and yet children are not required to study a set book for CSE or 'O' level GCE, it is probably more fruitful for the teacher to whet the children's appetites – by telling them about books, reading extracts, starting them off by reading two or three chapters of a wide range of books – rather than by plodding all the way through one, except perhaps in a rare case where a book is relatively short *and,* after the first two or three chapters, the entire class *wants* to hear the rest.

6   I believe that comprehension exercises should be kept totally separate from children's reading and from class readers if they are used – even partially. Obviously at the end of a reading session the teacher might wish to discuss vocabulary or hypothesize as to what will happen next, or to recap at the beginning of a lesson; what should *not happen* is compulsory comprehension, or essay writing on books read for pleasure. A child might *wish* to write a story, or a

project based on personal reading, but should not be forced to do so, particularly as the less-able pupil will then associate reading books with general school failure. In any case, there are many other sources of material for comprehension and essay work without utilizing the reading book. Several case study children, and others, admitted to reading far more slowly than they were able if faced by the prospect of written work when they finished.

7 Some of the case study children, particularly boys, who were added on the teachers' recommendations, were avid readers of non-fiction. This revealed an inadequacy in the design of the Reading Record Form in that it was not particularly well-suited to non-fiction books that a child is unlikely to finish, and ones that a child finds it difficult to say whether he wanted to read another book by the same author. It is my intention to analyse the results for fiction and non-fiction separately, as I have set up the computer file in such a way that this can be done easily, given time. However, if teachers are keeping records of children's reading, they could bear these differences in mind, and possibly use differently coloured record sheets for fiction and non-fiction.

8 Several of the case study children, without actually using the word, said they read for 'escapism' and therefore preferred fiction. I do not think we should use the word 'escapism' in a derogatory sense. These children obviously had a need to get away from their immediate environment and found that they could do so through fiction. This does not mean to say that they were escaping into impossible worlds. *Realism is not the same as naturalism. Mrs Frisby and the Rats of NIMH, Charlotte's Web*, or *Freaky Friday* are not *naturalistic* stories, but they do say *real* things about people and experiences; thus the children are extending their experience and discovering new possibilities. Even if they are reading *Winnie the Pooh* or *Asterix* what a wealth of language and humour they are going to discover. Don't let us make the mistake of equating non-fiction with worth-while facts about life, and fiction with frills and fripperies.

9 Discussions with case study children revealed a greater awareness of authors among children in both experimental schools than in both control schools, with the exception of one child in the inner city control school. Even though the case study children in the outer city experimental school actually decreased the amount of reading that they did in school during the course of the experiment (unlike those in the inner city experimental school – *all* of whom increased the amount) they were still, on their own admission, positively affected in terms of awareness of a wider variety of authors, and they read a great deal at home. Children in both

experimental schools also exhibited a remarkable degree of awareness of their reading deficiencies and difficulties as well as of the
skills and deficiencies of their peers. The 'flood', in conjunction
with visits from researchers and the use of the Reading Record
Form, had had a consciousness-raising effect.

Chapter 5

Common factors among avid and among infrequent readers

A   *Quantitative findings*

1   *Sociological factors*
Although this study concerned such a small number of subjects, it
is nevertheless interesting to note that our findings lend support to
those of larger scale studies, and this despite the sociological
homogeneity of the sample:

(a)   Parents of avid readers spent longer in full-time education
than parents of infrequent readers.
(b)   Several parents of avid readers were involved in further
education, while none of the parents of infrequent readers
received any education after they left school.
(c)   The occupations of the parents of avid readers tended to be
skilled and to involve responsibility, whereas the occupations of
the parents of infrequent readers were more likely to be unskilled.
(d)   Avid readers belonged to smaller families than infrequent
readers and were usually either the first-born or an only child.

2   *Reading – related factors*

(a)   Avid readers had far more books available in their homes
than did the infrequent readers.
(b)   Avid readers and their parents were more likely to belong
to public libraries than were infrequent readers and their parents.

B   *Qualitative findings*
1   Although there were exceptions, avid readers were more likely
than infrequent readers to have rooms of their own. The parents,
none of whom had a great deal of money to spare, often went to
considerable lengths to provide desks, bookshelves, adequate
heating and lighting, and often a typewriter or television set. This
was indicative of their respect for children's individuality and
consideration for their needs.

2 'For years, the popular conception of a book reader was that of an introverted person, often described as a "Bookworm"' (*Reading in America 1978*, 1979). The American researchers, in their large-scale survey, found, as I did, that the opposite is more likely to be the case, and that the reader is usually a socially integrated and highly active person. Certainly our study bears out their statement: 'The doers are the readers!'. Although there was a tendency for the activities of the avid readers to include a preponderance of indoor activities, there were quite a few sportsmen and women among them; the infrequent readers, although they spent more time out of doors than the avid readers, tended to indulge in purposeless activity and, apart from one child, did not show a great deal of interest in anything. Avid readers used their time to the full and crammed a phenomenal amount of activity into their lives.

Avid readers were described by parents and teachers as being unusually mature and trustworthy for their age.

3 Although all the parents of both avid and reluctant readers cared for and were concerned about their children, the avid readers were deliberately planned and consciously wanted, parents often spacing their families so that each child could receive the maximum attention. This was typical of the *degree of control* that parents of avid readers exercised over their own lives and the lives of their children. The parents of the infrequent readers gave the impression that large families had *happened to them* and that, therefore, they could not help the fact that they had little time to devote to each child. The parents of avid readers were *aware* of the importance of spending time with each child and, in any case, enjoyed the time thus spent.

4 None of the parents of avid readers described discipline problems with their children. They conveyed the impression that a well-established system of values was in operation and that, although there was discussion and disagreement between members of the family, it took place within clear guidelines. The parents of infrequent readers, on the other hand, had considerable difficulty controlling their children. There was a lack of communication between parents and children and no mutually accepted system of values. Parents of avid readers were often quite strict but this was seen by the children as indicative of love and concern.

5 While, on the agreement of parents and children, *none* of the infrequent readers had had stories read to them when they were small, *all* of the parents of avid readers read to their children or told them stories, many continuing to do so long after the children could read for themselves. The avid readers almost all had books bought for them at an early age, their parents regarding this as the

norm. Parents of avid readers obviously believed that they were introducing their children to an enjoyable and worth-while experience.

6   Several of the avid readers enjoyed drawing, and more particularly writing, a few of them even considered the possibility of writing as a career. The kinds of writing undertaken by these children included voluntary project work, short stories, full-length stories, poems and plays.

7   Parents of avid readers talked to their children before the children themselves were able to talk, and gave their children ample opportunity for conversation with adults once they were able to converse; the respect accorded to their opinions made verbal communication a rewarding activity for these children. Parents of avid readers did not talk down to them. With one exception, the parents of infrequent readers had little time for listening to, or conversation with, their children, and, in some cases, rarely saw them.

8   The parents, and often grandparents, of the avid readers were for the most part keen readers themselves. Sometimes, in addition, avid readers were influenced by aunts and uncles or elderly neighbours who were keen readers. The parents of avid readers who were not particularly keen readers themselves, demonstrably encouraged whatever interests or abilities their children manifested. Parents of infrequent readers rarely mentioned reading at all and, certainly, it played no significant part in any of their lives, whereas it was obviously a vital part of the lives of some of the parents of the avid readers, and of their grandparents' lives also.

9   It could be logically argued that other leisure-time activities – especially television – would interfere or compete with the time available for book reading or any types of reading. The findings of this study, however, clearly show quite the opposite. Book readers are considerably the most active people in terms of their participation in a great number of leisure-time activities (*Reading in America 1978*, 1979). In our study also we found that avid readers watched a good deal more television than did infrequent readers. They had learnt to accommodate television, to integrate it into their lives, they had developed mental strategies that would allow them both to read and to watch television. In some instances, avid readers had found stimulation for creative writing in television. Infrequent readers expressed very little interest in television, whereas avid readers often knew a great deal about particular programmes, and demonstrated the ability to select and discriminate; this was frequently facilitated by parents providing two television sets in the home.

10   Although avid readers were more likely than infrequent readers to be members of public libraries, they usually preferred to *own* books rather than to borrow them (although their experience of public libraries was almost always limited to small local libraries with limited stock). The exogenous children were more likely to use public libraries extensively than were the indigenous children.

The reasons given for wanting to own books were: they liked to re-read them from time to time; they did not like time limits on borrowing; they liked to *collect* authors or series; and, in some instances, they liked the books as artefacts, although not ornaments – they were read. Avid readers often had rather adult tastes in literature, finding the books in the middle school and in the children's section of the public library 'babyish'. The majority of infrequent readers did not have books at home; some parents made it quite clear to their children that they did not think money spent on books was money *well* spent.

11   We saw earlier that the avid readers did not enjoy having the teacher's choice of book imposed upon them at school. This may have been partly because the parents had considerable respect for their offsprings' choice of reading material, even if it was not to their personal taste. The mother who made no bones about her attempt to influence her son's reading was very well-read herself, particularly in the classics, but probably had not read the best of modern children's fiction. Her son did not appear to resent the intervention as he realized that it was indicative of caring and was mature enough to understand that his mother's stance was concerned with style and aesthetics rather than morality.

12   Parents of avid readers were more knowledgeable about the educational system than were the parents of infrequent readers; they also understood the mechanics of effective intervention. They held strong, often highly critical, views about education generally, and about their own children's education in particular. They believed that they had the right to have 'a say' in their children's education and were not overawed by authority.

The parents of avid readers, some of whom had had a poor education themselves, wanted better things for their children. They were well aware of the connection between academic achievements and career prospects and were quite happy to influence their children directly, several of them confessing that they had not received sufficient guidance from *their* parents. They gave their children active practical help with their education and usually involved themselves in the life of the school in some way.

Mostly the parents of infrequent readers had aspirations for their children but not high expectations. They did not know how to intervene effectively in their children's education and were inadequate, although willing, at helping them with their school-work. They were not prepared to influence their children's decisions about staying on at school and choice of career.

The main strand that runs throughout all these aspects of the home lives of the avid readers is that they know they are wanted, respected, cared for and considered. Their parents are prepared to 'put themselves out' for their children. The parents of avid readers saw themselves as having considerable *control* over their own lives and the lives of their children. Via the written and spoken word, they and their children had found that they were able to manipulate their environment, obviously within the limits of income and other circumstances. Also I noticed an improvement in the academic achievement and social status of these families over several generations, or improvements that the parents clearly intended should continue through future generations.

The avid readers, although they were happy about the Book Flood, were not greatly impressed by it, since they had so many books at home. The infrequent readers tended to be overawed by such an influx of books into their class-rooms. What they needed above all was individual help with the mechanics of reading, combined with care and attention to boost their confidence and self-esteem. This suggests that children who are most likely to be influenced by a book flood are those who are capable as readers but do not come into contact with books at home.

Epilogue

Was the Bradford Book Flood Experiment worth while? Did the supply of a substantial amount of additional reading material to certain groups of children have a differential and beneficial effect on their reading attainments, attitudes to reading and their reading habits? While the design of the experiment does not enable the second of these questions to be answered unequivocally, this does not mean that the answer to the first question is 'No'. The descriptive material that has been collected and, in part, presented, provides an important longitudinal account of the amount and variety of books read by children under somewhat contrasting educational regimes.

In the event, the results obtained using the various tests of reading attainments and of attitudes to reading will disappoint readers who either hoped or considered that the increased provision of books was both a necessary and sufficient condition to achieve significant differential improvement. One weakness in the research design was the relative crudity of the attainment and attitude tests available. This could have obscured differences that more sensitive measures might have revealed. While such a statement may be seen as a rationalization, it is not a completely unsupported defence. The Reading Record Forms provided an important additional means of appraising the extent and variety of children's reading habits. While the findings based on the analyses of these returns are complex, they offer interesting insights into the amount and variety of reading undertaken by the children over a three-year period.

The evidence presented in relation to reading attainments, attitudes and habits is admittedly restricted in its generalizability. It is also open to many interpretations. One of these is that the supply of additional appropriate books is a necessary but not sufficient condition for differential improvement. The *actual uses* made by teachers of the opportunity presented by a book flood is a key issue towards which this study directs our attention. The piano in our home does not, by itself, make our children competent pianists who enjoy playing the instrument.

Argument by analogy is often suspect but can be illuminating. If we measure temperature using a thermometer, we can find ice at 0°C; a considerable amount of heat is required before it becomes water at 0°C. When this does occur, the qualitative change in the characteristics of the substance is unmistakable. However, *as measured by the thermometer*, nothing has changed: both ice and water are at the same temperature. It is possible that in the attempt to improve children's reading attainments and attitudes and to extend the amount and scope of their reading, we have a situation that is, in part, like the input of heat to ice when wishing to effect a change of state. While recognizing the manifest category error in the analogy, the typical tests used to measure changes in reading attainments and attitudes may be as incapable of measuring the change in quality of children's reading habits as the thermometer in the situation outlined above.

Latent heat is a phenomenon well known to the physicist. Latent learning is an established psychological phenomenon and the learning that takes place before it becomes manifest in performance is largely dependent on variety in and availability of stimulation in the environment. The teacher and what he or she does is an integral part of the child's developmental reading environment. A plentiful supply of books is another. The techniques and strategies devised by the teacher in order to optimize the involvement of his or her pupils with books and the satisfactions these both give and develop, are crucial. It is towards the description and professional control of this complex interaction that Mrs Ingham's report points us.

The information obtained from the Reading Record Forms is interesting and valuable in its own right. The further development and use by schools of such cumulative recording and evaluation procedures will sensitize all parties involved to the contribution that the number, variety and availability of reading books can help make to the amount and range of children's reading.

Yes, on reflection, the Bradford Book Flood Experiment was well worth while.

P. D. Pumfrey

Appendix I

The Reading Record Form

What I Think About My Book

Your name .... Your class ....

Title of book ....

Author ....

Date you began this book ....

ANSWER THE FIRST TWO QUESTIONS WHEN YOU CHOOSE A BOOK TO READ

1 *Where did you get this book from?* Tick one box below.

The public library	. . . .	1
The school library	. . . .	2
The books in the class	. . . .	3
It belongs to me	. . . .	4
It belongs to a brother or sister	. . . .	5
I borrowed it from a friend	. . . .	6

2 *Why did you choose this book?*

ANSWER THE REST OF THE QUESTIONS WHEN YOU HAVE FINISHED WITH YOUR BOOK

Date you finished with this book ....

3   *Did you take this book home to read* . . . .   Yes/No

4   *How much of the book did you read?* Tick one box which applies to you.

I read all of it   1

I read over half of it   2

I read less than half of it   3

I read a few pages   4

5   *What did you think of this book?* Tick one box which applies to you.

It was one of the best books I have ever read   1

I liked it very much   2

I quite liked it   3

I did not like it much   4

I did not like it at all   5

6   *How difficult was it to read?* Tick one box which applies to you.

Very difficult   1

Quite difficult   2

Not difficult but not easy   3

Easy   4

Very easy   5

Did you talk to anyone about this book? If you did, put a tick against the people you talked to.

Your class teacher 1

Another teacher in school 2

Your friends 3

Your parents 4

Your brothers and sisters 5

I did not talk to anyone about it 6

8 *Have you told your friends that this is a good book?* . . . . Yes/No

9 *Would you like to read another book by the same author?* . . Yes/Don't Know/No

10 *If there is anything else you would like to say about your book, write it here.*

Appendix II

Final category system for coding children's reasons for book choice

1 Child has read other books by the same author (or books edited by a particul. person) or mentions the author's name as a factor affecting his/her choice.
2 Child has read other books in the same series, or mentions that there are oth books of 'the same kind', e.g. *Narnia, Secret Seven, Famous Five, Mrs Pepperpot.*
3 Child has read part of the book before choosing and found it interesting, e.g contents, jacket, first page, etc.
4 Child interested in an activity or object or certain type of story. (If child does n specify the interest or type of story he must use the expression 'type of story' to included in this category.)
5 The book's appearance, title, cover, typography, level of difficulty, et influenced choice.
6 Child knows something of the story before reading the book (but has not rea books in the same series if one exists – or *other* books by the same author – althoug he may have read the book under consideration before), e.g. child has read boo before, seen/heard it on television as a story read or serialization, has heard some of read by a teacher before, etc.
7 Book recommended by someone.
(No category 8.)
9 Miscellaneous reasons.
10 Information given but *no reason.*
11 Compulsory reading.

0 No information given at all.

Appendix III

Reasons and final comments from the Reading Record Forms

a) Typical reasons for book choice
(Original spelling and punctuation preserved.)

1 (a) I chose this book because I know the author rights good books (a *Nancy Drew* book by Carolyn Keene).
   (b) Because I like Enid Blyton books.
   (c) Because I had a book by the same make and I liked it (W. H. Chalk).
2 (a) I like *Famous Five* books and I have not read this one.
   (b) Because I read another *Jackie* book.
      Final Comment: I wish there were more *Jackie* books in class.
   (c) I chose this book because I like reading *Hardy Boys* books.
3 (a) I chose this book because when I read the ilastration it sounded very exciting and there would be a lot of adventure to share with the children in the book (*A Green Wishbone* by Ruth Tomalin).
   (b) I chose this book because I read the editors blub and it sounded very exciting.
   (c) I chose this book because I read the first page and it was good.
4 (a) I chose this book because I like playing with string (*Why Don't You? String Games – BBC*).
   (b) I had just drawn a map of the barrier reef of Australia and I got a book about diving in the barrier reef (*Diving Adventure* by Willard Price).
   (c) Because I like cowboys.
5 (a) I chose this book because I liked the title *Journey to Jupiter* and the cover looked good (by Hugh Walters).
   (b) I chose this book because the written looked hard so I chose it.
   (c) The picter took my eye (*Charlie and the Chocolate Factory* by Roald Dahl).
6 (a) I chose this book because once a teacher only read part of the book and that part of the book was very good so I disided to read the rest of it (*Nurse Matilda Went to Town* by Christianna Brand).
   (b) Be cassi saw it on tellevigan.
   (c) Because I have read it befor.

7   (a)   I chose this book because Amanda recommended it to me.
    (b)   I chose this book because my friend Susan said it was a good book so I thought I would choose it.
          Final Comment: I think my friend was right it was a good book (*The Kingdom Under the Sea* by Joan Aiken).

More than one reason

(a)   I chose this book because I read the introduction and it sounded good. I chose this book for another reason which is that this story has been on television and when I watched it, it looked and sounded good (*Ballet Shoes* by Noel Streatfield: coded 3,6).
(b)   I chose this book because it was a mystery book. I also chose it because of the picture at the front (*The Mystery of the Brass Bound Trunk* by Carolyn Keene: coded 4,5).
(c)   I chose this book because Alfred Hitchcock is a well-known author, and his stories are always mysterious (*Sinister Spies* by Alfred Hitchcock: coded 1,4).

(b) Unusual reasons or usual reasons expressed in unusual ways, and some interesting final comments

(Original spelling and punctuation preserved.)

1   Final Comment: I enjoid the book very much because I have read it three times before I would recommend the book to any boy but not a girl (*North Against the Sioux* by Kenneth Ulyatt).
2   Final Comment: It was a super book and when I picked it up I couldn't put it down. It was the best book I have ever read the writer captured the scene so well (*The Girl in the Opposite Bed* by Honor Arundel).
3   Final Comment: It was not as good as Bettinas Secret because I could put this down when it was teatime but I read Bettinas secret over tea (*The Family That Came Back* by Doris B. White).
4   Final Comment: It was a fantastic book by a very creative author. I read it from cover to cover in 2 nights and an afternoon (*Hidden Staircase* by Carolyn Keene).
5   Reason: I chose this book because the teacher read it to us and I enjoyed it so much that I wanted to read it again (*Charlie and the Chocolate Factory* by Roald Dahl).
    Final Comment: I am going to read *Charlie and the Great Glass Elevator* by Roald Dahl.
6   Reason: I chose this book because I thought it would be good because it was a new version (*A Child's Bible: Old Testament* ed. by Anne Edwards, Piccolo).
    Final Comment: I did not like it because it seemed to go on and on about the same thing.
7   Reason: Joan Lingard is a very good writer and I like the way she makes me feel as though I was there (*Into Exile* by Joan Lingard).
8   Final Comment: The book is very funny and it is easy to get into the situation that the boy is in (*More Adventures of the Great Brain* by John D. Fitzgerald).
9   Reason: I chose this book because I think I'm rather romantic so I like love stories (*Two Love Stories* by Julius Lester).

Reason: I chose this book because I am a schoolboy so I got a book on school-boys to see how they behaved.

Final Comment: There was some bad language in this book. There was something happening all the time (*Us Boys of Westcroft* by Petronella Breinberg).

One boy's reasons:

Because I like Dogs	Because I like dogs
Because I like Dogs	Because I like <u>DOGS</u>
Because I like Dogs	<u>BECAUSE I LIKE DOGS</u>

Final Comment: The sort of thing it had in the book was

accountant – insect who is good with figures

abundance – a waltz for cakes (*Professor Branestawm's Dictionary* by Norman Hunter).

Reason: Because I like poimes and words that rhyme.

Final Comment: I like the Song of the Jellicles and the Rum Tum Tugger Best (*Old Possum's Book of Practical Cats* by T. S. Eliot).

Reasons: Whell Miss Ashby wrede chumley so it simde just my tiyp of reding (*Dear Zoo* by Joan Crammond).

Reason: I pit it because we were erin abote muscles (*The Human Body* published by Macdonald Educational).

Reason: I got it because my friend recommended it to me.

Final Comment: This book was rubish and I did not like it attal becase it was not ecsiting and it is not my tipe of book (child read it all – *Amazon Adventure* by Willard Price).

Reason: I like Bears they are Interesting.

Final Comment: My sister gets Paddington books and she has read all of them (*More About Paddington* by Michael Bond).

I wred it on and off evenings but I have started to read more now the wether is colder (*Nurse Matilda* by Christianna Brand).

I chose this book because I thought it would be a good book because I wondered what an acre was (*Mr Broom's Wonderful One Acre Farm* by Sid Fleischman).

Because I have seen it at the pictures and liked it very much. Because it's about a 18 foot gut crunching man eating terror. I also like Bears. I also like blood thirsty books (*Grizzly* by Will Collins).

Appendix IV   Descriptive statistics

Boys

	Outer city experimental						Outer city control					
	2nd year			4th year			2nd year			4th year		
	N	Mean	s.d.	N	Mean	s.d.	N	Mean	s.d.	N	Mean	s.d.
Cattell A	38	95·211	15·127	—	—	—	44	89·091	16·030	—	—	—
B	38	102·921	14·261	—	—	—	44	99·500	16·324	—	—	—
full	38	99·079	13·613	—	—	—	44	94·045	15·336	—	—	—
Teachers' R. Att.[1]	37	4·162	1·740	37	4·459	1·346	44	4·614	1·104	42	4·476	1·110
BBFR Att.[2]	38	7·237	1·881	37	7·243	1·992	44	7·545	1·886	43	7·279	2·207
Askov	38	6·263	4·253	38	8·026	5·206	44	7·000	4·861	44	8·523	5·785
Sharples–Reid	38	5·105	2·115	35	5·286	1·840	43	5·581	2·130	42	4·881	2·109
Schonell: words	38	57·474	19·159	37	79·378	12·266	44	48·318	16·726	43	77·558	12·229
R. age	38	10·911	2·158	37	13·797	2·056	44	9·852	1·705	43	13·426	1·903
Age	38	(10·589)	(·255)	37	(12·959)	·276	44	(10·730)	(·285)	43	(13·073)	(·299)
Edinburgh RQ	38	92·737	13·809				44	89·833	10·936			
raw score	38	60·316	29·319				42	55·048	23·916			
AD Test	35	94·971	14·462	37	104·054	29·047	44	92·273	11·772	43	90·837	31·319

Girls

	Outer city experimental						Outer city control					
	2nd year			4th year			2nd year			4th year		
	N	Mean	s.d.	N	Mean	s.d.	N	Mean	s.d.	N	Mean	s.d.
Cattell A	35	97·800	17·595	—	—	—	34	83·147	14·020	—	—	—
B	35	106·171	14·074	—	—	—	34	93·206	16·807	—	—	—
full	35	102·000	14·586	—	—	—	34	88·294	14·848	—	—	—
Teachers' R. Att.[1]	35	4·886	1·728	32	5·344	1·359	34	5·176	1·058	32	4·938	1·105
BBFR Att.[2]	35	8·143	1·593	32	8·406	1·214	34	8·265	·994	32	8·125	2·060
Askov	35	10·057	4·633	35	10·571	5·315	34	9·147	4·620	34	12·853	5·609
Sharples–Reid	35	6·114	1·967	32	5·781	1·518	34	6·853	1·579	32	5·625	2·152
Schonell: words	35	60·114	18·024	32	84·656	10·548	34	48·588	13·246	32	78·344	9·721
R. age	35	11·157	1·969	32	14·569	1·916	34	9·868	1·351	32	13·441	1·454
Age	35	(10·611)	(·289)	32	(12·961)	(·313)	34	(10·537)	(·254)	32	(12·894)	(·262)
Edinburgh RQ	35	96·029	14·247				33	89·727	8·232			
raw score	35	66·914	30·976				33	52·636	16·513			
AD Test	35	95·000	13·427	32	107·719	33·435	34	92·735	8·502	32	82·969	29·745

Inner city experimental

Boys

	2nd year N	2nd year Mean	2nd year s.d.	4th year N	4th year Mean	4th year s.d.
Cattell A	49	93·755	14·400		—	—
B	49	103·755	13·281		—	—
full	49	98·857	12·332		—	—
Teachers' R. Att.[1]	35	4·306	1·122		4·050	1·300
BBFR Att.[2]	46	6·837	1·897		7·087	1·930
Askov	50	5·360	4·989		6·280	4·755
Sharples–Reid	46	5·082	2·110		5·109	1·449
Schonell: words	46	50·600	18·514		78·478	15·130
R. age	50	10·154	2·019		13·780	2·396
Age	50	(10·630)	(·305)		13·000	0·324
Edinburgh RQ	49	92·245	14·481		—	—
raw score	49	60·122	31·787		96·609	32·015
AD Test	46	92·265	12·020		—	—

Girls

	2nd year N	2nd year Mean	2nd year s.d.	4th year N	4th year Mean	4th year s.d.
Cattell A	39	92·769	14·673		—	—
B	39	102·359	11·858		—	—
full	39	97·513	12·206		—	—
Teachers' R. Att.[1]	39	4·487	·970	26	4·676	1·313
BBFR Att.[2]	40	7·700	1·454	37	7·757	2·033
Askov	40	8·850	5·066	40	10·050	5·905
Sharples–Reid	40	5·750	1·864	40	5·595	1·739
Schonell: words	40	50·950	15·785	38	80·368	9·925
R. age	40	10·163	1·693	38	13·951	1·895
Age	40	(10·626)	(·272)	38	12·958	(·260)
Edinburgh RQ	39	94·205	10·235		—	—
raw score	39	62·744	23·105	37	104·514	27·183
AD Test	37	94·750	9·818		—	—

Inner city control

Boys

	2nd year N	2nd year Mean	2nd year s.d.	4th year N	4th year Mean	4th year s.d.
Cattell A	35	86·000	16·022		—	—
B	35	95·171	17·73		—	—
full	35	90·600	15·812		—	—
Teachers' R. Att.[1]	35	4·486	1·380	33	3·879	1·536
BBFR Att.[2]	35	6·886	2·011	32	7·000	2·095
Askov	35	5·943	4·569	35	8·829	6·506
Sharples–Reid	35	4·771	2·073	31	5·129	1·607
Schonell: words	35	48·800	19·015	34	82·324	10·873
R. age	35	9·960	2·084	34	14·224	1·916
Age	35	(10·510)	(·253)	34	(12·863)	(·247)
Edinburgh RQ	35	89·857	9·804		—	—
raw score	35	53·229	20·145	32	92·844	36·358
AD Test	35	90·914	11·268		—	—

Girls

	2nd year N	2nd year Mean	2nd year s.d.	4th year N	4th year Mean	4th year s.d.
Cattell A	49	92·306	16·466		—	—
B	49	98·224	17·517		—	—
full	49	95·082	15·899		—	—
Teachers' R. Att.[1]	49	4·571	1·369	45	4·178	1·230
BBFR Att.[2]	48	7·938	1·359	45	8·267	2·224
Askov	49	8·521	4·212	49	12·327	4·432
Sharples–Reid	48	5·551	1·926	47	6·128	1·329
Schonell: words	48	50·688	18·738	47	81·681	11·071
R. age	48	10·140	1·998	47	14·045	1·736
Age	48	(10·682)	(·320)	47	(13·017)	(·314)
Edinburgh RQ	47	91·447	8·856		—	—
raw score	47	56·745	20·039	46	87·413	27·891
AD Test	49	91·673	10·473		—	—

[1] Teachers' Assessment of Reading Attitude. [2] Bradford Book Flood Reading Attitude Scale.

Appendix V

Favourite authors and titles

Table 3·1 Favourite authors: outer city experimental school: 10+

Authors	No. of books supplied	No. of times books rated as one of the best ever read or as liked very much			Additional information
		Boys and girls	Boys	Girls	
Blyton, Enid	89	52	27	15	
Dahl, Roald★	11	19	10	9	
Smith, Dodie★★	14	17	8	9	
Beresford, Elisabeth	38	11		8	Wombles Series
Price, Willard	20	11	11		Adventure Series
Hunter, Norman	65	9	9		
Nesbit, E.	14	9		6	
Wilder, Laura I.	23	8		7	Little House Series
Chambers, Aidan★	12	7			
Palmer, G. and Lloyd, N.	4	7		6	
Price, Roger★	17	7	7		The Tomorrow People
Rackham, Arthur★	3	7			Aesop's Fables
Bond, Michael	18	6		5	
Harrison, David L.	4	6			
Jansson, Tove	35	6			
Lewis, C. S.	27	6		5	
Tison, A. and Taylor, T.	9	6		5	
Baxter, B. and Gill, R.★		5			Blue Peter Book of Limericks
Cunningham, S. A.★	3	5			The Piccolo Book of Riddles
Dickinson, Peter	16	5			
Green, Roger L.	11	5	5		
Hitchcock, Alfred	13	5			Alfred Hitchcock Series
King, Clive★	3	5			Stig of the Dump
Kingsley, Charles★	3	5		5	
Schwartz, Alvin	6	5			Witcracks 3; Tomfoolery 3
Sewell, Anna	9	5			
Stevenson, Robert L.	23	5			

★★ Authors whose books were rated five or more times as one of the best ever read or as liked very much.

★ Authors who have a book in the corresponding list of favourite titles.

Favourite titles*: outer city experimental school: 10+

Titles	Boys and girls
Charlie and the Chocolate Factory by Roald Dahl	10
The Starlight Barking by Dodie Smith	10
The 101 Dalmatians by Dodie Smith	7
Hans Andersen's *Fairy Tales*	7
Blue Peter Book of Limericks by B. Baxter and R. Gill (eds.)	5
Great Ghosts of the World by Aidan Chambers	5
The Piccolo Book of Riddles by S. B. Cunningham	5
Stig of the Dump by Clive King	5
The Water Babies by Charles Kingsley	5
A Brew of Witchcraft by Geoffrey Parker and Noel Lloyd	5
The Tomorrow People by Roger Price	5
Aesop's Fables by Arthur Rackham	5
Back Beauty by Anna Sewell	5

* Titles that were rated as one of the best ever read or as liked very much five or more times.

Table 3·II   Favourite authors: outer city experimental school: 11+

Authors	No. of books supplied	No. of times books rated as one of the best ever read or as liked very much Boys and girls	Boys	Girls	Additional information
Hitchcock, Alfred	13	25		23	
Norton, Mary	25	18		14	
McCullagh, Sheila	68	8		5	Reading scheme
Blyton, Enid	89	7			
Hunter, Norman	65	7	5		
Allan, Esther Mabel	24	5			Wood Street
Goscinny, R. and Uderzo, M.	25	5			
Lewis, C. S.	27	5		5	
Zim, Herbert S.	9	5	5		Science Books: World's Work Series

Favourite titles: outer city experimental school: 11 +

Titles	Boys and girls
The Borrowers by Mary Norton	6
The Borrowers Afield by Mary Norton	5

Favourite authors: outer city experimental school: 12 +

Authors	No. of books supplied	No. of times books rated as one of the best ever read or as liked very much Boys and girls	Boys	Girls	Additional information
Blyton, Enid	89	10		6	
Goscinny, R. and Uderzo, M.	25	9	9		*Asterix* Series
Willans, G. and Searle, R.	3	7	6		
Von Daniken, E.	0	5	5		
Wilder, Laura Ingalls	23	5		5	

Table 3·III   *Favourite authors: outer city control school: 10 +*

Authors	No. of times books rated as one of the best ever read or as liked very much Boys and girls	Boys	Girls	Additional information
Blyton, Enid	16	11	5	
Bond, Michael	8	5		
Bird, Bettina	6			
Kennett, John (ed.)	6	6		
McCullagh, Sheila K.	6	5		*Dragon Pirates* and *Adventures in Space*
Warren, Mary	6	5		
Clewes, Dorothy	5			Series: Reindeer, H. Hamilton, Antelope, Gazelle
Dickens, Charles	5			

Favourite titles: outer city control school: 10 +

Titles	Boys and girls
The Boy with a Sling by Mary Warren	6

Favourite authors: outer city control school: 11 +

Authors	No. of times books rated as one of the best ever read or as liked very much Boys and girls	Boys	Girls	Additional information
Webster, James	47	17	30	Reading scheme
Hitchcock, Alfred	16	11	5	
Butterworth, Ben and Stockdale, Bill	11	8		Jim Hunters by Methuen of adult literacy derivation. *The Island of Helos, The Temple of Mantos, The Ship-wreckers*
Keene, Carolyn	10	6		Nancy Drew Series
Blyton, Enid	8		5	
Dahl, Roald	8		5	
McCullagh, S. K.	8	5		Dragon Pirates
Dixon, Franklin W.	6	6		Hardy Boys Series
Owen, Evan	6	6		Checkers Reading Scheme, e.g. Birdy Jones, Series in Macmillan 'Topliners', Jim Starling, Various Publishers
Hildick, E. W.	5			
Tomlinson, Jill	5			Methuen Read Aloud, first real book after picture books, e.g. The Aardvark Series

Favourite titles: outer city control school: 11 +

Titles	Boys and girls
The Night I Heard a Noise by James Webster	6
The Ghost Train by James Webster	5

Table 3·IV   Favourite authors: outer city control school: 12+

Authors	No. of times books rated as one of the best ever read or as liked very much Boys and girls	Boys	Girls	Additional information
Blyton, Enid	25	11	14	
Keene, Carolyn	14	6	8	Nancy Drew
Serraillier, Ian	11	8		
Crosher, G. R.	6			Anchor Series
Ward, Richard and Gregory, Thomas Gerald	6	6		Les Books, Hutton Inswinger Series and Popswinger Series
Arthur, Robert (Alfred Hitchcock Series)	5			
Garner, Alan	5			
Havilano, Virginia	5			Fairy Tales
Hunter, Norman	5			
Mackay, Margaret	5			
Dickens, Charles	6			
Dickenson, Christine	6			*Dark Horses* in Macmillan Topliners and *Siege of Robbins Hill*

Favourite titles: outer city control school: 12+

Titles	Boys and girls
David Copperfield by Charles Dickens	6
Fairy Tales Told in Japan by Virginia Haviland	5
The Dolphin Boy by Margaret Mackay	5
Hercules the Strong by Ian Serraillier	5
The Silver Sword by Ian Serraillier	5
Les Signs On by Richard Ward and Gerald T. Gregory	5

Table 3·V Favourite authors: inner city experimental school: 10+

Authors	No. of books supplied	No. of times books rated as one of the best ever read or as liked very much Boys and girls	Boys	Girls	Additional information
Blyton, Enid	97	91	45	46	
Goscinny and Uderzo	24	13	13		Asterix Series
Hunter, Norman	56	12	6	6	Branestawm Series
Tison, A. and Taylor, T.	9	9		8	Barbapapa Series
Chambers, Aidan	12	7		5	
Dahl, Roald	13	7			
Lewis, C. Day	25	7	5		
McKee, David	9	7			*Mark and the Monocycle; The Magician Who Lost His Magic; The Man Who Was Going to Mind The House* (Abelard–Schuman: Picture)
Edwards, Anne (ed.)	3			6	*A Child's Bible* (Old Testament)
Hardcastle, Michael	17	6			Football mainly
Harrison, David L.	4	6			Giant Stories
Bond, Michael	19	5			Paddington
Lord, John Vernon	3	5	5		*The Giant Jam Sandwich; The Runaway Roller Skate*
Price, Roger	18	5	5		*Tomorrow People*

Favourite titles: inner city experimental school: 10+

Titles	Boys and girls
Five Go Adventuring Again by Enid Blyton	9
The Otterbury Incident by C. Day Lewis	7
Good Old Secret Seven by Enid Blyton	6
Five Go To Smugglers Top by Enid Blyton	6
A Child's Bible A. Edwards (ed.)	6
The Book of Giant Stories by David L. Harrison	6
Shock For The Secret Seven by Enid Blyton	5
Asterix in Britain by Goscinny and Uderzo	5

Table 3· V—continued
Favourite authors: inner city experimental school: 11+

Authors	No. of books supplied	No. of times books rated as one of the best ever read or as liked very much			Additional information
		Boys and girls	Boys	Girls	
McCullagh, Sheila K.	31	33	14	19	Dragoon Pirates
Blyton, Enid	97	22	11	11	
Dahl, Roald	13	12	8		
Serraillier, Ian	66	12	5	7	
Goscinny and Uderzo	24	9	9		Asterix Series
Smith, Dodie	13	9	7		
Keene, Carolyn	8	8		8	Nancy Drew
Dixon, Franklin W.	7				Hardy Boys
MacDonald	183	7	5		(pub. – Non-fictional Visual Library Series
Bond, Michael	19	6	5		Paddington
Fitzgerald, John D.	6	5			Great Brain
Hughes, Ted	10	5			
Lewis, C. S.	24	5			
Morris and Goscinny		5	5		
Norton, Mary	25	5	5		Borrowers

Favourite titles: inner city experimental school: 11+

Titles	Boys and girls
Charlie and the Chocolate Factory by Roald Dahl	6
The Silver Sword by Ian Serraillier	5

Table 3· VI   Favourite authors: inner city experimental school: 12+

Authors	No. of books supplied	No. of times books rated as one of the best ever read or as liked very much			Additional information
		Boys and girls	Boys	Girls	
Blyton, Enid	97	69	8	61	
Jackson, Anita	8	42	24	18	Spirals
Hardcastle, Michael	17	25	25		Football Fiction

Table 3·VI—continued

Authors	No. of books supplied	No. of times books rated as one of the best ever read or as liked very much			Additional information
		Boys and girls	Boys	Girls	
MacDonald		19		17	Visual Library non-fiction
rice, Willard	21	19	19		Adventure Series
Owen, Evan	6	16	16		Checkers' Evans Bros.
Dixon, Franklin W.	7	10		10	Hardy Boys
Oates, Anne		10	10		Crown Street Kings Macmillan Educational
Hoke, Helen	3	9	6		Riddles, etc.
eene, Carolyn	8	9		9	Nancy Drew
ate, Joan	10	9		8	Anchor Series
errisford, Judith	4	8		8	Ponies
ond, Michael	19	7		7	
oyers, Barbara		7		6	Checkers (e.g. *Lost and Found*
rand, Christianna	6	7		7	Nurse Matilda (Large Print)
Chambers, Aidan	12	6			
Dahl, Roald	13	6			
Ward, R. and Gregory, G. T.		7	7		Hulton Inswinger, Cassell/Onward
Fleming, Ian	1	6	6		Goldfinger
ohns, Capt. W. E.	28	6	6		Biggles
eslie, Steven	6	6			Tracker Series pub. by Transworld, e.g. *Codebreaker, Skyjacker, Three Men in a Maze*
mith, Dodie	13	6	6		
Chalk, W. H.	25	5			22 of which were *Escape From Bondage* Booster Books, Heinemann Educ.
ewis, C. S.	24	5			
McCann, S.		5	5		Football Fiction
Thorpe, John		5	5		
Verne, Jules		5			

Table 3·VI—continued
Favourite titles: inner city experimental school: 12+

Titles		Boys and girls
The Austin Seven	Anita Jackson	12
The Ear		11
A Game of Life and Death		10
Pentag		5

Table 3·VII   Favourite authors: inner city control school: 10+

Authors	No. of times books rated as one of the best ever read or as liked very much Boys and girls	Boys	Girls	Additional information
Jackson, Anita	31	6	25	
Macdonald (series pub.)	17	12	5	Publisher
Blyton, Enid	9		6	
Serraillier, Ian	8		8	
Chalk, W. H.	7		5	Instant Readers Heinemann Educ.
Gregory, O. B.	6		6	Read About It Series by Wheaton
Smith, John	6		6	*My Kind of Rhymes* pub. Burk
Hughes, Ted	5			*Tom Brown's School Days*

Favourite titles: inner city control school: 10+

Titles	Boys and girls
Dreams by Anita Jackson	9
A Game of Life and Death by Anita Jackson	8
The Ear by Anita Jackson	7
(pub. by Hutchinson for the Inner London Ed. Auth. Media Resources Centre – Spirals)	

able 3· VII—continued
avourite authors: inner city control school: 11 +

uthors	No. of times books rated as one of the best ever read or as liked very much Boys and girls	Boys	Girls	Additional information
lyton, Enid	51		47	
rraillier, Ian	51	16	35	
ickens, Charles (abridged)	26	6	20	
ates, Anne	26	11	15	Crown Street Kings Macmillan Educ.
rontë, Charlotte	10		9	*Jane Eyre*
umas, Alexandre	8		5	*Count of Monte Cristo*
yre, Antony	7		6	Longman, Structural Readers'
lacdonald, Trend	7		7	
anon, Lexie (F. W. Cheshire)	6			Trend/Cheshire
cia, Gertrude	6			Adventures in Reading OUP
enchley, Peter	5		5	
ewell, Anna	5			

avourite titles: inner city control school: 11 +

Titles	Boys and girls
The Silver Sword by Ian Serraillier	45
Oliver Twist by Charles Dickens	10
Jane Eyre by Charlotte Brontë (abridged)	10
The Count of Monte Cristo by Alexandre Dumas	8
The Secret Seven by Enid Blyton	7
The Naughtiest Girl in School by Enid Blyton	6
Shark in the Surf by L. Canon	6
There's No Escape by Ian Serraillier	6
Black Beauty by Anna Sewell	5

Table 3·VIII   Favourite authors: inner city control school: 12+

Authors	No. of times books rated as one of the best ever read or as liked very much Boys and girls	Boys	Girls	Additional information
Blyton, Enid	47	24	23	
Bird, Bettina and Falk, Ian		19	14	Trend/Cheshire
Oates, Anne	26	6	20	Crown Street Kings Macmillan Educ.
Alcott, Louisa M.	26		23	
Orwell, George	25	14	11	*Animal Farm* as class reader
Serrailler, Ian	23			*The Silver Sword* as class reade
Crosher, Geoffrey R.	22	9	13	Cassell's Anchor Series
Dickens, Charles (abridged)	19	5	14	
Higgins, A. L. and D. S.	17		13	Cassell's Anchor Series
London, Jack	16	6	10	
Marryat, Capt. Frederick	13	7	6	
Stevenson, Robert Louis	12	8		
Samuda, Mike	9	9		Headline Series, Headline Publications, E. J. Arnold
Sewell, Anna	9		8	
Fleming, Ian	8			*Goldfinger* Bull's Eye Hutchinson, abridged
Cliffe, A.	7		5	Cassell's Banjo Series
Beddington, Roy	6		6	*The Pigeon and the Boy* as class reader
Dugan, Michael	6			Poetry, Trend
Seawell, Lawrie	6			
Brontë, Charlotte	5		5	
Coolidge, Susan M.	5		5	*Katy*
Hitchcock, Alfred (series)	5			
Verne, Jules	5		5	

Favourite titles: inner city control school: 12+

Titles	Boys and girls
Little Women by L. M. Alcott	27
Animal Farm by George Orwell	25
A Real City Kid by Bird and Falk	15
Katy at School by Ian Serraillier	14
Children of the New Forest by Capt. F. Marryat	13
Call of the Wild by Jack London	11
I Bet You by Bird and Falk	10

able 3· VIII—continued

Titles	Boys and girls
Daredevils by Mike Samunda	9
Katy at Home by Ian Serraillier	9
Black Beauty by Anna Sewell	9
Lonely Girl by A. L. and D. S. Higgins	8
David Copperfield by Charles Dickens (abridged)	7
Goldfinger by Ian Fleming	7
The Dark House by Lawrie Seawell	7
The Pigeon and the Boy by R. Beddington	6
Danger Ride by Bird and Falk	6
Great Expectations by Charles Dickens (abridged)	6
My Old Dad by M. Dugan (poetry)	6
No Time to Scream by A. L. and D. S. Higgins	6
Jane Eyre by Charlotte Brontë	5
White Fang by J. London	5
Leather Jacket Boys by A. Oates	5

References

ASKOV, Eunice N. *Primary Pupil Reading Attitude Inventory* (Dubuque: Kendall Hunt Publishing Co).

BAGLEY, C., VERMA, G. K., MALLICK, K., and YOUNG, L. (1979) *Personality, Self-esteem and Prejudice* (Saxon House).

BERG, L. (1977) *Reading and Loving* (Routledge & Kegan Paul).

BLACK, M., and SOLOMON, F. (1968) 'A tutorial programme to develop abstract thinking in socially disadvantaged pre-school children', *Child Development*, vol. 39, pp. 379–89.

BLIGH, D. A. (1972) *What's the Use of Lectures?* (Harmondsworth: Penguin).

BRUNER, J. (1980) *Under Five in Britain* (Oxford pre-school research project, Grant McIntyre).

BULLOCK, A. (Chairman) (1975) *A Language for Life: Report of the Committee of Enquiry* (London: HMSO).

BURT, C. (1938 to 1955) (revised by P. E. Vernon) *Burt (rearranged) Word Reading Test* (Hodder & Stoughton).

BUTTS, D. (1963) 'What do some boys and girls read and why?' *Use of English*, vol. XV (2), pp. 87–90.

CARSLEY, J. D. (1957) 'The interest of children (10–11 years) in books', *British Journal of Educational Psychology*, vol. XXVII, pp. 13–23.

CATTELL, R. B., and A.K.S. (1961) *Test of 'g' Culture Fair* (NFER).

CLARK, M. M. (1976) *Young Fluent Readers* (Heinemann Educational Books).

CLAY, M. M. (1972) *A Diagnostic Survey* (Auckland: Heinemann).

CLIFT, S. (1976) 'Book-flood reading attitude scale' (University of Bradford, Postgraduate School of Studies in Research in Education, unpublished).

COOPERSMITH, S. (1967) *Antecedents of Self-esteem* (San Francisco: W. H. Freeman).

DANIELS, J. C., and DIACK, H. (1958) *The Standard Reading Tests* (London: Chatto & Windus).

DAVIE, R., BUTLER, N., and GOLDSTEIN, H. (1972) *From Birth to Seven* (Longman, in association with the National Children's Bureau).

DICKINSON, P. (1970) 'A defence of rubbish', *Children's Literature in Education*, Nov., no. 3 (Ward Lock Educational).

DURKIN, Dolores (1966) *Children Who Read Early: Two Longitudinal Studies* (New York: Teachers College Press).

ELLEY, W. B., COWIE, C. R., and WATSON, J. E. (1975) *The Impact of a 'Book Flood': Interim Report prepared for the New Zealand Book Council* (Wellington, May).

ELLEY, W. B., and REID, N. A. (1969) *Progressive Achievement Tests: Reading Comprehension and Vocabulary* (Wellington, NZ: CER).

ELLEY, W. B., and REID, N. A. (1971) *Progressive Achievement Tests: Listening Comprehension* (Wellington, NZ: CER).

FADER, D. N. and McNEIL, E. B. (1968) *Hooked on Books: Program and Proof* (New York: Putnam).

FRANCE, N. and FRASER, I. (1975) *The Richmond Test of Basic Skills.* British adaptation of *The Iowa Test of Basic Skills* by A. N. Hievonymous and E. F. Lindquist (Thomas Nelson).

GORDON, I. J. (1972) *Infant Intervention Project: Progress Report to the Children's Bureau etc.* (University of Florida, Institute for Development of Human Resources).

GRAY, J. (1979) 'Reading progress in English infant schools: some problems emerging from a study of teacher effectiveness', *British Educational Research Journal*, vol. 5 (2), pp. 141–57.

HARTLEY, J. (1974) 'Programmed instruction 1954–74: a review', *Programmed Learning and Educational Technology*, vol. II (6), pp. 273–321.

HIMMEWEIT, H. T., OPPENHEIM, A. N., and VINCE, P. (1958) *Television and the Child* (Oxford University Press).

HOLLINDALE, Peter (1974) *Choosing Books for Children* (London: Paul Elek).

INGHAM, J. (1980) 'Recording children's responses to books in the Bradford Book Flood Experiment', in Bray, G., and Pugh, A. K. (eds), *The Reading Connection* (London: Ward Lock) pp. 122–34.

INGHAM, J. (1982) 'Middle School Children's Responses to Enid Blyton in the Bradford Book Flood Experiment' in *Journal of Research in Reading,* vol. 5 (1), pp. 43–56.

INGLIS, F. (1969) *The Englishness of English Teaching* (London: Longman).

JENKINSON, A. J. (1940) *What Do Boys and Girls Read?* (Methuen).

LOEWENTHAL, K., and KOSTREVSKI, B. (1973) 'The effects of training in written communication of verbal skills', *British Journal of Educational Psychology*, vol. 43 (1), pp. 82–6.

LOMBARD, A. D. (1973) *Home Instruction Programme for Pre-School Youngsters* (National Council of Jewish Women: School of Education, The Hebrew University of Jerusalem).

MORAY HOUSE COLLEGE OF EDUCATION (1972) *Edinburgh Reading Tests, Stage 3* (Hodder & Stoughton).

READING IN AMERICA 1978 (1979) (Washington: Library of Congress) pp. 43–4.

SCHONELL, F. J., and F. E. (1942 to 1955) *Schonell Reading Tests* (Oliver & Boyd).

SHARPLES, D. and REID, I. (1972) 'Attitudes towards subjects and activities' (University of Bradford, Postgraduate School of Studies in Research in Education, unpublished).

SHEARER, E. (1975) 'A re-standardization of the Burt–Vernon and Schonell graded word reading tests', *Educational Research*, vol. 18 (1), pp. 67–73.

SMITH, W. H. and HARRAP, G. G. (1957) *A Survey of Boys' and Girls' Reading Habits* (London: Harrap).

TIZARD, B., MORTIMORE, J., and BURCHELL, B. (1981) *Involving Parents in Nursery and Infant Schools* (Grant McIntyre).

TORREY, Jane (1969) 'Learning to Read Without a Teacher' article in: *Elementary English,* 40, pp. 550–6.

TUCHMAN, B. (1979) in *Reading in America 1978* (Washington: Library of Congress) p. 8.

VERNON, P. E. (1938) *Graded Word Reading Test* (Hodder & Stoughton).

WATTS, A. F. (1948) *Holborn Reading Scale* (G. G. Harrap).

WATTS, A. F. (1954) *NFER Reading Test AD* (NFER).

WEINBERG, C. B. (1979) in *Reading in America 1978* (Washington: Library of Congress) p. 14.

WELLS, G. (1981) *Learning Through Interaction.*

WHITEHEAD, F., CAPEY, A. C., MADDREN, W., and WELLINGS, A. (1977) *Children and Their Books* (Schools Council Research Studies, Macmillan Education).

YARLOTT, G., and HARPIN, W. S. (1970–1) '1,000 responses to English literature (1)/(2)', *Educational Research*, vol. 13, pp. 3–11, 87–97.

YOUNG, D. (1968) *Group Reading Test* (Hodder & Stoughton).

Index

advisers, 11
Alcott, Louisa M., 104
analysis of co-variance, 211, 215–16, 219–22
Animal Farm (Orwell), 105
Antecedents of Self-Esteem (Coopersmith), 151, 167
Asimov, Isaac, 132
Askov, Eunice N., 7
Askov Non-Verbal Reading Inventory, 12, 13, 20–1, 210, 211, 212, 221, 222, 224, 256, 257
Asterix (Goscinny and Uderzo), 36, 101, 103, 107, 109, 231, 241
authors
    awareness of, 62, 74, 89, 140–1, 143, 146, 241
    favourite, 93, 96–108, 123, 140–1, 146, 230, 258–68
avid readers, 113–14, 116, 117–18, 126–8, 134–5, 143–4, 151–2
    and arrival of Book Flood, 120
    books: at home, 157, 158, 246; choice, 126, 133, 143, 196–9, 245; ownership, 79, 189–94, 245; peer group discussion of, 122, 124; supply, 121, 131
    career prospects, 203–5, 244
    conversation with adults, 175–7, 244
    discipline, 168, 169–70, 243
    drawing, 173, 174, 244
    early reading, 170–2, 173, 243–4
    family: position in, 156, 157; reading habits of, 178–83, 244; size of, 156, 243
    homes of, 159–61
    illness and disability, 157, 158
    interests, 161, 162–3, 243
    and libraries, 79, 157, 189–94, 245
    parents: attitude to child-rearing, 167, 168, 169–70, 242, 243; attitude to school and education, 199–205, 245; reading to children, 170–2, 243; socio-economic factors, 153–6
    personality, 163
    reading habits, 121, 125–6, 184–9
    and television, 184–9, 244
    truancy, 157, 158
    writing, 173–5, 244

B.B., 122
Bagley, C., 116
Baked Beans Again (Oates), 147
Beano, 195
Benchley, Peter, 104, 146
Berg, Leila, 4, 88, 151, 164, 175
Beresford, Elizabeth, 101
Berrisford, Judith M., 141
Bernstein, B., 55
Best Sellers, 187, 197
Biggles, 108, 141
Billion for Boris (Rodgers), 111
Bird, B., 104
Black, M., 215
Bi⋅ck Jack (Garfield), 35, 132
Blah (Kent), 109
Blake's Seven, 129
Blue Peter, 187
Blume, Judy, 96, 111, 123, 147
Blyton, Enid, 101–106, 109, 110, 121, 129, 141–2, 170, 173, 194, 195, 196, 231
Bobsey Twins, 146
book(s)
    accessibility, 80, 92, 120
    appearance, 98, 133, 142
    awareness of, 38, 62, 74, 89, 114, 140–1, 143, 146, 227, 241
    buying, 171, 172, 173, 178, 243
    children's recorded opinion of, 85
    choice, 5, 8, 38, 60, 62, 74, 80–2, 89, 97–8, 107, 122, 123, 126, 133, 139, 141, 142, 143, 196–9, 215, 229, 230–1, 233, 245, 252, 253–5
    display, 35, 38, 46, 47, 52–3, 60, 66, 71, 137, 230–1, 235, 238
    early experience of, 170–3, 243–4
    exhibitions, 34, 236
    favourite, 93, 94–5, 96–108, 230, 259–64, 266–9
    at home, 121, 146, 157, 158, 245, 246
    ownership, 79, 114, 119, 130, 136, 145, 189–95, 245
    series, 107, 108
    shops, 190, 191, 192, 194, 199, 237, 238; school, 28, 41, 53, 66, 79, 195, 237–8
    supply, 22–3, 27–8, 40–1, 43–4, 46, 48–9, 50–1, 61, 64–5, 66, 67, 75, 79,

92, 94, 101, 103, 104–105, 119–20, 121, 126, 131, 137, 143, 217, 227, 228, 236, 238, 239, 248
taken home, 40–1, 47, 48, 65, 80, 82–3, 128, 131, 137, 138, 191, 229–30
Borrowers series, 101
Borrowers Aloft (Norton), 107
Bradford Book Flood Experiment, 2–3, 5–6, 8, 9, 11, 12–15, 20, 21, 22–3
Bradford Central Library, 124, 190, 237
Bradford Libraries, 22, 23, 28, 237
Bradford Reading Attitude Test, 12, 13, 21, 210, 211, 221, 222, 223, 224, 256, 257
Bradford Schools' Library Assistants, 70
Bristol Longitudinal Language Development Research Programme, 4
Bruner, J., 215
Buckeridge, Anthony, 141
Burt, C., 12
Burt Graded Word Reading Test, 30, 31, 42, 43
Butler, N., 3, 4, 165
Butts, D., 74
Byars, Betsy, 96, 111

Carsley, J. D., 8, 74
Carrie's War (Bawden), 129
case studies, 24, 113–16
homes and children, 3, 5–6, 13, 25, 150–208, 242–6
reading in school, 13, 34, 113–49, 228, 238–42
see also avid readers, infrequent readers
Cattell's Culture Fair Test, 12, 13, 15, 116, 143, 209, 210, 213–14, 215, 217, 218, 219, 221, 222, 223, 224, 256, 257
Centennial (Michener), 146
Certificate in School Library Studies, 45, 235
Chambers, Aidan, 107
Charlie and the Chocolate Factory (Dahl), 103, 111, 150
Charlie and the Great Glass Elevator (Dahl), 91, 110
Charlotte's Web (White), 109, 241
Chaucer, 109
Checkers series, 104
'Child's Place', 237

Children of the New Forest (Marryat), 148
Children's Literature in Education, 71, 236
Children and their Books (Whitehead et al.), 3
Chip Club, 53, 194, 195
Christie, Agatha, 141
Clark, Margaret M., 4, 7, 151, 158
class readers, 91, 105, 123–4, 125, 138–9, 147, 240
classics, 103, 104, 198
Cleary, Beverley, 96, 123, 147
Clift, Stephen, 21, 24
comprehension exercises, 214–15, 240–1
conversation, of children with adults, 4, 5, 55–6, 58, 59, 71, 87, 88, 175–7, 227, 229, 235, 243, 244
Coopersmith, Stanley, 151, 167–8, 170
Coopersmith Self-esteem Inventory, 12, 116, 117, 127, 128, 134, 143
Crompton, Richmal, 141
Crosher, G. R., 104, 146
Crown Street Kings series, 104

Dahl, Roald, 101, 102, 103, 104, 107, 109–111, 141, 150, 197
Dandy, 195
Danny, Champion of the World (Dahl), 110, 111
Daredevils (Samuda), 148
Davie, R., 3, 4, 165
Deep (Benchley), 146
diary, children's, 114, 125–6
Dickens, Charles, 102, 104, 196, 198
Dickinson, Peter, 89
discipline, at home, 167–70, 243
Dixon, Franklin W., 102, 103, 104, 105, 109, 131, 141, 143
drawing, 173–5, 244
Durkin, Dolores, 4

Edinburgh Reading Test, 12, 13, 15, 17–20, 116, 153, 210, 211, 213–14, 215, 216, 218, 220, 221, 222, 223, 224, 227, 256, 257
education officers, 11
English
head of, 24, 27, 28–9, 30, 31, 33, 44, 51, 53, 54, 55, 57, 58, 63, 65, 67, 70, 71–2, 104, 123, 196
non–specialist teachers, 29–30, 34–7, 42–3, 44–5, 46, 47–8, 68, 84–5, 102, 136, 236
specialist, 66–7, 68, 69, 82, 140, 147, 148, 149, 236, 239

teaching: method, 35, 36, 38, 42,
129–30; organization, 28–30, 41–2,
53–6, 58, 66–8
Enormous Crocodile (Dahl), 110
ethnic minorities, 2, 26, 39, 49, 50, 61,
63–9 passim, 72, 105, 114, 134,
135, 143, 144, 145, 148, 149, 151–9
passim, 165, 167, 170, 172–3, 183,
189, 193–4, 197, 200, 205, 216, 220

Falk, I., 104
family
discussion of books with, 86, 88, 124,
229
reading habits, 177–83, 244
size, 156, 165–6, 242, 243
see also case studies (homes and
children), grandparents, home
environment, parents, siblings
Famous Five (Blyton), 45, 105, 106, 197
fiction, 2, 27, 34, 39, 40, 48, 50–1, 64,
65, 66, 70, 71, 72, 74, 79, 80, 91,
92, 93, 94, 98, 99, 100, 131, 141,
143, 146, 173–4, 179, 198, 232, 233,
234, 241
Fifteen (Cleary), 123
finance, for school books, 34, 43, 49,
59, 66, 72, 80, 82, 93, 149, 230, 238
Fisk, Nicholas, 141
Fleming, Ian, 141, 142, 196
Foundation (Asimov), 132
Freaky Friday (Rodgers), 111, 241
From Birth to Seven (Davie et al.), 165

Game of Life and Death (Jackson), 109
Garfield, Leon, 35, 132
Garner, Alan, 102, 111, 123–4
Ghost of Thomas Kempe (Lively), 123
Goals in the Air (Hardcastle), 36
Goldfinger (Fleming), 142
Goldman, William, 146
Goldstein, H., 3, 4, 165
Gordon, I. J., 215
Goscinny, R., 104, 109, 110, 231
grandparents, 170, 175, 176, 177, 178,
182, 183, 244
Growing Point, 71

Hardcastle, Michael, 103, 141, 197
Hardy Boys series, 104, 106, 107, 108
*Hardy Boys: the Mystery of the Aztec
Warrier* (Dixon), 106
Harpin, W. S., 8, 9, 74

Harrap, G. G., 9, 74
headteacher, 11, 24, 25, 27–8, 29–30,
31–3, 42, 43, 51, 53, 54, 57–9, 64,
66–7, 68, 69–70, 74, 201, 226, 230,
231, 232, 236
Heim's AH5 verbal intelligence test, 215
Hidden Staircase (Keene), 107
Himmelweit, H. T. 6
Hitchcock, Alfred, 101-109 passim,
121, 131, 141, 143, 194
Holborn Sentence Reading Test, 57, 68
Hollindale, Peter, 9
home environment, 3–7, 32, 43, 46, 47,
49, 59, 63–4, 70, 103, 111, 115–16,
126–7, 133, 137, 144, 148, 149, 153,
156–208, 219, 230, 236, 237, 239,
242, 243–4, 245–6; *see also* family,
parents
How, 188
Hunter, Norman, 101, 102, 103, 104,
109

I Never Loved Your Mind (Zindel), 123
infrequent readers, 113–14, 116, 117–18,
126–8, 134–5, 143–4, 152, 153
and arrival of Book Flood, 120
books, at home, 157, 158, 245;
choice, 126; ownership, 194–5, 245
career prospects, 205–206, 246
conversation with adults, 177, 244
discipline, 168–9, 243
early reading, 170, 172
family: position in, 156, 157; reading
habits, 177, 183, 244; size, 156, 157,
243
homes of, 159–61, 242
illness and disability, 157, 158
interests, 161–2, 163, 243
and libraries, 157, 194–5, 245
parents: attitude to child rearing,
165–6, 168–9, 243, 244; attitude to
school and education, 199–200,
205–207, 245–6; reading to
children, 170, 243; socio-economic
factors, 153, 154, 155
television, 189, 244
truancy, 157, 158, 168
writing, 173
Ingham, J., 73, 74
Inglis, F., 9, 74
Innes, Michael, 9
in-service training, 57, 68, 70, 84, 237,
238

intelligence test, 12, 116, 117, 118, 126, 127, 134, 135, 144, 151, 152, 153, 218
interviews, 11–12, 24, 31, 74, 113, 114–16, 118
It's Not the End of the World (Blume), 8, 96

Jackanory, 187
Jackie, 93
Jackson, Anita, 103, 104, 107, 108–109, 111
James Bond, 196, 199
Jaws (Benchley), 104, 146, 164, 174, 197
Jenkinson, A. J., 8, 9, 74
Jennings, 146
jokes, 74, 91, 92, 98, 99, 100, 233
Jones, Diana Wynne, 96, 109, 123, 147
Journeying Boy (Innes), 9

Keene, Carolyn, 102, 103, 104, 105, 109, 141, 143
Kennett Library, 102
Kent, Jack, 109
King, Clive, 109
Kipling, Rudyard, 198
Kostrevski, B., 215

Ladybird series, 171, 195
language development, 4, 55, 56, 61–2, 111
Leather Jacket Boys (Oates), 147
le Guin, Ursula, 96, 147
less able children, 12, 32, 36, 37–8, 44, 57, 61, 102, 104, 107, 108, 110, 111, 141–2, 148, 214, 218–19, 228, 229, 230, 231, 241
Lewis, C. S., 36
library
   class, 11, 26–8, 33–42 passim, 45, 48, 50–3, 58, 61, 62, 64–6, 67, 77, 79, 80, 82, 91, 92, 94, 96, 118, 119, 120, 121, 126, 128, 130–7 passim, 145, 146, 147, 191, 227, 232, 234, 238, 239
   lesson, 56, 62, 65, 67, 70, 137, 138, 235
   mobile, 195
   public, 43, 77, 79, 82, 96, 119, 121, 125, 130, 135, 136, 145, 157, 173, 181, 189–95, 234, 238, 242, 245
   school, 24, 26–8, 33–41 passim, 48, 49, 50–3, 58, 60, 62, 64–6, 70, 72, 77, 79–80, 92, 94, 96, 119, 120, 121, 128, 130–8 passim, 145, 192, 227, 232, 234–5, 238, 239

Line, David, 141
Lively, Penelope, 123
Lion, the Witch and the Wardrobe (Lewis), 36
local education authority, 25, 201, 236
Loewenthal, K., 215
Lombard, A. D., 215
London, Jack, 104
Look-in, 93, 147
Lucky Scoop club, 53

McCullagh, Sheila, 101, 103, 104, 107, 108, 109
Mackay, 102
McKee, David, 109
magazines, 93, 96, 147
Magic (Goldman), 146
Magic Finger (Dahl), 110
Marathon Man (Goldman), 146
Marryat, Frederick, 104
Meet Harry King (Oates), 147
Michener, James A., 146
Milligan, Spike, 141
Milton, John, 109
Moomintrolls (Jansson), 107
Moon of Gomrath (Garner), 124, 129
Moonstone Castle Mystery (Keene), 107
more able children, 14, 32, 44, 48, 87, 148, 217, 218–19
Mrs Frisby and the Rats of NIMH (O'Brien), 109, 132–3, 241
My Naughty Little Sister (Edwards), 142
Mystery of the Coughing Dragon (West), 106, 107
Mystery of the Flaming Footprints (West), 107

Nancy Drew series, 107, 108
National Book League, 22, 23
National Child Development Study, 3
Nesbit, E., 101
News of the World, 109
NFER
   EH2 Test, 210, 216–17
   Reading Test AD, 12, 13, 15, 16–17, 210, 218, 256, 257
non-fiction, 2, 27, 39, 40, 48, 50–1, 64, 65, 72, 74, 80, 91, 92, 93, 94, 98, 99, 100, 104, 118, 120, 127, 131, 142–3, 146, 174, 179, 198, 232, 233, 234, 241
Norton, Mary, 101, 107

Oates, Anne, 104, 146–7
O'Brien, Robert, 109, 132
observation, 11, 24–5
Ogre Downstairs (Jones), 96, 109, 111
Oppenheim, A. N., 6
Orwell, George, 104
Owen, Evan, 104
Owl Service (Garner), 123, 187

Paddington (Bond), 107, 111
Paradise Lost (Milton), 109
Pardoner's Tale (Chaucer), 109
parents
    attention given to children, 5, 164–7
    attitude: to child rearing, 6, 32, 59,
        165–6, 167–70, 176, 180, 242, 243–
        4; to child's career prospects, 203,
        205, 245–6; to school and
        education, 6, 59, 199–208, 245–6
    and buying books, 66, 190, 237, 245
    and children's book choice, 196–9,
        245
    and discipline, 167–70, 243
    education, 153, 154, 242
    encouraging children to read, 5, 57,
        142, 143, 153, 159–61, 171–2,
        180–1, 203, 243–4
    interviews with, 24, 115–16, 158–9
    library membership, 157, 191–2, 195,
        242
    occupations, 154–5, 156
    reading: to children, 5, 170–2, 243;
        habits, 5, 6, 177–83, 192, 195, 244
    talking to children, 4, 5, 59, 88,
        175–7, 243, 244
    and television, 184–5, 186, 244
    see also family, home environment,
        socio-economic status
peer group
    book borrowing among, 77, 96, 119,
        130, 136, 145
    discussion of books, 56, 61, 62, 86,
        87, 88, 90, 123, 124, 140, 142, 229
Peppermint Pig (Bawden), 186
picture books, 231–2
Pigman (Zindel), 123
Plague Dogs (Adams), 86, 141, 199
plays, 91, 173
poetry, 74, 91, 92, 98, 99, 100, 173, 174,
    233
Pollard, Michael, 141, 197
Pool of the Black Witch (B.B.), 122
Power of Three (Jones), 123
Price, Roger, 101

Price, Willard, 101, 104, 141, 142, 194,
    197
Prince and the Pauper (Twain), 122
Professor Branestawm's Dictionary
    (Hunter), 91
Professor Branestawm series, 107
project work, 241, 244
PTA, 202, 203
publishers' involvement in Book Flood,
    22, 23
pupil librarians, 52, 135, 137, 235
puzzles, 74, 91, 98

questionnaire, 159; *see also* Reading
    Record Form

reading
    developing skills, 60, 61, 122, 126,
        129, 138, 143, 144, 148–9, 153, 221,
        224, 226, 227–8, 229
    difficulty, 16, 86, 87, 121–2, 126, 129,
        135, 141–2, 143, 148
    record, 8–11, 73–112, 241; *see also*
        Reading Record Form
    schemes, 27, 39, 42, 48, 61, 64, 65,
        66, 67, 91, 94, 101, 102, 103, 104,
        108, 109, 131
    in school case studies, 113–49
    silent, 38, 45, 47, 56, 61, 65, 71, 80,
        84, 91, 116, 125–6, 130, 131, 132,
        138, 147–8, 227, 228, 230, 239–40
    success, 1, 3, 4, 5, 225–6; *see also* avid
        readers
    tests, 15–20, 56–7, 126, 127, 134, 143,
        144, 151, 152, 209, 218, 227–8
    time in school, 118, 124, 125–6,
        128–30, 131, 132, 138, 148, 227,
        228, 230, 239–40
Reading and Loving (Berg), 4, 151
Reading in America, 7, 161, 184, 189–90,
    243, 244
Reading Record Form, 7, 9–10, 13, 38,
    73–4, 75, 78, 81, 83, 85, 87, 88, 90,
    94, 107, 114, 116, 117, 127, 128,
    130, 134, 143, 144, 151, 152, 227,
    228, 229, 230, 232, 241, 242, 247,
    248, 249–51, 253–5
Real City Kid (Bird and Falk), 147
reasoning skills, 214–15
Record Breakers, 187
reference books, 59, 238; *see also*
    non-fiction
regression analysis, 211, 222–4
remedial

provision, 27, 29, 30–1, 42–3, 48, 53, 54, 56–7, 65, 66, 67, 68, 129, 237, 239
readers, 27, 110
service, 56, 158
see also less able children
research
difficulties of, 24–5, 209–10, 211, 225
methods, 7, 8–12, 73–4, 118
Richards, Frank, 141
Richardson, Elizabeth, 11
Richmond Test of Basic Skills, 57
Rodgers, Mary, 96, 111, 123, 147
Run for Your Life (Line), 141

Sampson's Circus (Spring), 122
Savery, Constance, 141
Scholastic Publications, 53
Schonell, F. J., 16
Schonell Graded Word Reading Test, 12, 13, 14–15, 16, 42, 210, 212–13, 220–1, 222, 223, 227
Schonell Reading Age, 117, 127, 134, 144, 147, 151, 152, 153, 210, 212, 213, 218, 226, 227, 256, 257
school(s), 2, 11–12, 13, 24–72, 209, 217, 234–5, 237, 239
bookshop, 28, 41, 53, 66, 79, 195, 237–8
inner city control, 50, 63–72; homes and children case study, 151, 152; reading in schools case study, 143–9, 241; reading record, 74–105 passim, 228, 230, 232, 233, 266–9; and tests, 210–14, 215–16, 217, 218–19, 220, 222, 223–4, 257
inner city experimental, 49–62, 72; homes and children case study, 151, 152; reading in schools case study, 134–43, 241; reading record, 74–105 passim, 228, 230, 233, 263–6; and tests, 210–14, 215–16, 217, 218–19, 220, 222, 223–4, 257
librarians, 30, 31, 34, 38, 41, 45, 51, 54, 58, 59–61, 64, 65, 66, 70, 80, 86, 93, 128, 235, 236, 237
outer city control, 39–49; homes and children case study, 151, 152; reading in schools case study, 126–33, 241; reading record, 74–105 passim, 228, 229, 230, 233, 260–2; and tests, 210–14, 215–16, 217, 218–19, 220–1, 222, 223–4, 256
outer city experimental, 26–38, 48–9, 51; homes and children case study, 151, 152; reading in schools case

study, 116–26, 241; reading record 74–105 passim, 228, 230, 233, 258–60; and tests, 210–14, 215–16, 217, 218–19, 220–1, 222, 223–4, 256
School Library Association, 45
School Psychological Service, 158
Schools Council, 6
Schools' Library Service, 52, 65
Screen Test, 187
Secret Seven series, 105
Serraillier, Ian, 102, 104
setting, 53, 72
sex
differentiation, 8, 68, 78, 82, 86, 93, 94, 95, 98, 100, 101, 103–104, 211, 213, 214, 215–16, 217, 218, 221, 222–4, 226, 233, 241, 256–7, 258–68
stereotypes, 10, 107
Sharples-Reid Self Assessment of Reading Interest, 12, 13, 15, 20, 210, 211, 223, 224, 256, 257
Shearer, E., 12, 16
siblings, books borrowed from, 119, 130, 136, 145
silent reading, *see* reading
Silver Sword (Serraillier), 105
Smith (Garfield), 131
Smith, Dodie, 101, 104
Smith, W. H., 9, 74
Snowdroppers (Scanlon), 148
socio-economic status, 3–4, 25, 26, 32, 39, 43, 49–50, 63–4, 209, 230, 242, 246; *see also* home environment, parents
Solomon, F., 215
SPA schools, 25, 49
Spirals series, 103
sport, 161, 162
Spring, Howard, 122
SRA, 67
Star Wars, 129
Stevenson, Robert L., 104, 131
Stig of the Dump (King), 91, 109, 111
streaming, 29, 31, 41–2, 48, 53, 67, 72
Swallows and Amazons (Ransome), 45
Sutcliffe, Rosemary, 35

teacher
assessment of children's reading interest, 12, 15, 20, 21; *see also* Teachers Reading Attitude Assessment
and children's book choice, 35, 36, 38, 121, 123, 124, 126, 129, 132,

136, 137, 139, 140, 142

discussion of books with children, 25, 37–8, 61–2, 74, 84, 86, 87, 88–9, 91, 139–40, 142, 229, 235, 240

encouraging children to read, 74, 86, 91, 111–12, 123, 153, 228–9, 235, 238, 240

fourth-year class, 31, 34–7, 44, 45–8, 70, 148

knowledge of children's books, 62, 82, 84, 93, 102, 105, 123, 126, 140, 141, 143, 147, 149, 235–7, 239

-pupil ratio, 238

reading to children, 91, 98, 125, 139, 147–8, 230, 232, 240

second-year class, 31, 54–5, 123, 136, 140, 148

third-year class, 70, 140, 148

training, 33, 34–6, 43, 45, 46, 47, 103, 236, 237, 238; in-service, 57, 68, 70, 84, 237, 238

see also English, headteacher, teaching

Teacher, the School and the Task of Management (Richardson), 11

Teachers' Reading Attitude Assessment, 210, 211–12, 256, 257

teaching approach and method, 129–30, 131, 132–3, 139–40, 221, 230–1, 236

television, 1, 5, 6–7, 91, 98, 103, 129, 142, 146, 150, 163, 175, 178, 183–9, 230, 235, 244

tests

attitude, 20–1, 210, 211–12, 218, 223

intelligence, 12, 116, 117, 118, 126, 127, 134, 135, 144, 151, 152, 153, 218

limitations of, 68, 248

programme, 12–15; post-testing, 2, 15, 211–16; pre-testing, 2, 12–14, 209–211, 218, 222

reading, 15–20, 56–7, 126, 127, 134, 143, 144, 151, 152, 209, 218, 227–8

results, 209–16, 225–6, 247, 256–7

self-esteem, 12, 116, 117, 126, 127, 144, 151, 152

see also Askov Non-Verbal Reading Inventory, Bradford Reading Attitude Test, Burt Graded Word Reading Test, Cattell's Culture Fair Test, Coopersmith Self-esteem Inventory, Edinburgh Reading Test, Heim's AH5 verbal intelligence test, Holborn Sentence Reading Test, NFER EHs Test, NFER Reading Test AD, Richmond Test of Basic Skills,

Schonell Graded Word Reading Test, Sharples-Reid Self Assessment of Reading Interest, Vernon Graded Reading Test, Young's Group Reading Test

T. F. Davies Centre for Teachers, 70

There's No Such Thing as a Dragon (Kent), 109

Tizard, Barbara, 4

Tomorrow's World, 188

Torrey, Jane, 4

Tryon, Thomas, 146

truancy, 157, 158, 166, 168, 207

Tuchman, Barbara, 161

Twain, Mark, 122, 198

Uderzo, M., 104, 110, 231

UKRA Conference 1979, 73, 74

US reading attitude tests, 20

Von Daniken, E., 101

Verma, Gajendra, 24

Verne, Jules, 141

Vernon, P. E., 12

Vernon Graded Reading Test, 30

Vince, P., 6

Visual Library series, 104

Wallace, Irving, 146

Waltons, 175

Warrior Scarlet (Sutcliffe), 35

Watts, A. F., 16

Weinberg, Charles B., 184

Weirdstone of Brisingamen (Garner), 124

Wells, Gordon, 4, 5

West, Nick, 106, 107

White, E. B., 109

White, T. H., 131

Whitehead, Frank, 3, 4, 6, 8, 9, 74, 184

Wilder, Laura Ingalls, 101, 104

Wilkes, R., 27

Winnie the Pooh (Milne), 111, 241

writing, 125, 133, 163, 173–5, 186, 187–8, 192, 240–1, 244

Wombles (Beresford), 107, 111

Worzel Gummidge, 186

Yarlott, G., 8, 9, 74

Yorkshire Joint Library Services School Library Book Exhibition Collection, 23

Young Fluent Readers (Clark), 151

Young's Group Reading Test, 56, 57, 68

Zindel, Paul, 96, 123, 147